Study Guide
for use with

MARKETING
Fourth Canadian Edition

Eric N. Berkowitz
University of Massachusetts

Frederick G. Crane
QMA Consulting Group Limited

Roger A. Kerin
Southern Methodist University

Steven W. Hartley
University of Denver

William Rudelius
University of St. Thomas

Prepared by

William J. Carner
Frederick G. Crane

McGraw-Hill
Ryerson

Toronto Montréal New York Burr Ridge Bangkok Bogotá Caracas Lisbon London Madrid
Mexico City Milan New Delhi Seoul Singapore Sydney Taipei

McGraw-Hill
Ryerson Limited

A Subsidiary of The McGraw-Hill Companies

Study Guide for use with
Marketing
Fourth Canadian Edition

ISBN: 0-07-086046-7

1 2 3 4 5 6 7 8 9 10 CP 0 9 8 7 6 5 4 3 2 1 0

Printed and bound in Canada

Care has been taken to trace ownership of copyright material contained in this text; however, the publisher will welcome any information that enables them to rectify any reference or credit for subsequent editions.

Sponsoring Editor: Lenore Grey Spence
Senior Marketing Manager: Jeff MacLean
Production Coordinator: Madeleine Harrington
Cover Design: Greg Devitt
Printer: Canadian Printco

Introduction

Business can be defined by its two most vital functions – production and marketing. You have to make something and you have to be able to sell it. What makes marketing the best part of business is that it is also the fun part. Figuring out why people buy what they do and using that information to sell your product is a creative endeavour that should be enjoyed. With that in mind, this study guide has been designed not only to help you succeed in this course, but to increase your enjoyment of it as well.

The format of this study guide has come from the input of students just like yourself who want to do their best in every course they take. Focus groups with Business and Marketing majors have showed that they wanted a study guide designed to enhance their existing study habits. These students reported that as they study their first task was most often to outline the chapter. Their next step was then to relate the material in the book to real life situations. Some used flashcards to remember terms, definitions, and concepts while others wanted to use realistic sample tests to help their learning process. These approaches to learning form the basis of what I hope will be your best study guide in your favourite course.

This study guide is a direct response to what students have said they do to learn better. It comprehensively approaches the ways in which we learn and is an intensely efficient companion to the text. Using the study guide along with the book maximizes both the amount of what you learn and the effectiveness of the time you spend studying. You will find that as you begin to use the study guide, you'll be almost effortlessly reinforcing what you learn in the book in a myriad of ways. Here's how it works. First and foremost, read the assigned chapter in the text. Read it straight through as you might read a magazine article, or a chapter of a novel. Remember to pay particular attention to the examples, especially the ones in the boxes. Once you have read an entire chapter, grab the study guide and go back over the material using the chapter outlines. This is a good way to pick up the terms and concepts that may have slipped past you in the first reading. Next, to remember the relevant cases in the book, you should answer the discussion questions. By answering these questions in the study guide you can better relate the material in the book to real life situations. Finally, take the sample tests in the study guide to simulate a testing situation and also to approach learning the material in still another way. Using the flash cards is another good way to remember the terms and concepts for your exams.

Good luck and remember to enjoy what you do.

William J. Carner, Ph.D.
University of Texas at Austin

Frederick G. Crane
QMA Consulting Group

TABLE OF CONTENTS

CHAPTER 1

Marketing: A Focus on Customer Relationships and Value

<u>Why is Chapter 1 important</u>? This is the overview; the chapter to let you know what this term is going to cover. What is marketing? Why is it important to business and consumers? What are the components of marketing? How did it begin and how has it progressed? What affects marketing? What are the benefits of good marketing programs? You will see examples of how marketing affects everything you do—from marketing yourself to get a date or a job to the reputation of the school you are attending.

Marketing: The <u>process</u> of planning and executing the conception, pricing, promotion, and distribution of ideas, goods, and services to create <u>exchanges</u> that <u>satisfy</u> individual and organizational objectives.

CHAPTER OUTLINE

I. WHAT IS MARKETING?

    A. Definition
        1. Process
        2. Exchange
        3. Need Satisfaction

    B. Influencing Factors
        1. Organizational Factors
        2. Environmental Factors
            a. Internal
            b. External
        3. Societal Factors

    C. Requirements
        1. Two or more parties with unsatisfied needs.
        2. Desire and ability to be satisfied.
        3. Way to communicate.
        4. Something to exchange.

II. DISCOVERING AND SATISFYING CONSUMER NEEDS

    A. Discovering Consumer Needs and Wants
        1. Market
            a. People
            b. Desire
            c. Ability to buy
        2. Needs
        3. Wants

    B. Satisfying Consumer Needs and Wants
        1. Controllable Factors--Marketing Mix
            a. Product
            b. Price
            c. Promotion
            d. Place
        2. Uncontrollable Factors--Environmental Factors
            a. Social
            b. Technological
            c. Economic
            d. Competitive
            e. Regulatory
        3.   Customer Value
        4.   Relationship Marketing
        5. The Marketing Program

III. EVOLUTION OF THE MARKETING ORIENTATION

    A. Production Era
    B. Sales Era
    C. Marketing Concept Era
    D. Marketing Orientation Era
        1. Continuous collection of information.
        2. Sharing information across departments.
        3. Using information to create customer value.
    E. Ethics
    F. Social Responsibility
        1. Societal Marketing Concept
        2. Macromarketing
        3. Micromarketing

IV. BREADTH AND DEPTH OF MARKETING

    A. Who Markets?
        1. Organizations
            a. For profit
            b. Nonprofit
        2. Places
        3. Individuals
    B. What is Marketed?
        1. Goods
        2. Services
        3. Ideas
    C. Who Buys and Uses What is Marketed?
        1. Ultimate consumers
            a. Individuals
            b. Households
        2. Organizations

D. Who Benefits?
    1. Consumers who buy
        a. Form utility
        b. Place utility
        c. Time utility
        d. Possession utility
    2. Organizations who sell
    3. Society as a whole.

You should be able to place these key terms in the outline and be able to discuss them.

customer value	market	mass customization	target market
environmental factors	market orientation	micromarketing	ultimate consumers
ethics	marketing	organizational buyers	utility
exchange	marketing concept	relationship marketing	
macromarketing	marketing mix	social responsibility	
	marketing program	societal marketing concept	

QUESTIONS & PROBLEMS

MARKETING: A DEFINITION TO FOCUS ON NEEDS

To serve both buyers and sellers, marketing seeks (1) to discover the needs and wants of prospective customers and (2) to satisfy them.

Decide which of the following statements demonstrate discovering needs, and which statements demonstrate satisfying needs:

1. A restaurant designates part of its seating as a "nonsmoking" section._____

2. A dentist starts office hours at 6:30 a.m. for patients who work "nine to five"._____

3. A new laundry product comes with the offer of a 50 cents-off coupon upon the completion of a mail-in questionnaire._____

4. An ice cream parlor has its patrons vote for their favourite ice cream flavour._____

5. A major studio looks at the most popular television series this season to decide what type of television shows to produce for next season._____

REQUIREMENTS FOR MARKETING TO OCCUR

List the four elements necessary for marketing to occur:

1._____

2._____

3._____

4._____

Identify how each requirement is being met when a consumer buys a new car? When a citizen votes for a political candidate? When a person chooses where to vacation?

TARGET MARKETS

List at least two possible target markets and the need or want to be satisfied for each product below:

1. Low salt, low fat baked potato chips.

Target markets: (for example: wives who want their husbands to lose weight)

Needs:_____

Wants:_____

2. Hotels rooms with computer terminal and hookups for modems and printers.

Target markets:_____

Needs:_____

Wants:_____

List at least two products (goods or services) that can satisfy these target markets:

1. Market: people who exercise
Target market: young mothers with small children

Products: (for example: in-house trainers)

_____

_____

2. Market: pet owners
Target market: extensive travelers

Products

_____

_____

MARKETING MIX - FOUR Ps

"The marketing mix elements are called controllable factors because they are under the control of the marketing department in an organization." The four elements of marketing mix include: Product, Price, Promotion, and Place.

The fast food business has been dominated by hamburger restaurants since its inception. Over the last ten years, inroads have been made by fast food franchises specializing in chicken, Mexican food, pizza, and "deli" sandwiches. The chicken and "deli" restaurants have emphasized their healthy menus, while the Mexican restaurants have emphasized the different taste of their product plus its low cost and the pizza franchises have made their entry with home delivery. Meanwhile, McDonald's and Burger King have run large ad campaigns and signed with Disney and other entertainment companies for special giveaways and events. Identify and discuss the 4 P's as they relate to the fast food industry.

UNCONTROLLABLE ENVIRONMENTAL FACTORS

Assume you are the head of a major television network. Social trends indicate that the public is becoming more and more concerned with sex and violence on television. If you don't do something to react to this trend, chances are that the government will come in and regulate the industry for you. In addition, certain groups are organizing boycotts against your sponsors and many major sponsors are threatening to pull advertising on some of your most popular programs. At the same time, more viewers are moving to cable TV, which offers more variety and less "censorship." What environmental factors are involved here and how would you respond?

MARKETING PROGRAM

After discovering what prospective customers need, the marketing manager must translate the ideas from consumers into some concepts for products the firm might develop. These ideas must then be converted into a tangible marketing program - a plan that integrates the marketing mix to provide a good, service, or idea to prospective buyers.

Assume you are an intelligent, enterprising ten year old. You have been asked by the National Hockey League to identify the needs of their customers and design a program to meet those needs.

Use the following grid to design a simple but thorough marketing program to meet at least three identified customer needs or wants.

Customer Need or Want	Product	Promotion	Place	Price
1._____	_____	_____	_____	_____
2._____	_____	_____	_____	_____
3._____	_____	_____	_____	_____

CAN YOU PASS THE TEST?

OVERVIEW OF CHAPTER 1: TERMS AND DEFINITIONS (multiple choice)

1. People who use the goods and services purchased for a household comprise the _____.
    a. Macromarketing
    b. Market
    c. Target market
    d. Marketing
    e. Ultimate consumers

2. The process of planning and executing the conception, pricing, promotion, and distribution of ideas, goods, and services to create exchanges that satisfy individual and organizational objectives is known as _Marketing_
    a. Macromarketing
    b. Market
    c. Target market
    d. Marketing
    e. Ultimate consumers

3. _____ is the study of the aggregate flow of a nation's goods and services to benefit society.
    a. Macromarketing
    b. Market
    c. Target market
    d. Marketing
    e. Ultimate consumers

4. A plan that integrates the marketing mix to provide a good, service, or idea to prospective consumers is a _____.
    a. Marketing concept
    b. Marketing program
    c. Marketing mix
    d. Marketing orientation
    e. Customer value

5. _____ are units such as manufacturers, retailers, or government agencies that buy for their own use or for resale.
    a. Marketing program
    b. Organizational buyers
    c. Exchange
    d. Societal marketing concept
    e. Utility

6. The benefits or customer value received by users of the product is known by the economic term _____.
    a. Marketing program
    b. Organizational buyers
    c. Exchange
    d. Societal marketing concept
    e. Utility

7. The _____ are uncontrollable factors involving social, economic, technological, competitive, and regulatory forces.
   a. Consumerism
   b. Environmental factors
   c. Micromarketing
   d. Ethics
   e. Social marketing concept

8. The _____ takes the view that an organization should discover and satisfy the needs of its customers in a way that also provides for society's well-being.
   a. Consumerism
   b. Environmental factors
   c. Micromarketing
   d. Ethics
   e. Social marketing concept

9. _____ are made up of one or more specific groups of potential consumers toward which an organization directs its marketing program.
   a. Macromarketing
   b. Market
   c. Target market
   d. Marketing
   e. Ultimate consumers

10. The marketing concept is a focus on the _____.
   a. Environment
   b. Competition
   c. Consumer
   d. Government
   e. Society

11. People with the desire and ability to buy a specific product make up the _Market_
   a. Macromarketing
   b. Market
   c. Target market
   d. Marketing
   e. Ultimate consumers

12. The _____ is the idea that an organization should (1) strive to satisfy the needs of consumers (2) while also trying to achieve the organization's goals.   _marketing concept_
   a. Marketing concept
   b. Marketing program
   c. Marketing mix
   d. Marketing orientation
   e. Customer value

13. A marketing manager's controllable factors, known as the _____, consists of product, price, promotion, and place.
   a. Marketing concept
   b. Marketing program
   c. Marketing mix
   d. Marketing orientation
   e. Customer value

14. Exchange is the trade of things of value between buyer and seller so that each is better off after the trade.
- a. Macromarketing
- b. Market
- c. Target market
- d. Marketing
- e. Exchange

15. _____ are the moral principles and values that govern the actions and decisions of an individual or group.
- a. Consumerism
- b. Environmental factors
- c. Micromarketing
- d. Ethics
- e. Social responsibility

16. The idea that organizations are part of a larger society and are accountable to society for their actions is known as _____.
- a. Consumerism
- b. Environmental factors
- c. Micromarketing
- d. Ethics
- e. Social responsibility

17. To practice the _____ *Marketing orientation* a company (1) actively tries to understand customers' needs and the factors affecting them, (2) shares this information across departments, and (3) utilizes the information to meet these customer needs.
- a. Marketing concept
- b. Marketing program
- c. Marketing mix
- d. Marketing orientation
- e. Customer value

18. How an individual organization directs its marketing activities and allocates its resources to benefit its customers is known as _____.
- a. Macromarketing
- b. Market
- c. Target market
- d. Marketing
- e. Micromarketing

19. _____ is the unique combination of benefits received by targeted buyers that includes quality, price, convenience, on-time delivery, and both before-sale and after-sale service.
- a. Marketing concept
- b. Marketing program
- c. Marketing mix
- d. Marketing orientation
- e. Customer value

20. Linking the organization to its individual customers, employees, suppliers, and other partners for their mutual long-term benefits is called:
- a. Product marketing
- b. Customer value
- c. Relationship marketing
- d. Mass customization

    e. Positioning

21. Tailoring goods or services to the tastes of individual customers in high volumes at a relatively low cost is referred to as:
    a. Product differentiation
    b. Mass marketing
    c. Mass selling
    d. Mass customization
    e. Positioning

For questions 22-27, please indicate which marketing mix element is described:

22. An art museum suggests a donation of $2 at the door.
    a. Product
    b. Price
    c. Promotion
    d. Place
    e. Positioning

23. A manufacturer of clothespins claims in its 30-second radio spots to keep your clothes "hanging in there."
    a. Product
    b. Price
    c. Promotion
    d. Place
    e. Positioning

24. A greeting card company markets over 300 different birthday cards.
    a. Product
    b. Price
    c. Promotion
    d. Place
    e. Positioning

25. A playing card company prices its deluxe line of playing cards $0.75 higher than its competitors' cards.
    a. Product
    b. Price
    c. Promotion
    d. Place
    e. Positioning

26. A chocolate bar company offers one line of its candy bars "without nuts."
    a. Product
    b. Price
    c. Promotion
    d. Place
    e. Positioning

27. A maker of lingerie decides to use the "party-plan" method of selling the product line.
    a. Product
    b. Price
    c. Promotion
    d. Place
    e. Positioning

For questions 28-32, please indicate which environmental factor is described:

28. Many people refuse to purchase products manufactured in countries that violate human rights.
    a. Social
    b. Technological
    c. Economic
    d. Competitive
    e. Regulatory

29. The advent of a good, inexpensive disposable razor has had an effect on the "shaving" industry.
    a. Social
    b. Technological
    c. Economic
    d. Competitive
    e. Regulatory

30. The value of the Canadian dollar on the foreign exchange market is constantly changing.
    a. Social
    b. Technological
    c. Economic
    d. Competitive
    e. Regulatory

31. There is legislation requiring children to be placed in car seats or seat belts.
    a. Social
    b. Technological
    c. Economic
    d. Competitive
    e. Regulatory

32. Crest lost market share when Colgate came out with toothpaste in a pump dispenser instead of a tube.
    a. Social
    b. Technological
    c. Economic
    d. Competitive
    e. Regulatory

For questions 33-40, which marketing era is described:

33. First era of North American marketing history; it extended into the 1920s.
    a. Production era
    b. Sales era
    c. Marketing concept era
    d. Marketing orientation era
    e. Societal Marketing era

34. Began in the 1980s and is expected to extend past the year 2000.
    a. Production era
    b. Sales era
    c. Marketing concept era
    d. Marketing orientation era
    e. Societal Marketing era

35. This era began in the 1920s and extended for many firms into the 1960s.
   a. Production era
   b. Sales era
   c. Marketing concept era
   d. Marketing orientation era
   e. Societal Marketing era

36. This era began in the late 1950s and continues today for many Canadian firms.
   a. Production era
   b. Sales era
   c. Marketing concept era
   d. Marketing orientation era
   e. Societal Marketing era

37. We are in the business of satisfying needs and wants of consumers. (but firms may not specifically have departments designed to discover these needs)
   a. Production era
   b. Sales era
   c. Marketing concept era
   d. Marketing orientation era
   e. Societal Marketing era

38. Production capabilities exceeded regular demand, competition increased, reaching new markets became more complex
   a. Production era
   b. Sales era
   c. Marketing concept era
   d. Marketing orientation era
   e. Societal Marketing era

39. Businesses have one or more departments specifically designed to understand consumers' needs and readily share this knowledge across departments
   a. Production era
   b. Sales era
   c. Marketing concept era
   d. Marketing orientation era
   e. Societal Marketing era

40. Goods were scarce and buyers were willing to accept virtually any goods that were produced and make do with them as best they could
   a. Production era
   b. Sales era
   c. Marketing concept era
   d. Marketing orientation era
   e. Societal Marketing era

Use the following statement for questions 41-44:

A survey shows three out of ten mothers do not use exercise facilities for lack of child care.   Which marketing eras are being described?

41. Too bad. We're the only place in town. If they want to work out, they'll work out here.
    a. Production era
    b. Sales era
    c. Marketing concept era
    d. Marketing orientation era
    e. Societal Marketing era

42. We should examine the feasibility of opening a room and hiring a babysitter.
    a. Production era
    b. Sales era
    c. Marketing concept era
    d. Marketing orientation era
    e. Societal Marketing era

43. We should direct our advertising more toward single or childless women.
    a. Production era
    b. Sales era
    c. Marketing concept era
    d. Marketing orientation era
    e. Societal Marketing era

44. Have the marketing department contact promotions. See if we can develop a video tape to rent to mothers for use at home.
    a. Production era
    b. Sales era
    c. Marketing concept era
    d. Marketing orientation era
    e. Societal Marketing era

45. Denny's restaurants will spend over $1 billion over the next seven years to improve hiring, and training of minority executives, and to improve work relationships with minority-owned businesses. This is representative of _____
    a. Production era
    b. Sales era
    c. Ethics
    d. Social responsibility
    e. Societal marketing concept

46. Whirlpool recently won a contest for developing the most energy efficient environmentally friendly refrigerator. This represents _____
    a. Production era
    b. Sales era
    c. Ethics
    d. Social responsibility
    e. Societal marketing concept

47. There is significant controversy concerning whether genetically engineered growth hormones should be given to children to make them grow. This would be a question of _____
    a. Production era
    b. Sales era
    c. Ethics
    d. Social responsibility
    e. Societal marketing concept

48. Coca Cola sells the syrup to local bottlers who deliver and sell it to the retailers who sell it to you. What market does the local bottle represent?
    a. ultimate consumers
    b. organizational buyer
    c. goods
    d. services
    e. ideas

49. What type of product is the retailer of Coca Cola selling?
    a. ultimate consumers
    b. organizational buyers
    c. goods
    d. services
    e. ideas

50. A local group is trying to get an ordinance passed and hires a public relations firms to design a campaign to convince voters to approve their initiative. What type of product does the public relations firm offer?
    a. ultimate consumers
    b. organizational buyers
    c. goods
    d. services
    e. ideas

51. What is the product of the local group backing the ordinance?
    a. ultimate consumers
    b. organizational buyers
    c. goods
    d. services
    e. ideas

52. The voter is the _____
    a. ultimate consumers
    b. organizational buyers
    c. goods
    d. services
    e. ideas

53. A restaurant buys popular music CDs to play in the evenings at the bar. During the hours the music is played, customers pay a cover charge. What type of consumer is the restaurant?
    a. ultimate consumers
    b. organizational buyers
    c. goods
    d. services
    e. ideas

54. A retail outdoor store decides to offer catalogues so its customers can order by mail. This represents the utility of _____
       a. time
       b. form
       c. possession
       d. place ✓
       e. all of the above

55. Canadian Airlines has a competitive advantage in a particular market by offering multiple flights throughout the day in that market. This represents the utility of _____

       a. time ✓
       b. form
       c. possession
       d. place
       e. all of the above

56. Burger King's most famous promotion was "Have it your way!" This represents the utility of
_____

       a. time
       b. form
       c. possession
       d. place
       e. all of the above

57. Little Caesar's offers your choice of pizza delivered directly to you at your home in 30-45 minutes. This represents the utility of _____.

       a. time
       b. form
       c. possession
       d. place ✓
       e. all of the above

Chapter 1—Answer Key

Discussion Questions

Marketing: A Definition to Focus on Needs

1. Satisfying needs
2. Satisfying needs
3. Discovering needs
4. Discovering needs
5. Discovering needs

Requirements for Marketing to Occur

1. Two or more parties with unsatisfied needs
2. Desire and ability to be satisfied
3. Way to communicate
4. Something to exchange

Example: New car

1. Buyer and dealer
2. Buyer has desire for new car and dealer has new cars to sell
3. Advertising communicates "deal" Dealer communicates personal sales pitch
4. Buyer exchanges money and trade-in; dealer exchanges new car

Target Markets

Example: Low salt, low fat baked potato chips

Target market: health conscious consumers
Need: healthy foods including snacks
Wants: healthy snack food without guilt

Marketing Mix-4 P's

Product--sandwiches
Place--convenient location
Price--low
Promotion--advertising, sales promotion

Uncontrollable Environmental Factors

Social culture environment
Legal/political environment
Separate "adult" themes to later in evening

Hockey: (example)

need or want--entertainment
product--more exciting games
promotion--prizes for goals scored
place--at the arena or on TV or radio
price--seat prices

Sample Tests

1. e	20. c	39. d
2. d	21. d	40. a
3. a.	22. b	41. a
4. b	23. c	42. c
5. b	24. a	43. b
6. e	25. b	44. d
7. b	26. a	45. d
8. e	27. d	46. d
9. c	28. a	47. c
10. c	29. b	48. b
11. b	30. c	49. c
12. a	31. e	50. d
13. c	32. d	51. e
14. e	33. a	52. a
15. d	34. d	53. b
16. e	35. b	54. d
17. d	36. c	55. a
18. e	37. c	56. b
19. e	38. b	57. d

CHAPTER 2

Linking Marketing and Corporate Strategies

<u>Why is Chapter 2 important?</u> This chapter will show you how a company decides which products to offer and to whom. You will see why marketing planning is important, what the planning process consists of, and how the each part of the organization is involved. You will learn how marketing strategies are determined, measured, and adjusted. It will show you what to expect from each product based on its market position and how not to have surprises.

Marketing Strategy: The means by which a marketing goal is to be achieved, usually characterized by a specified target market and a marketing program to reach it.

CHAPTER OUTLINE

I. LEVELS OF STRATEGY IN ORGANIZATIONS

    A. Kinds of Organizations
        1. Profit
        2. Nonprofit

    B. Levels in Organizations
        1. Corporate Level Strategy
            a. Corporate vision
            b. Corporate goals
                i. profit
                ii. sales revenue
                iii. market share
                iv. unit sales
                v. quality
                vi. employee welfare
                vii. social responsibility
            c. Corporate philosophy and culture
        2. Business Unit Strategy
            a. Business mission (definition)
            b. Business (unit) goals
                i. Boston Consulting Group (BCG) business portfolio analysis
                    --cash cow
                    --star
                    --question mark (problem children)
                    --dogs

        c. Business (unit) competencies (Competitive Advantage)
           i. quality
           ii. time
           iii. cost
           iv. innovation
           v. customer intimacy

      3. Functional Level Strategy

II. STRATEGIC MARKETING PROCESS--MARKETING PLAN

    A. Situation Analysis (SWOT Analysis)
      1. Strengths
      2. Weaknesses
      3. Opportunities
      4. Threats

    B. Market Product Focus and Goal Setting
      1. Market Segmentation
      2. Measurable Marketing Objectives

    C. Marketing Program
      1. Product Strategy
      2. Price Strategy
      3. Promotion Strategy
      4. Place (Distribution) Strategy

    D. Implementation
      1. Obtaining Resources
      2. Designing Marketing Organization
      3. Developing Schedules
      4. Executing Marketing Program

    E. Control
      1. Comparing Results with Plan to Identify Deviations
      2. Acting on Deviations
        a. exploiting positive deviations
        b. correcting negative deviations

You should be able to place these key terms in the outline and be able to discuss them.

business unit	corporate culture	market segmentation	profit
business unit competencies	corporate level	market share	quality
business unit goal	corporate philosophy	marketing plan	SWOT analysis
business unit level	corporate vision	marketing strategy	situation analysis
business unit mission	functional level	marketing tactics	
strategic marketing process			

QUESTIONS & PROBLEMS

STRATEGIC MARKETING PROCESS

There are three main phases in the strategic marketing process:

Planning
Implementation
Control

Match the proper phase of the strategic marketing process with the situations below:

1. The three steps of situation analysis, goal setting, and marketing program development are highly interrelated._____

2. In this phase, the marketing manager compares the results of the marketing program with the goals in the written plan to identify deviations and to act on deviations - correcting negative deviations and exploiting positive ones._____

3. This phase includes executing the program described in the marketing plan and designing the marketing organization needed._____

4. Pillsbury assigns the responsibility for a new Hungry Jack Biscuit promotion to a marketing manager. Above him in the chain of command is the Group Marketing Manager for biscuits. Below him are the Associate Marketing Manager and the Marketing Assistant._____

5. Coca-Cola decides to produce products for target markets wanting sugar and/or nonsugar and caffeine and/or noncaffeine products._____

MARKETING PLAN

There are three steps in the planning phase of the strategic marketing process:

Situation analysis
Goal setting
Marketing program

Match the correct term with the statements listed below:

1. Organizing potential resources into a coherent marketing program that uses the four marketing mix elements (4Ps) to reach the targeted goal._____

2. Taking stock of where the firm or product has been recently, where it is now, and where it is likely to end up using present plans._____

3. Setting measurable marketing objectives to be achieved._____

BUSINESS MISSION

An organization's business, or mission, is a statement that specifies the markets and product lines in which the business will compete, i.e., the scope of the business unit. The "mission" can dramatically narrow or broaden the range of marketing opportunities available.

Give a possible "business" or "mission" statement for each of the companies below:

1. Bell Canada
2. Molson Breweries
3. Xerox Canada
4. NHL (National Hockey League)
5. Nabisco

SITUATION ANALYSIS

The letters in the SWOT acronym stand for:

1. S = _____

2. W = _____

3. 0 = _____

4. T = _____

Using the Rollerblade, Inc.'s example in the text, write out your version of a SWOT analysis for Rollerblade.

THE BCG GROWTH SHARE MATRIX

The growth-share matrix helps in evaluating individual SBUs (strategic business units) as if they were separate, independent businesses. They are plotted on a matrix with market growth rate on the vertical axis and relative market share on the horizontal axis. The matrix is divided into four quadrants based on the amount of cash each generates for the firm or requires from it. The quadrants are called:

Cash cows
Stars
Question marks (or problem children)
Dogs

Match the correct BCG quadrant name to the products listed below:

1. Coca-Cola_____
2. Netscape_____
3. Pepsi One_____
4. Gillette Sensor_____
5. Tab_____
6. Kellogg's Frosted Flakes_____
7. IMac_____
8. Windows 98_____

MARKET-PRODUCT FOCUS AND GOAL SETTING

There are four market-product strategies:

Market penetration
Market development
Product development
Diversification

Match the correct product strategy to the statements below:

1. There is no change in product line offered but increased sales are made possible through better advertising, more retail outlets, and/or lower prices._____

2. The sale of existing products to new markets._____

3. This involves developing new products and selling them in new markets._____

4. The product changes, but it is sold to existing markets._____

5. Tide laundry detergent, sold for years in powder form, now is available in liquid laundry detergent.
_____

6. Proctor & Gamble now manufactures diaper products for adults, as well as for babies.
_____

7. White Castle Hamburgers had an ad campaign, "Hamburgers for breakfast? Why not?"
_____

8. Sara Lee Corporation has a division that includes "non-edibles" such as Bali, Hanes, and L'eggs products._____

MARKETING PROGRAM

Using the Rollerblade, Inc.'s example in the text, develop a strategy for each of the elements of the Marketing Mix (examples of items to be considered below):

Product	Price	Promotion	Place
Features	List price	Advertising	Outlets
Accessories	Discounts	Personal selling	Channels
Options	Allowances	Sales promotion	Coverage
Line breadth	Credit terms	Public relations	Transportation
Brand name	Payment period		Stock level
Service			
Warranty			
Returns			

IMPLEMENTATION

Two key elements of the implementation stage are (1) executing the program described in the marketing plan, and (2) designing the marketing organization needed.

There are two main aspects to executing the marketing program:

> Marketing strategies
> Marketing tactics

Which of the following would most likely be a marketing strategy decision and which would be a marketing tactic decision?

1. The best way to reach our target market will be to advertise on country music radio stations._____
_____

2. Select the best country music station in the metropolitan listening area._____

CONTROL

The control phase of the strategic marketing process seeks to keep the marketing program moving in the direction set for it. Accomplishing this requires the marketing manager (1) to compare the results of the marketing program with the goals in the written plans to identify deviations, and (2) to act on these deviations - correcting negative deviations and exploiting positive ones.

The Ocean Spray Cranberries Company has to decide whether to sell its new Mauna La'i Hawaiian Guava Drink nationally or not. The marketing plan target market was older children through older adults with average income and education. Goals were set for both "first trial" and "repeat purchases." Although "first trial" results were good, "repeat purchase" results were not. Research showed that the highest buying group was not the targeted market but upscale buyers (YUPPIES). Research also showed that upscale buyers consumed larger quantities than expected.

Using the information above, demonstrate your knowledge of the control phase of the strategic marketing process. Describe which steps you would take next:

CAN YOU PASS THE TEST?

OVERVIEW OF CHAPTER 2: TERMS AND DEFINITIONS (multiple choice)

1. _____ consists of the steps taken at the product and market levels to allocate marketing resources to viable marketing positions and programs; and involves phases of planning, implementation and control.
   a. Quality
   b. Business unit competency
   c. Strategic marketing process
   d. Marketing tactics
   e. Marketing strategy

2. _____ is a business firm's reward for the risk it undertakes in offering a product for sale.
   a. Market development
   b. Product development
   c. Market penetration
   d. Profit
   e. Market segmentation

3. The difference between the projection of the path to reach a new goal and the projection of the path of the results of a plan already in place is known as_____.
   a. Organization's goals
   b. Diversification
   c. Planning gap
   d. Goal setting
   e. Product development

4. _____ is the process of forming submarket, or market segments, by either aggregating individual potential buyers or subdividing large markets.
   a. Market development
   b. Product development
   c. Market penetration
   d. Profit
   e. Market segmentation

5. An organization that carries on economic activity to earn a profit is called a_____
   a. Benchmarking
   b. Nonprofit organization
   c. Business firm
   d. Organization's business (mission)
   e. Business unit competency

6. An organization's special capabilities, or_____ , result from its personnel, resources, or functional units.
   a. Benchmarking
   b. Nonprofit organization
   c. Business firm
   d. Organization's business (mission)
   e. Business unit competency

7. The ratio of sales revenue of the firm to the total sales revenue of all firms in the industry, including the firm itself is known as _____.
    a. Quality
    b. Market share
    c. Situation analysis
    d. Marketing plan
    e. Strategic marketing process

8. A(n) _____ is a statement about the type of customer an organization wishes to serve, the specific needs of these customers, and the means or technology by which it will serve these needs.
    a. Benchmarking
    b. Nonprofit organization
    c. Business firm
    d. Organization's business (mission)
    e. Business unit competency

9. A nongovernmental organization that serves its customers but does not have profit as an organizational goal is known as a _____.
    a. Benchmarking
    b. Nonprofit organization
    c. Business firm
    d. Organization's business (mission)
    e. Business unit competency

10. The detailed day-to-day operational decisions, or _____, are essential to the overall success of marketing strategies.
    a. Quality
    b. Business unit competency
    c. Strategic marketing process
    d. Marketing tactics
    e. Marketing strategy

11. The means by which a marketing goal is to be achieved, is known as _____, and is characterized by (1) a specified target and (2) a marketing program to reach it.
    a. Quality
    b. Business unit competency
    c. Strategic marketing process
    d. Marketing tactics
    e. Marketing strategy

12. Specific, measurable objectives, also known as the _____, state what the organization seeks to achieve and by which measures it can judge its performance.
    a. Organization's goals
    b. Diversification
    c. Planning gap
    d. Goal setting
    e. Product development

13. Taking stock of where the firm or product has been recently, where it is now, and where it is likely to end up using present plans is included in the _____.
    a. Quality
    b. Market share
    c. Situation analysis
    d. Marketing plan
    e. Strategic management process

14. _____is the setting measurable marketing objectives to be achieved.
    a. Organization's goals
    b. Diversification
    c. Planning gap
    d. Goal setting
    e. Product development

15. The _____ is a written statement that identifies the target market; specific marketing goals such as units sold, sales revenue, and profit; and the budget and timing for the marketing mix elements that make up the marketing program.
    a. Quality
    b. Market share
    c. Situation analysis
    d. Marketing plan
    e. Strategic management process

16. A strategy of selling a new product to existing markets is known as _____.
    a. Market development
    b. Product development
    c. Market penetration
    d. Profit
    e. Market segmentation

17. A strategy of developing new products and selling them in new markets is known as _____.
    a. Organization's goals
    b. Diversification
    c. Planning gap
    d. Goal setting
    e. Product development

18. _____ is a strategy of selling existing products to new target markets.
    a. Market development
    b. Product development
    c. Market penetration
    d. Profit
    e. Market segmentation

19. _____is a strategy of increasing sales of present products in their existing markets.
    a. Market development
    b. Product development
    c. Market penetration
    d. Profit
    e. Market segmentation

20. Discovering how other firms do something better than your firm so it can imitate or leapfrog their technique is called _____.
      a. Benchmarking
      b. Nonprofit organization
      c. Business firm
      d. Organization's business (mission)
      e. Business unit competency

21. _____ includes the totality of features and characteristics of a product and service that bear on its ability to satisfy stated or implied needs.
      a. Quality
      b. Distinctive competency
      c. Strategic marketing process
      d. Marketing tactics
      e. Marketing strategy

22. Under the _____ strategy, a firm may choose to maintain or increase its market share sometimes at the expense of greater profits if industry status or prestige is at stake.
      a. Profit
      b. Sales revenue
      c. Market share
      d. Unit sales
      e. Survival

23. Those following a _____ strategy respond to advocates of corporate responsibility and seek to balance conflicting goals of consumers, employees, and stockholders to promote overall welfare of all these groups, even at the expense of profits
      a. Profit
      b. Sales revenue
      c. Market share
      d. Unit sales
      e. Social responsibility

24. A _____ strategy seeks to achieve as high a financial return on its investment as possible.
      a. Profit
      b. Sales revenue
      c. Market share
      d. Unit sales
      e. Survival

25. Companies choosing a safe action with reasonable payoff instead of one with a large return that may endanger its future follow a _____ strategy.
      a. Profit
      b. Sales revenue
      c. Market share
      d. Unit sales
      e. Survival

26. If profits are acceptable, a firm may elect to maintain or increase its sales level even though profitability may not be maximized. This is an example of a _____ strategy.
      a. Profit
      b. Sales revenue
      c. Market share
      d. Unit sales
      e. Survival

27. Sales revenue may be deceiving because of the effects of inflation; therefore, a firm may choose to maintain or increase the number of units it sells. This is known as a _____ strategy.
   a. Profit
   b. Sales revenue
   c. Market share
   d. Unit sales
   e. Survival

28. The point in the planning process where you segment the market is called the _____.
   a. Control phase
   b. Implementation phase
   c. Marketing program
   d. Goal setting
   e. Situation analysis

29. The point at which you design the marketing organization and execute the marketing program is known as the _____..
   a. Control phase
   b. Implementation phase
   c. Marketing program
   d. Goal setting
   e. Situation analysis

30. The _____ is the point at which you measure results and compare with plans.
   a. Control phase
   b. Implementation phase
   c. Marketing program
   d. Goal setting
   e. Situation analysis

31. The point at which you select the target market is part of the _____.
   a. Control phase
   b. Implementation phase
   c. Marketing program
   d. Goal setting
   e. Situation analysis

32. The point at which you correct negative deviations; exploit positive deviations is known as _____.
   a. Control phase
   b. Implementation phase
   c. Marketing program
   d. Goal setting
   e. Situation analysis

33. The _____ is the point at which you identify alternative marketing opportunities.
   a. Control phase
   b. Implementation phase
   c. Marketing program
   d. Goal setting
   e. Situation analysis

34. The point at which you find out where you have been, where you are now, and where you will be if you stay with existing plans is called the _____.
    a. Control phase
    b. Implementation phase
    c. Marketing program
    d. Goal setting
    e. Situation analysis

35. The point at which you develop the marketing mix is known as _____.
    a. Control phase
    b. Implementation phase
    c. Marketing program
    d. Goal setting
    e. Situation analysis

36. _____ are SBUs with a low share of low-growth markets - they may generate enough cash to sustain themselves, but they do not hold the promise of ever becoming real winners for the firm.
    a. Cash cows
    b. Stars
    c. Question marks
    d. Dogs
    e. Obsolete products

37. SBUs with a high share of high-growth markets that may not generate enough cash to support their own demanding needs for future growth are known as _____.
    a. Cash cows
    b. Stars
    c. Question marks
    d. Dogs
    e. Obsolete products

38. _____ are SBUs that typically generate large amounts of cash, far more than can be invested profitably in their own product line - they have a dominant share of a slow-growth market and provide cash to pay large amounts of company overhead and to invest in other SBUs.
    a. Cash cows
    b. Stars
    c. Question marks
    d. Dogs
    e. Obsolete products

39. SBUs with a low share of high-growth markets - they require large injections of cash just to maintain their market share, much less increase it. Their name implies management's dilemma for these SBUs: finding the right ones to bet on and phasing out the rest are known as _____.
    a. Cash cows
    b. Stars
    c. Question marks
    d. Dogs
    e. Obsolete products

Chapter 2--Answers

Discussion Questions

Strategic Marketing Process

1. planning
2. control
3. implementation
4. implementation
5. planning

Marketing Planning

1. marketing program
2. situation analysis
3. goal setting

Business Mission

1. communication (example)

Situation Analysis

S = strengths
W = weaknesses
O = opportunities
T = threats

The BCG Growth Share Matrix

1. cash cow
2. stars
3. ?
4. stars
5. dogs
6. cash cow
7. ?
8. star

Market-Product Focus and Goal Setting

1. market penetration
2. market development
3. diversification
4. product development
5. product development
6. market development
7. market penetration
8. diversification

Marketing Program

Example:

Product: features
Price: premium
Promotion: advertising
Place: specialty sporting goods outlets

Implementation

1. marketing strategies
2. marketing tactics

Control

Example: Adjust target market to upscale buyers and retest.

Sample Tests

1. c	20. a	39. c
2. d	21. a	
3. c	22. c	
4. e	23. e	
5. c	24. a	
6. e	25. e	
7. b	26. b	
8. d	27. d	
9. b	28. e	
10. d	29. b	
11. e	30. a	
12. a	31. b	
13. c	32. a	
14. d	33. e	
15. d	34. e	
16. b	35. c	
17. b	36. d	
18. a	37. b	
19. c	38. a	

CHAPTER 3

The Changing Marketing Environment

<u>Why is Chapter 3 is important?</u> This chapter illustrates all of the environmental factors which affect the marketing of products. It will show you how changes in the external environment dictate changes in the marketing mix.

Environmental Scanning: The process of continually acquiring information on events occurring outside the organization in order to identify and interpret potential trends.

CHAPTER OUTLINE

I. ENVIRONMENTAL FORCES

    A. Social Forces
        1. Demographics
            a. population size
            b. population growth rate
            c. gender
            d. marital status
            e. education
            f. ethnicity
        2. Culture
            a. values
            b. ideas
            c. attitudes

    B. Economic Forces
        1. Macroeconomic conditions
            a. inflation
            b. recession
         2. Microeconomic conditions
            a. gross consumer income
            b. disposable consumer income
            c. discretionary consumer income

    C. Technological Forces
        1. Impact on customer value
        2. Information technology

    D. Competitive Forces
        1. Types of competition
            a. pure competition
            b. monopolistic competition
            c. oligopoly
            d. monopoly
        2. Components of competition
            a. ease of entry
            b. power of buyers and suppliers
            c. existing competitors and substitutes

E. Regulatory Forces
1. Protecting competition and consumers
2. Self-regulation

You should be able to place these key terms in the outline and be able to discuss them.

baby boomers	consumerism	environmental scanning	restructuring
baby boomlet	culture	Generation X	self-regulation
barriers to entry	demographics	gross income	social forces
blended family	discretionary income	mature household	technology
census metropolitan areas	disposable income	regional marketing	value consciousness
competition	economy	regulation	
Competition Act			

QUESTIONS & PROBLEMS

SOCIAL FORCES

Demographics

Grocery stores have progressed from general stores to Mom-and-Pop neighbourhood stores to giant supermarkets. Now, the trends in grocery stores include operating 24 hours a day, ethnic foods, fresh bakeries, deli's, salad bars and pre-prepared meals, plus delivery, acceptance of credit cards and specialization in exotic or natural foods. Discuss how these changes have been influenced by demographics and what current or future changes could be in store.

Culture

Which of the three cultural influences, changing role of women and men, changing attitudes, or changing values is best demonstrated by the statements below?

1. They purchase almost half of all new cars and over 20 percent of new trucks, spend billion of dollars a year on vehicles for their own use and influence 80 percent of all new car sales._____

2. Nestlé replaces a picture of a woman with that of a man on the label of Taster's Choice decaffeinated coffee._____

3. Del Monte has added a 14-item product line of no-salt vegetables to appeal to the more health-conscious consumer._____

4. Work is seen as a means to an end--recreation, leisure, and entertainment--which has contributed to a growth in sales of products such as videocassette recorders, sports equipment, and easily prepared meals.
_____

ECONOMIC FORCES

Ted Jones earns $36,000 a year and his wife Rebecca earns $30,000 a year. Both are paid monthly and have the following deductions:

Federal taxes	$550
Provincial taxes	$150
Social insurance	$400

Their average monthly bills and expenses:

Rent	$900
Food	$350
Utilities	150
Clothing	100
Medical	50
Insurance	50
Transportation	100
Car payment	350

Using the information above answer the following questions:

1. What is their gross monthly income?_____

2. What is their monthly disposable income?_____

3. What is their monthly discretionary income?_____

4. What percent of their gross income does their discretionary income represent?_____

TECHNOLOGY

What technological development(s) affected the following products?

1. Straight razor_____

2. Slide rule_____

3. 8 Tracks tapes_____

4. Atari Video games_____

5. Vinyl records (LPs)_____

6. Typewriters_____

REGULATORY FORCES

Consumerism is a movement to increase the influence, power, and rights of consumers in their dealings with institutions of all types. This movement was responsible for the creation of many of the laws. Interestingly, much of the momentum for these laws was generated by popular literature (fiction, non-fiction, and speeches). What current regulation of business (proposed regulation) can you name that has been influenced by popular culture?

CAN YOU PASS THE TEST?

OVERVIEW OF CHAPTER 3: TERMS AND DEFINITIONS (multiple choice)

1. The characteristics of the population, its values, and its behaviour in a particular environment are known as _____.
        a. Culture
        b. Demographics
        c. Technology
        d. Regulation
        e. Social forces

2. _____ consists of the laws placed on business with regard to the conduct of its activities.
        a. Culture
        b. Demographics
        c. Technology
        d. Regulation
        e. Self-regulation

3. _____ is the total amount of money earned in one year by a person, family, or household.
        a. Consumerism
        b. Discretionary income
        c. Disposable income
        d. Ecology
        e. Gross income

4. Acquiring information on events occurring outside the company and interpreting potential trends is called _____.
        a. Environmental scanning
        b. Value consciousness
        c. Regional marketing
        d. Barriers to entry
        e. Social forces

5. Distribution of a population, or _____, is based on selected characteristics, such as where people live, their numbers, and who they are in terms of age, gender, income, or occupation.
        a. Culture
        b. Demographics
        c. Technology
        d. Regulation
        e. Self-regulation

6. The over-50 age group in Canada is also known as _____.
        a. Consumers
        b. Demographers
        c. Baby boomlet
        d. Mature households
        e. Generation X

7. _____ are two families from prior marriages merged into a single household as spouses remarry.
     a. Baby boomers
     b. Blended families
     c. Mature households
     d. Generation X
     e. Strategic alliances

8. Business practices or conditions, or _____, make it difficult for a new firm to enter the market.
     a. Environmental scanning
     b. Value consciousness
     c. Regional marketing
     d. Barriers to entry
     e. Social forces

9. The _____ are the generation of children born between 1946 and 1964.
     a. Baby boomers
     b. Blended families
     c. Mature households
     d. Generation X
     e. Strategic alliances

10. The set of alternative firms, known as _____, that could provide a product to satisfy a specific market's needs.
     a. Competition
     b. Outsourcing
     c. Restructuring
     d. Economy
     e. Global competition

11. The set of values, ideas, and attitudes of a homogeneous group of people, that are transmitted from one generation to the next is known as _____.
     a. Culture
     b. Demographics
     c. Technology
     d. Regulation
     e. Self-regulation

12. _____ is the money that remains after taxes and necessities have been paid for.
     a. Consumerism
     b. Discretionary income
     c. Disposable income
     d. Ecology
     e. Gross income

13. An environmental force, known as _____, includes inventions or innovations from applied science or engineering research.
     a. Culture
     b. Demographics
     c. Technology
     d. Regulation
     e. Self-regulation

14. _____ is an industry policing itself rather than relying on government controls.
  a. Culture
  b. Demographics
  c. Technology
  d. Regulation
  e. Self-regulation

15. _____ is the money a consumer has left after taxes to use for food, shelter, and clothing.
  a. Consumerism
  b. Discretionary income
  c. Disposable income
  d. Ecology
  e. Gross income

16. One of the major reasons there is a new look in Canadian corporations is due to: _____.
  a. Capitalism
  b. Internet
  c. Power of buyers
  d. Discretionary income
  e. Taxes

17. A movement, known as _____, has as its goal to increase the influence, power, and rights of consumers in their dealings with institutions.
  a. Consumerism
  b. Discretionary income
  c. Disposable income
  d. Ecology
  e. Gross income

18. _____ are households headed by people over 50.
  a. Baby boomers
  b. Blended families
  c. Mature households
  d. Generation X
  e. Strategic alliances

19. The development of marketing plans to reflect specific area differences in taste preference, perceived needs, or interests is known as _____.
  a. Environmental scanning
  b. Value consciousness
  c. Regional marketing
  d. Barriers to entry
  e. Social forces

20. The income, expenditures, and resources, or _____, affect the cost of running a business and household.
  a. Consumerism
  b. Discretionary income
  c. Disposable income
  d. Economy
  e. Gross income

21. _____ is striving for more efficient corporations that can compete globally by selling off unsatisfactory product lines and divisions, closing down unprofitable plants, and laying off employees.
    a. Competition
    b. Outsourcing
    c. Restructuring
    d. Economy
    e. Global competition

22. Consumer concern, known as _____, means trying to attain the best quality, features, and performance for a given price of a product or service.
    a. Environmental scanning
    b. Value consciousness
    c. Regional marketing
    d. Barriers to entry
    e. Social forces

23. The Internet is changing the structure of many organizations resulting in network organizations or: _____.
    a. Competitive organizations
    b. Outsourcing corporations
    c. Traditional corporations
    d. Economic organizations
    e. E-corporations

24. One approach to corporate restructuring that has become very popular recently is_____.
    a. Environmental scanning
    b. Acquisitions
    c. Regional alliances
    d. Efficiency evaluation
    e. Socialism

25. The label _____ is often given to persons born between 1965 and 1976 (children of baby boomers).
    a. Baby boomers
    b. Blended families
    c. Mature households
    d. Generation X
    e. Strategic alliances

26. More employment in Internet-based businesses is an example of a(n) _____ force.
    a. Social
    b. Economic
    c. Technological
    d. Competitive
    e. Regulatory

27. Increased use of massive computer databases is an example of a(n) _____ force.
    a. Social
    b. Economic
    c. Technological
    d. Competitive
    e. Regulatory

28. Canadian population shifts from rural to urban areas is an example of a(n) _____ force.
    a. Social
    b. Economic
    c. Technological
    d. Competitive
    e. Regulatory

29. More Canadian firms looking to foreign markets is an example of a(n) _____ force.
    a. Social
    b. Economic
    c. Technological
    d. Competitive
    e. Regulatory

30. More protection for Canadian consumers when dealing with corporations is an example of a(n) _____ force.
    a. Social
    b. Economic
    c. Technological
    d. Competitive
    e. Regulatory

31. A decline in real per capita income is an example of a(n) _____ force.
    a. Social
    b. Economic
    c. Technological
    d. Competitive
    e. Regulatory

32. Growing number and importance of older Canadians is an example of a(n) _____ force.
    a. Social
    b. Economic
    c. Technological
    d. Competitive
    e. Regulatory

33. Restructuring of many corporations is an example of a(n) _____ force.
    a. Social
    b. Economic
    c. Technological
    d. Competitive
    e. Regulatory

34. Biotechnology and superconductivity breakthroughs is an example of a(n) _____ force.
    a. Social
    b. Economic
    c. Technological
    d. Competitive
    e. Regulatory

35. Renewed emphasis on self-regulation is an example of a(n) _____ force.
    a. Social
    b. Economic
    c. Technological
    d. Competitive
    e. Regulatory

36. The increased number of Canadian consumers living in census metropolitan areas is an example of _____.
    a. Economic trends
    b. Baby boomers
    c. Canadian family composition
    d. Population shifts
    e. Ethnic diversity

37. Close to 3 out of 10 Canadians are of neither French nor British descent. This is an example of _____.
    a. Economic diversity
    b. Baby boomer growth
    c. Canadian family composition
    d. Population movement
    e. Ethnic diversity

38. The over-50 age group, or mature household is a fast-growing age segment in Canada. This is an example of a _____.
    a. Age waves
    b. Baby boomers and Generation X
    c. Canadian family
    d. Population decline
    e. Ethnic diversity

39. The population of Canada is growing by slightly over 1 percent per year. This represents an example of: _____.
    a. Population growth
    b. Baby boomers and Generation X
    c. Canadian family
    d. Mature households
    e. Ethnic diversity

40. About 50 percent of all marriages now end in divorce. The majority of divorced people eventually remarry, which has given rise to the blended family. This represents an example of: _____.
    a. Population growth
    b. Baby boomers and Generation X
    c. the changing Canadian family
    d. Population shifts
    e. Ethnic diversity

41. Procter & Gamble develops Attends adult-size diapers. This was done in response to a _____.
    a. Population trend
    b. Regional marketing
    c. Canadian family
    d. Population decline
    e. Ethnic diversity

42. Hallmark Cards now has special cards and verses that are designed for stepparents and stepchildren. This was done in response to a _____.
    a. Population trend
    b. Regional marketing
    c. a change in the Canadian family
    d. Population shifts
    e. Ethnic diversity

43. Street signs are being made larger and easier to read. This was done in response to _____.
    a. The greying of Canada
    b. Regional marketing
    c. Canadian family
    d. Gender differences
    e. Ethnic diversity

44. Club Med is now offering special vacation packages for families with children. This was done in response to _____.
    a. Population decline
    b. Regional marketing
    c. a changing Canadian family
    d. Population shifts
    e. Ethnic diversity

45. Campbell's changes the spiciness of its soups depending on where the soups are sold. This was done in response to a _____.
    a. Population trend
    b. Regional marketing
    c. Canadian family
    d. Population shifts
    e. Ethnic diversity

46. One-third of Generation X gets at least some of their political information from comedy shows like Jay Leno, David Letterman, and Mad TV. This is an example of _____.
    a. Population trend
    b. Regional marketing
    c. Canadian family
    d. Population shifts
    e. Ethnic diversity

47. Apartments are designed with two master bedrooms. This was done in response to a _____.
    a. Population trend
    b. Regional marketing
    c. Canadian family
    d. Population shifts
    e. Ethnic diversity

48. An Ontario company opens a distribution centre in British Columbia. This was done in response to a _____.
    a. Population trend
    b. Regional marketing
    c. Canadian family
    d. Population shifts
    e. Ethnic diversity

49. New Minute Rice "Rice-ipies" include dishes such as pork fried rice, fajita rice, and spicy beans and rice. This was done in response to a _____.
    a. Population trend
    b. Regional marketing
    c. Canadian family
    d. Population shifts
    e. Ethnic diversity

50. In Canada, visible minorities represent close to 18 percent of the population. This is an example of _____.
    a. Population growth
    b. Regional marketing
    c. Canadian family
    d. Population shifts
    e. Ethnic diversity

51. Close to 20 percent of the population living in Canadian census metropolitan areas register their native language as something other than English or French. This is an example of _____.
    a. Population growth
    b. Regional marketing
    c. Canadian family
    d. Population shifts
    e. Ethnic diversity

52. MacLean's Magazine carries the same basic articles nationwide, but the cover usually features a more "local" hero. This was done in response to a _____.
    a. Population trend
    b. Regional marketing
    c. Canadian family
    d. Population shifts
    e. Ethnic diversity

For questions 53-56 which form of competition best fits the statements below?

53. The many sellers compete with their products on a substitutable basis and coupons or sales are frequently used marketing tactics.
    a. Pure competition
    b. Monopolistic competition
    c. Oligopoly
    d. Global competition
    e. Monopoly

54. Occurs when only one firm sells the product and marketing plays a small role.
    a. Pure competition
    b. Monopolistic competition
    c. Oligopoly
    d. Global competition
    e. Monopoly

55. Every company has a similar product and distribution is important, but other elements of marketing have little impact.
    a. Pure competition
    b. Monopolistic competition
    c. Oligopoly
    d. Global competition
    e. Monopoly

56. A common industry structure that occurs when a few companies control the majority of industry sales and in which price competition among firms is not desirable.
    a. Pure competition
    b. Monopolistic competition
    c. Oligopoly
    d. Global competition
    e. Monopoly

57. By keying on market niches and "radical" styling, Chrysler has remained a major player in the automobile market. This is an example of _____.
    a. Barriers to entry
    b. Power of buyers
    c. Power of suppliers
    d. Existing competition
    e. Substitutes

58. One company has been able to attract competitors customers by offering substantially lower prices and special services which are attractive to those customers. This is an example of _____.
    a. Barriers to entry
    b. Power of buyers
    c. Power of suppliers
    d. Existing competition
    e. Substitutes

59. Difficulties exist for potential competitors because of capital requirements, advertising expenditures, access to distributors, switching costs, and product identity. This is an example of _____.
    a. Barriers to entry
    b. Power of buyers
    c. Power of suppliers
    d. Existing competition
    e. Substitutes

60. When coffee prices skyrocketed, people began buying more tea and cocoa. This is an example of
_____.
    a. Barriers to entry
    b. Power of buyers
    c. Power of suppliers
    d. Existing competition
    e. Substitutes

Chapter 3--Answers

Discussion Questions

Social Forces--Culture

1. role of men and women
2. changing attitudes
3. changing values
4. changing values

Economic Forces

1. $5500
2. $4400
3. $2350
4. 42.7%

Technology

Example:

1. Straight razor--safety razor (currently like Sensor) or electric razor

Regulatory Forces

Example: telemarketing regulation

Sample Tests

1. e	28. a	55. a
2. d	29. d	56. c
3. e	30. e	57. d
4. a	31. b	58. b
5. b	32. a	59. a
6. d	33. b	60. e
7. b	34. c	
8. d	35. e	
9. a	36. d	
10. a	37. e	
11. a	38. a	
12. b	39. a	
13. c	40. c	
14. e	41. a	
15. c	42. c	
16. b	43. a	
17. a	44. c	
18. c	45. b	
19. c	46. a	
20. d	47. c	
21. c	48. b	
22. b	49. e	
23. e	50. e	
24. b	51. d	
25. d	52. b	
26. c	53. b	
27. c	54. e	

CHAPTER 4

Ethics and Social Responsibility in Marketing

<u>Why is Chapter 4 important</u>? This chapter illustrates the necessity of operating a business in an ethical fashion. It also shows the rewards of exercising social responsibility in the workings of a business enterprise.

Ethics: The moral principles and values that govern the actions and decisions of an individual or group.

CHAPTER OUTLINE

I. NATURE AND SIGNIFICANCE OF MARKETING ETHICS

    A. Ethical/Legal Framework
        1. Ethics
        2. Laws

    B. Current Perceptions of Ethical Behaviour
        1. Dilemma
        2. Reasons for perceptions
            a. increased pressure from diverse value systems
            b. public judgment
            c. increased expectations
            d. ethical business conduct declining

II. UNDERSTANDING ETHICAL MARKETING BEHAVIOUR

    A. Societal Culture and Norms
    B. Business Culture and Industry Practices
        1. Ethics of exchange
            a. caveat emptor
            b. consumer rights
                 i. safety
                ii. be informed
                iii. choice
                iv. be heard
        2. Ethics of competition
            a. industrial espionage
            b. bribes and kickbacks
    C. Corporation Culture and Expectations
        1. code of ethics
        2. ethical behaviour of management and co-workers
    D. Personal Moral Philosophy
        1. moral idealism
        2. utilitarianism

III. SOCIAL RESPONSIBILITY IN MARKETING

    A. Concepts of Social Responsibility
        1. profit responsibility
        2. stakeholder responsibility
        3. societal responsibility
            a. "green" marketing
            b. cause-related marketing

    B. Social Audit
        1. recognition and rationale
        2. identification
        3. determination
        4. specification
        5. evaluation

    C. Consumer Ethics

You should be able to place these key terms in the outline and be able to discuss them.

cause-related marketing	code of ethics	ISO 14000	social responsibility
caveat emptor	ethics	laws	sustainable development
	green marketing	moral idealism	utilitarianism
		social audit	whistleblowers

QUESTIONS & PROBLEMS

ETHICAL/LEGAL FRAMEWORK IN MARKETING

1. What is the key difference between legality and ethically?_____

2. Using examples from your own personal reference, define and explain an action to fit in each of the quadrants of the ethical-legal continuum._____

CURRENT STATUS OF ETHICAL BEHAVIOUR

List four possible reasons and cite examples of why the state of perceived ethical business conduct is at its present level.

1._____

2._____

3._____

4._____

ETHICS OF EXCHANGE

Consumers have four basic rights when dealing with businesses and institutions:

      The right to safety
      The right to be informed
      The right to choose
      The right to be heard

Match the correct right to the example or statement below:

_____   1.   A medical device company markets a product that it knows is potentially dangerous to some patients.

_____   2.   A supermarket refuses to stock a new product that consumers are demanding.

_____   3.   Customers have a complaint about a new snowboard but the company that produces it refuses to answer the customers' letters or return customers' telephone calls.

_____   4.   An investment firm sells a new mutual fund but does not provide all the necessary that a customer would need to make a judgment about the risks involved.

ETHICS OF COMPETITION

Two kinds of unethical behaviours among competitors are most common: industrial espionage and bribery.

1. Many companies regularly buy their competitors products or ask there customers to buy them so they can test and evaluate the products. In a slightly different version, a employee of a competitor will pose as a potential customer to receive literature and other sales information. A major consumer products company monitors the test markets of its largest competitor and rolls national with the product months before the competitor without doing test marketing of their own. Are these examples ethical? How can you ethically get information on your competitors?_____

_____

_____

2. General Motors charged Volkswagen of hiring away one of its top executives and receiving privileged information he had taken with him? A regional bank had spent 18 months and several million dollars planning a new product when their executive vice president in charge of the product development left, taking the information to a major competitor which introduced the product first. How do you protect yourself against this type of industrial espionage?_____

_____

_____

3. Foreign makers of defense related material regularly bribe government officials in third world countries to sell their products. How do you compete against this type of competition?_____

_____

_____

PERSONAL MORAL PHILOSOPHY AND ETHICAL BEHAVIOUR

Ultimately, ethical choices are based on the moral philosophy of the decision maker.
Moral philosophy consists of two major types:

Moral idealism
Utilitarianism

Match the correct moral philosophy to the example or statement below:

_____1. In 1991 there was a major controversy over the drug Prozac. In some cases there were reports of extremely dangerous side effects. However, the company did not withdraw the drug because of the extremely effective job it did with most patients.

_____2. This philosophy is favoured by consumer advocates.

_____3. This philosophy is favoured by moral philosophers.

_____4. When several people died as the result of the tampering of a handful of Tylenol bottles, literally millions of bottles were withdrawn from shelves to avoid even the slightest risk of endangering anyone else.

_____5. This philosophy considers certain individual rights or duties to be universal .

_____6. A personal moral philosophy which focuses on "the greatest good for the greatest number."

SOCIAL AUDIT

A social audit is a systematic assessment of a firm's objectives, strategies, and performance in the domain of social responsibility.

List the five basic steps in a social audit:

1._____.

2._____

3._____

4._____

5._____

SOCIETAL RESPONSIBILITY

Two aspects of societal marketing include:

Green marketing
Cause-related marketing

Match the correct term to the definition or statement below:

_____1. Oxydol laundry detergent now comes in a highly concentrated form in order to reduce waste in packaging.

_____2. Every time you buy Daily's frozen yogourt pops money is donated to save the penguins.

_____3. Tying the charitable contributions of a firm directly to the customer revenues produced through the promotion of one of its products

_____4. Marketing efforts to produce, promote, and redeem environmentally sensitive products

CONSUMER ETHICS AND SOCIAL RESPONSIBILITY

1. There is a practice which many retailers are familiar with but seldom do very much about. A consumer will come into a store and ask to take an expensive evening outfit out on approval or will actually buy it. After wearing to the "event," it will be returned as "unacceptable." The store is then stuck with a garment which has been worn. The store usually does nothing about this because the consumer is a good customer throughout the year. How would you handle this situation?_____
_____

2. Some consumers will shop establishments for deals for new customers. An example would be a free cellular phone and one month's with the sign-up for service of one year. Shortly after they get the free phone, they cancel the service saying they are moving and repeat the process with another company. Most times they end up with the phone and the first month's service. How should this be handled?_____
_____
_____

CAN YOU PASS THE TEST?

OVERVIEW OF CHAPTER 4: TERMS AND DEFINITIONS (multiple choice)

1. Tying the charitable contributions of a firm directly to the customer revenues produced through the promotion of one of its products is called _____.
   - a. cause-related marketing
   - b. green marketing
   - c. Code of Ethics
   - d. consumer rights
   - e. promotional marketing

2. The Latin term, _____, means "let the buyer beware."
   - a. caveat emptor
   - b. laws
   - c. moral idealism
   - d. utilitarianism
   - e. ethics

3. _____ are marketing efforts to produce, promote, and reclaim environmental products .
   - a. cause-related marketing
   - b. green marketing
   - c. Code of Ethics
   - d. consumer rights
   - e. promotional marketing

4. _____ are society's values and standards that are enforceable in the courts.
   - a. caveat emptor
   - b. laws
   - c. moral idealism
   - d. utilitarianism
   - e. ethics

5. A formal statement of ethical principles and rules of conduct is the company's _____.
   - a. cause-related marketing
   - b. green marketing
   - c. Code of Ethics
   - d. consumer rights
   - e. practice rights

6. A personal moral philosophy that considers individual rights or duties as universal regardless of the outcome is known as _____.
   - a. caveat emptor
   - b. laws
   - c. moral idealism
   - d. utilitarianism
   - e. ethics

7. The clandestine collection of trade secrets or proprietary information about a company's competitors.
  a. cause-related marketing
  b. green marketing
  c. competitive intelligence
  d. kickbacks
  e. industrial espionage

8. _____ are the moral principles and values that govern the actions and decisions of an individual or group.
  a. caveat emptor
  b. laws
  c. moral idealism
  d. utilitarianism
  e. ethics

9. The rights of consumers in the exchange process including the right to safety, to be informed, to choose, and to be heard are called _____.
  a. cause-related marketing
  b. green marketing
  c. Code of Ethics
  d. consumer rights
  e. consumer ethics

10. A _____ is a systematic assessment of a firm's objectives, strategies, and performance in the domain of social responsibility.
  a. cause-related marketing
  b. green marketing
  c. values and principles
  d. social responsibility
  e. social audit

11. The idea that organizations are part of a larger society and are accountable to society for their actions is called _____.
  a. cause-related marketing
  b. green marketing
  c. values and principles
  d. social responsibility
  e. social audit

12 A personal moral philosophy that focuses on the "greatest good for the greatest number" by assessing the costs and benefits of the consequences of ethical behaviour is known as _____.
  a. caveat emptor
  b. laws
  c. moral idealism
  d. utilitarianism
  e. ethics

13. A brokerage firm does not disclose all the information about the past performance of its mutual funds, only the best years performance. This violates your right to:
    a. cause-related marketing
    b. choose
    c. be informed
    d. be heard
    e. social auditing

14. Many insurance companies were specifying to auto repair shops that they should use "nongenuine" parts, when possible, to lower costs. Most car owners were not made aware that genuine replacement parts had not been used. This is an example of violating the consumer's _____.
    a. right to safety
    b. right to be informed
    c. right to choose
    d. right to be heard
    e. right to be ignored

15. A number of small towns have developed "master plans" stating their goals and wishes for future growth. New building permits must be consistent with these plans. This would be considered part of _____.
    a. The right to safety
    b. The right to be informed
    c. The right to choose
    d. The right to be heard
    e. The right to be ignored

16. _____ was evident when over 600,000 baby pacifiers were recalled when it was discovered the plastic guard and nipple separated under stress.
    a. The right to safety
    b. The right to be informed
    c. The right to choose
    d. The right to be heard
    e. The right to be ignored

17. A small bottler of real-fruit carbonated beverages could not pay the "slotting" fee to have his product access shelf space at a major grocery chain. As a result, the only place customers can find his product is at a local health food store. He is considering entering a lawsuit questioning the legality of slotting allowances. This is an example of _____.
    a. The right to safety
    b. The right to be informed
    c. The right to choose
    d. The right to be heard
    e. The right to be ignored

For questions 18-31, choose the element of the marketing mix affected by these ethical situations:

18. Not manipulating the availability of a product for purpose of exploitation
    a. Product development and management
    b. Promotion
    c. Distribution
    d. Pricing

19. Avoidance of false and misleading advertising
    a. Product development and management
    b. Promotion
    c. Distribution
    d. Pricing

20. Prohibiting selling or fund raising under the guise of conducting research
    a. Product development and management
    b. Promotion
    c. Distribution
    d. Pricing

21. Disclosing the full price associated with any purchase
    a. Product development and management
    b. Promotion
    c. Distribution
    d. Pricing

22. Disclosure of all substantial risks associated with product or service usage
    a. Product development and management
    b. Promotion
    c. Distribution
    d. Pricing

23. Not exerting undo influence over the reseller's choice to handle the product
    a. Product development and management
    b. Promotion
    c. Distribution
    d. Pricing

24. Identification of extra-cost added features
    a. Product development and management
    b. Promotion
    c. Distribution
    d. Pricing

25. Identification of any product component substitution that might materially change the product or impact on the buyer's purchase decision
    a. Product development and management
    b. Promotion
    c. Distribution
    d. Pricing

26. Treating outside clients and suppliers fairly
    a. Product development and management
    b. Promotion
    c. Distribution
    d. Pricing

27. Not practicing predatory pricing
    a. Product development and management
    b. Promotion
    c. Distribution
    d. Pricing

28. Rejection of high pressure manipulation or misleading sales tactics
    a. Product development and management
    b. Promotion
    c. Distribution
    d. Pricing

29. Not using coercion in the marketing channel
    a. Product development and management
    b. Promotion
    c. Distribution
    d. Pricing

30. Maintaining research integrity by avoiding misrepresentation and omission of pertinent research data
    a. Product development and management
    b. Promotion
    c. Distribution
    d. Marketing research

31. Avoidance of sales promotions that use deception or manipulation
    a. Product development and management
    b. Promotion
    c. Distribution
    d. Pricing

32. Obligations that organizations have to (1) the preservation of the ecological environment, and (2) the general public are known as _____
    a. profit responsibility
    b. stakeholder responsibility
    c. societal responsibility
    d. personal responsibility
    e. marketing responsibility

33. _____ states that companies have a simple duty, to maximize profits for its owners or stockholders.
    a. profit responsibility
    b. stakeholder responsibility
    c. societal responsibility
    d. personal responsibility
    e. marketing responsibility

34. _____ are the obligations an organization has to those who can affect achievement of its objectives.
    a. profit responsibility
    b. stakeholder responsibility
    c. societal responsibility
    d. personal responsibility
    e. marketing responsibility

35. Several companies involved in strip mining have begun to fill in mined sites, plant trees, and turn the sites into parks. This is an example of _____.
      a. profit responsibility
      b. stakeholder responsibility
      c. societal responsibility
      d. personal responsibility
      e. marketing responsibility

36. A number of residents in a small town complained about the mural on the outside of a skateboard shop. However, since none of the people airing their complaints were store patrons, the mural was left in place. This is an example of _____.
      a. profit responsibility
      b. stakeholder responsibility
      c. societal responsibility
      d. personal responsibility
      e. marketing responsibility

37. Because of a glut in the sugar market, a candy manufacturer was able to buy sugar for ten percent less than normal. The savings could have been passed on to the customer, but management felt that the cost savings outweighed any additional profits that would be made from increased sales. Management's position would best exemplify _____.
      a. profit responsibility
      b. stakeholder responsibility
      c. societal responsibility
      d. personal responsibility
      e. marketing responsibility

38. The _____ includes the shared values, beliefs, and purpose of employees that affect individual and group behaviours.
      a. business culture
      b. corporate culture
      c. societal culture
      d. marketing culture
      e. personal culture

39. The effective rules of the game, the boundaries between competitive and unethical behavior, [and] the codes of conduct in business dealings are part of the _____.
      a. business culture
      b. corporate culture
      c. societal culture
      d. marketing culture
      e. personal culture

40. An insurance company vetoed the acquisition of a tobacco company, even though it could have been highly profitable, because the employees believed the acquisition to be in conflict with the company's basic philosophy. This is an example of _____.
      a. business culture
      b. corporate culture
      c. societal culture
      d. marketing culture
      e. personal culture

41. The _____ affects ethical conduct both in the exchange relationships between sellers and buyers and in the competitive behaviour among sellers.
    a. business culture
    b. corporate culture
    c. societal culture
    d. marketing culture
    e. personal culture

42. _____ can be demonstrated in terms of dress, sayings, manner of work, and expectations of ethical actions of top management and coworkers.
    a. business culture
    b. corporate culture
    c. societal culture
    d. marketing culture
    e. personal culture

Chapter 4--Answers

Discussion Questions

Ethical/Legal Framework in Marketing

1. Legality is required by law and ethically is required by consumers.

Current Status of Ethical Behaviour

1. Increased pressure for diverse value systems
2. Public judgment
3. Increased expectations
4. Ethical business conduct declining

Ethics of Exchange

1. safety
2. choice
3. heard
4. informed

Ethics of Competition

1. Yes, these are ethical and utilized frequently.
2. Employment contracts are the most common protection.
3. High quality products with superior performance.

Personal Moral Philosophy and Ethical Behaviour

1. utilitarianism
2. moral idealism
3. moral idealism
4. moral idealism
5. utilitarianism
6. utilitarianism

Social Audit

1. recognition and rationale
2. identification
3. determination
4. specification
5. evaluation

Societal Responsibility

1. green marketing
2. cause-related marketing
3. cause-related marketing
4. green marketing

Consumer Ethics and Social Responsibility

1. Possibly develop a rental section of your formal wear.

2. Monitor and require deposit that is returned at the end of trial contract.

Sample Tests

1. a		28. b	
2. a		29. c	
3. b		30. d	
4. b		31. b	
5. c		32. c	
6. c		33. a	
7. e		34. b	
8. e		35. c	
9. d		36. d	
10. e		37. a	
11. d		38. b	
12. d		39. a	
13. c		40. b	
14. b		41. a	
15. d		42. b	
16. a			
17. c			
18. c			
19. b			
20. e			
21. d			
22. a			
23. c			
24. d			
25. b			
26. a			
27. d			

CHAPTER 5

Global Marketing And World Trade

<u>Why is Chapter 5 important</u>? Marketing worldwide involves environmental scanning to learn the culture, geography, and, perhaps more importantly, the history of a country. Adapting the marketing mix for the global market is the challenge of today's corporations.

Global Marketing Strategy: The practice of standardizing marketing activities when there are cultural similarities and adapting them when cultures differ.

CHAPTER OUTLINE

I. DYNAMICS OF WORLD TRADE

    A. World Trade Flows
        1. Global perspective
        2. Canadian perspective

    B. Competitive Advantage of Nations
        1. Factor conditions
        2. Demand conditions
        3. Related and supporting industries
        4. Company strategy, structure, and rivalry

II. EMERGENCE OF A BORDERLESS ECONOMIC WORLD

    A. Decline of Economic Protectionism
        1. Tariffs
        2. Quotas

    B. Rise of Economic Integration
        1. European Union
        2. North American Free Trade Agreement
        3. Asian free trade agreements

    C. Global Competition among Global Companies for Global Consumers
        1. Global competition
        2. Global companies
            a. international firms
            b. multinational firms
            c. transnational firms
        3. Global consumers

III. A GLOBAL ENVIRONMENTAL SCAN

    A. Cultural Diversity
        1. Values
        2. Customs
        3. Cultural symbols
        4. Language

        5. Cultural ethnocentricity
        6. Cultural change

    B. Economic Considerations
        1. Stage of economical development
            a. developed countries
            b. developing countries
        2. Economic infrastructure
        3. Consumer income and purchasing power
        4. Currency exchange rate

    C. Political-Regulatory Climate
        1. Political stability
        2. Trade regulations
        3. Trade incentives

IV. GLOBAL MARKET ENTRY STRATEGIES

    A. Exporting
        1. Indirect exporting
        2. Direct exporting
        3. Franchising

    B. Licensing
        1. Local manufacturing
        2. Local assembly

    C. Joint Ventures

    D. Direct Investment

V. CRAFTING A WORLDWIDE MARKETING EFFORT

    A. Product and Promotion Strategies
        1. Product extension
        2. Product adaptation
        3. Product invention

    B. Distribution Strategy

    C. Pricing Strategy
        1. Dumping
        2. Grey market

You should be able to place these key terms in the outline and be able to discuss them.

back translation	customs	global marketing strategy	quota
balance of trade	direct investment	grey market	semiotics
consumer ethnocentrism	dumping	gross domestic product	strategic alliances
countertrade	economic infrastructure	ISO 9000	tariffs
cross-cultural analysis	exporting	joint venture	trade feedback effect
cultural symbols	global competition	multidomestic marketing	values
currency exchange rate	global consumers	protectionism	World Trade Organization

QUESTIONS & PROBLEMS

WORLD TRADE FLOWS

Answer the following questions concerning world trade flows:

All nations and regions of the world do not participate equally in world trade.

1. What percentage of world trade involves services?_____

2. What percentage of world trade involves countertrade?_____

3. Is the trade feedback effect an argument for or against free trade among nations? Why?_____
_____

4. Canada exports over _____ percent of its gross domestic product.

5. Under which conditions does a country have a surplus in their balance of trade, and under which conditions does a country have a deficit in their balance of trade?_____

6. Who are the three largest importers of Canadian goods and services? _____

7. Canada's gross domestic product is valued at? _____

COMPETITIVE ADVANTAGE OF NATIONS

Professor Michael Porter suggests a "diamond" to explain a nation's competitive advantage and why some industries and firms become world leaders. He identified four key factors:

Factor conditions
Demand conditions
Related and supporting industries
Company strategy, structure, and rivalry

Match the correct factor with the examples listed below:

1. These factors include the conditions governing the way a nation's businesses are organized and managed, along with the intensity of domestic competition._____

2. Firms and industries seeking leadership in global markets need clusters of world-class suppliers that accelerate innovation._____

3. These include both the number and sophistication of domestic customers for an industry's product.
_____

4. These reflect a nation's ability to turn its natural resources, education, and infrastructure into a competitive advantage._____

5. The Dutch lead the world in cut flowers because of their research in cultivation, packaging, and shipping._____

6. The Italian shoe industry has become the world leader because of intense domestic competition that enhances quality and innovation._____

7. Japan's sophisticated consumers demand quality in their TVs and radios, thereby making Japan's producers the world leaders in the electronics industry._____

8. The German leadership in printing relates directly to the cluster of supporting German suppliers.
_____

EMERGENCE OF A BORDERLESS ECONOMIC WORLD

Answer the following questions:

1. What three challenges need response in the global marketplace?
_____
_____
_____

2. What is the difference between a tariff and a quota?_____

3. What does WTO stand for and why is it important?_____
_____

4. What does NAFTA stand for and why is it important?_____
_____

5. What is ISO 9000 and why is it important?_____
_____

Two other important factors when doing a cross-culture analysis are semiotics (the correspondence between symbols and their role in the assignment of meaning for people) and back translation (where a word or phrase is retranslated into the original language by a different interpreter to catch errors). Very often companies don't even know that there are questions about symbols, customs, values, or language to be asked.

Two other factors cultural ethnocentricity (the belief that aspects of one's culture are superior to another's) and consumer ethnocentricity (the tendency to believe that it is inappropriate, indeed immoral, to purchase foreign-made products) greatly inhibit global marketing.

CULTURAL DIVERSITY

A thorough cross-cultural analysis involves an understanding of and appreciation for the values, customs, symbols, and language of other societies.

Values
Customs
Cultural symbols
Language

Match the correct term to the appropriate example below:

1. In Japan, women give men chocolates for Valentine's Day._____

2. A door-to-door salesman would have difficulty in Italy because it is improper for a man to call on a woman if she is home alone._____

3. Canadians are superstitious about the number 13. Many hotels don't have a thirteenth floor.
_____

4. The brandname "Vicks," an American vapo-rub, means "sexual intimacy" in German; the name was changed to "Wicks."_____

ECONOMIC CONSIDERATIONS

Economic considerations important to marketers include:

Stage of economic development
Economic infrastructure
Consumer income and purchasing power
Currency exchange rate

Identify which consideration would be most important for the following countries:

1. Russia_____
2. Bosnia_____
3. Haiti_____
4. Uganda_____

GLOBAL MARKET ENTRY STRATEGIES

Companies utilize four strategies to enter the international marketplace. They are:

Exporting
Licensing
Joint Ventures
Direct investment

Identify which strategy would be best to use in the following situations:

1. A company receives a request for its product from a foreign retailer._____

2. General Electric buys a Hungarian lighting company._____

3. Paul Mueller Company, a producer of stainless steel dairy and brewery equipment, opens up the Dutch market but finds it necessary to manufacture there._____

4. A software firm with cash flow problems receives a request from Bull, the French computer manufacturer, to utilize their new software package._____

CRAFTING A WORLDWIDE MARKETING EFFORT

Strategies for bringing products to the worldwide marketplace include:

Product extension
Product adaptation
Product invention

Which of the strategies would be best in the following situation?

1. McDonald's entering the Australian market._____

2. Campbell Soups discovers that the English market has no knowledge of "condensed" soups.

_____

3. Saturn has to make right-hand drive cars for the Japanese market._____

CAN YOU PASS THE TEST?

OVERVIEW OF CHAPTER 5: TERMS AND DEFINITIONS (multiple choice)

1. The practice of shielding one or more sectors of a country's economy from foreign competition through the use of tariffs or quotas is known as _____.
   a. Consumer ethnocentrism
   b. Protectionism
   c. Countertrade
   d. Cross-cultural analysis
   e. Cultural ethnocentricity

2. In international marketing, _____ are a government tax on goods or services entering a country.
   a. Quota
   b. Semiotics
   c. World Trade Organization (WTO)
   d. Balance of trade
   e. Tariffs

3. A country's imports affect its exports and exports affect imports. This relationship is _____.
   a. Back translation
   b. Cultural symbols
   c. Trade feedback effect
   d. Customs
   e. Values

4. _____ is the monetary value of all goods and services produced in a country during one year.
   a. Quota
   b. Semiotics
   c. World Trade Organization (WTO)
   d. Balance of trade
   e. Gross domestic product

5. In international marketing, a restriction placed on the amount of a product allowed to enter or leave a country is known as _____.
   a. Quota
   b. Semiotics
   c. World Trade Organization (WTO)
   d. Balance of trade
   e. Gross domestic product

6. _____ are things that represent ideas and concepts.
   a. Back translation
   b. Cultural symbols
   c. Trade feedback effect
   d. Customs
   e. Values

7. _____ is the field of study which examines the correspondence between symbols and their role in the assignment of meaning for people.
   a. Quota
   b. Semiotics
   c. World Trade Organization (WTO)
   d. Balance of trade
   e. Gross domestic product

8. The practice of retranslating a word or phrase into the original language by a different interpreter to catch errors is known as _____.
   a. Back translation
   b. Cultural symbols
   c. Trade feedback effect
   d. Customs
   e. Values

9. _____ is the belief that aspects of one's culture are superior to another's.
   a. Consumer ethnocentrism
   b. Protectionism
   c. Countertrade
   d. Cross-cultural analysis
   e. Cultural ethnocentricity

10. _____ is the tendency to believe that it is inappropriate, indeed immoral, to purchase foreign-made products.
   a. Consumer ethnocentrism
   b. Protectionism
   c. Countertrade
   d. Cross-cultural analysis
   e. Cultural ethnocentricity

11. Using barter rather than money in making international sales is called _____.
   a. Consumer ethnocentrism
   b. Protectionism
   c. Countertrade
   d. Cross-cultural analysis
   e. Cultural ethnocentricity

12. _____ are the norms and expectations about the way people do something in a specific country.
   a. Back translation
   b. Cultural symbols
   c. Trade feedback effect
   d. Customs
   e. Values

13. _____ is the international trade organization intended to address a broad array of world trade issues including disputes.
   a. Quota
   b. Semiotics
   c. World Trade Organization (WTO)
   d. Balance of trade
   e. Gross domestic product

14. _____ is the study of similarities and differences between consumers in two or more nations or societies.
      a. Consumer ethnocentrism
      b. Protectionism
      c. Countertrade
      d. Cross-cultural analysis
      e. Cultural ethnocentricity

15. Personally or socially preferable modes of conduct or states of existence that are enduring are known as _____.
      a. Consumer ethnocentrism
      b. Values
      c. Countertrade
      d. Cross-cultural analysis
      e. Cultural ethnocentricity

16. _____ is the difference between the monetary value of a nation's exports and imports .
      a. Quota
      b. Semiotics
      c. World Trade Organization (WTO)
      d. Balance of trade
      e. Gross domestic product

Chapter 5--Answers

Discussion Questions

World Trade Flows

1. 25%
2. 20%
3. For. Because exports create higher incomes which create more demand for imports
4. 35%
5. When the monetary value of exports exceeds the monetary value of imports. The reverse, an excess of monetary value of imports over exports, yields a deficit balance of trade.
6. U.S.A., Japan, EU
7. $900 billion

Competitive Advantage of Nations

1. factor conditions
2. related and supporting industries
3. demand conditions
4. factor conditions
5. related and supporting industries
6. company strategy, structure, and rivalry
7. demand conditions
8. related and supporting industries

Emergence of a Borderless Economic World

1. gradual decline of economic protectionism
   formal economic integration and free trade among nations
   global competition among global companies for global customers
2. tariff--tax on imports
   quota--restrictions on amounts of imports allowed
3. World Trade Organization--successor to the GATT agreements that focuses on settled trade disputes
4. North American Free Trade Agreement--it brings the US, Canada, and Mexico into a one market trade area
5. the European Union's quality standards which require registration and certification of a company's quality management and quality assurance system.

Cultural Diversity

1. customs
2. values
3. cultural symbols
4. language

Economic Considerations

1. currency
2. economic infrastructure
3. consumer income and purchasing power
4. stage of economic development

Global Market Entry Strategies

1. exporting
2. direct investment
3. joint ventures
4. licensing

Crafting a Worldwide Marketing Effort

1. product extension
2. product invention
3. product adaptation

Sample Tests

1. b
2. e
3. c
4. e
5. a
6. b
7. b
8. a
9. e
10. a
11. c
12. d
13. c
14. d
15. b
16. d

CHAPTER 6

Consumer Behaviour

<u>Why is Chapter 6 important</u>? This chapter illustrates why consumers buy. Understanding consumer behaviour is vital to the successful implementation of the marketing mix. This chapter outlines the consumer decision process and shows how the marketing mix can relate to each step. It also shows the external and internal influences on that buying process and how they can be influenced.

Consumer Behaviour: The actions a person takes in purchasing and using products and services, including the mental and social processes that precede and follow these actions.

CHAPTER OUTLINE

I. CONSUMER PURCHASE DECISION PROCESS

    A. Problem Recognition

    B. Information Search
        1. Internal sources
            a. knowledge
            b. experience
        2. External information
            a. personal sources
            b. public sources
            c. market-dominated sources

    C. Alternative Evaluation
        1. Suggesting criteria to use for purchase
        2. Develop "evoked set" of brand names meeting criteria
        3. Develop consumer value perceptions

    D. Purchase Decision
        1. From whom to buy
        2. When to buy

    E. Postpurchase Behaviour

    F. Involvement and Problem Solving Variation
        1. High involvement
            a. expensive
            b. can have serious personal consequence
            c. could reflect on one's social image
        2. Low involvement
        3. Routine problem solving
        4. Limited problem solving
        5. Extended problem solving
    G. Situational Influences
        1. Purchase task
        2. Social surroundings
        3. Physical surroundings

        4. Temporal effects
        5. Antecedent states

II. PSYCHOLOGICAL INFLUENCES

    A. Motivation
        1. Physiological needs
        2. Safety needs
        3. Social needs
        4. Personal needs
        5. Self-actualization needs

    B. Personality

    C. Perception
        1. Selective perception
            a.   selective exposure
            b.   selective attention
            c.   selective comprehension
            d.   selective retention
        2. Perceived risk

    D. Learning
        1. Behavioural learning
            a. drive
            b. response
            c. reinforcement
            d. stimulus generalization
            e. stimulus discrimination
        2. Cognitive Learning
        3. Brand Loyalty

III. VALUES, BELIEFS AND ATTITUDES

    A. Values
    B. Beliefs
    C. Attitudes
    D. Lifestyle

IV. SOCIO-CULTURAL INFLUENCES

    A. Personal Influences
        1. Opinion leadership
        2. Word of mouth

    B. Reference Groups
        1. Membership group
        2. Aspiration group
        3. Dissociative group

    C. Family Influences
        1 Consumer socialization
        2. Family Life Cycle
        3. Family decision making

      a. information gatherer
      b. influencer
      c. decision maker
      d. purchaser
      e. user

D. Social Class

E. Culture and Subculture
    1. French Canadian
    2. Acadian
    3. Chinese Canadian

You should be able to place these key terms in the outline and be able to discuss them.

attitude	evaluative criteria	motivation	reference groups
beliefs	evoked set	national character	self-concept
brand loyalty	family life cycle	opinion leaders	situational influences
cognitive dissonance	involvement	personality	social class
computer-mediated buying		perceived risk	subcultures
consumer behaviour	learning	perception	subliminal perception
consumer socialization	lifestyle	purchase decision process	word of mouth

QUESTIONS & PROBLEMS

PROBLEM RECOGNITION

Problem recognition, the initial step in the purchase decision, is perceiving a difference between a person's ideal and actual situations big enough to trigger a decision. There are many ways a marketer can "activate" a consumer's decision process.

Discuss how problem recognition occurs (and which ones are aided by the marketer) for each of the following:

1. Gasoline_____

2. A new Mustang convertible_____

3. A birthday card_____

4. Lunch at Burger King_____

5. A Broadway play_____

6. A new Visa card_____

INFORMATION SEARCH

The information search stage clarifies the problem for the consumer by (1) suggesting criteria to use for the purchase, (2) yielding brand names that might meet the criteria, and (3) developing consumer value perceptions .

An information search can be internal (personal experience), or external (personal sources, public sources or marketer-dominated sources).

1. If you were looking for a fun time in Montreal, including meals, nightlife, and hotels plus shopping and sightseeing, trace your information search, both internal and external. Did it yield a criteria for selection and a list of items meeting that criteria?_____
_____
_____

2. Repeat the above exercise for buying a long distance service._____
_____
_____

ALTERNATIVE EVALUATION

Complete the following exercise for each of the following items:

coffee
personal computer
restaurant (evening meal)
running shoes
college

1. Select criteria to be used for the purchases (evaluative criteria):_____
_____

2. Select brands that might meet your criteria (evoked set):_____
_____

3. Develop consumer value perceptions; decide where and when to buy:_____
_____

4. Evaluate (hypothetically) your decision (How would you do this?):_____
_____

5. In what ways could the company manufacturer reduce your cognitive dissonance?_____
_____

PURCHASE DECISION

During the purchase decision, "two choices remain: (1) from whom to buy and (2) when to buy. These two issues can be affected by many factors, whether your preferred brand is on sale, whether you've just won the lottery, whether you're making a purchase in the company of a friend, whether the sales staff is rude, etc..

Think of the last time you purchased CD, a computer (or other major purchase), and airline ticket. Discuss what influenced your decision of when to buy and from whom to buy?_____
_____
_____

POST PURCHASE BEHAVIOUR

After buying a product, the consumer compares it with his or her expectations and is either satisfied or dissatisfied. If the consumer is dissatisfied, marketers must decide whether the product was deficient or if consumer expectations were too high.

List three ways each of these types of marketers can attempt to reduce cognitive dissonance in the postpurchase stage:

1. Automobile dealer_____

2. Expensive restaurant_____

3. Hotel_____

4. Clothing store_____

5. University_____

INVOLVEMENT

Involvement refers to "... the personal, social, and economic significance of the purchase to the consumer."

Discuss the difference, in terms of personal, social, and economic significance, the amount of involvement in buying gas for your car, purchasing T-shirt and selecting a college to attend.

SITUATIONAL INFLUENCES: MOTIVATION

Motivation is the energizing force that causes the behaviour that satisfies a need. There are five need classes:

physiological
safety
social
personal
self-actualization

Which needs do the following products meet?

1. LA Gear apparel_____

2. Dr. Pepper_____

3. First Alert smoke detectors_____

4. milk_____

5. Ph.D._____

PERCEPTION

There are four stages of selective perception:

Selective exposure
Selective attention
Selective comprehension
Selective retention

Match the type of selective perception with the statements below:

_____1. Consumers do not remember all the information they see, read, or hear.

_____2. Consumers pay attention to messages that are consistent with their attitudes and beliefs and ignore messages that are inconsistent.

_____3. The ad said something about a warranty, but I'm not sure if they said they had one or didn't have one.

_____4. The consumer interprets information so it is consistent with her attitudes or beliefs.

_____5. People thought Toro's SnowPup was a toy or too lightweight to do snow blowing even though it could do the job.

_____6. I watch programs on CTV but not on CBC.

LEARNING

Learning refers to those behaviours which result from repeated experience and thinking. Five variables are linked to learning:

Drive
Response
Reinforcement
Stimulus generalization
Stimulus discrimination

Match the learning variable to the correct statement:

_____ A person fires up the grill and throws on a steak.

_____ A person is hungry.

_____ A person slices into a thick, juicy, rare steak, eats it, and smiles.

_____ Weight Watchers, in addition to having a well-known weight loss program, also distributes a line of frozen foods, desserts, and cookbooks.

_____ Trident gum used an advertising slogan, "... the ONLY gum my mom lets me chew."

VALUES, BELIEFS, AND ATTITUDES

An attitude is a "learned" predisposition to respond to an object or class of objects in a consistently favourable or unfavourable way. Beliefs are a consumer's subjective perception of how well a product or brand performs on different attributes. Personal values affect attitudes by influencing the importance assigned to specific product attributes.

Match the correct term to the statements listed below:

_____1. My mother always said Hellman's was the smoothest mayonnaise.

_____2. Reliability, not style, is the most important function of a good watch.

_____3. All female doctors are more caring.

LIFESTYLE

According to Goldfarb Consultants, adult Canadians can be classified into six segments (Goldfarb Segments):

Structured
Discontented
Fearful
Resentful
Assured
Caring

Match the segment with its description below:

1. Not likely to describe themselves as happy with family, friends, or work. _____

2. Family is top priority, value relationships; and give back to society. _____

3. Leading edge group, self-confident and self-oriented. _____

4. Traditional value structure; religious and satisfied with life. _____

5. Quiet, reserved, and afraid of change._____

6. Loners, want power and money. _____

SOCIOCULTURAL INFLUENCES ON CONSUMER BEHAVIOUR

The effects of sociocultural influences are examined in terms of personal influence, reference groups, the family, social class, and culture and subculture.

PERSONAL INFLUENCE

Two aspects of personal influence are important to marketing: opinion leadership and word of mouth activity.

Opinion leadership
Word of mouth activity

Match the type of personal influence to the correct statement below:

_____ This type of influence is more likely to be important for products that provide a form of self-expression.

_____ Celebrities and sports figures are often used as spokespeople.

_____ This is perhaps the most powerful information source for consumers.

_____ This is a form of one-way directed influence.

_____ This form of influence often uses "teaser" advertising and toll-free numbers are sometimes used.

REFERENCE GROUPS

Reference groups are people to whom an individual looks as a basis for self-appraisal or as a source of personal standards. There are three important reference groups with marketing implications:

Membership group
Aspiration group
Dissociative group

Discuss which reference group to which each of these examples relate.

1. A young athlete buying a Montreal Expos shirt._____

2. A hockey player wearing his hockey team's jacket._____

3. An environmentalist not buying particular products._____

FAMILY INFLUENCE

Discuss the stage of the family life cycle for yourself, your parents, and your grandparents. When you graduate, how will this change your stage and your parents stage within the cycle?_____
_____

Five roles exist in the family decision-making process: Information gatherer, influencer, decision maker, purchaser, and user.

The Nelson family has decided to take a vacation this year. Mrs. Nelson looks in a travel guide and sends in the reply card for brochures from several provinces. Mr. Nelson and son, John, want to see a professional baseball game, while daughter, Kimberly, wants to go to a salt-water beach. Mrs. Nelson rules out any destination that does not have a coastline. After comparing prices, Mr. Nelson makes reservations for the South Shore of Nova Scotia. Which roles did each family member play? (Multiple roles expected)
_____
_____

SOCIAL CLASS

Social class may be defined as the relatively permanent, homogeneous divisions of society into which people sharing similar values, interests, and behaviour can be grouped. What criteria are used to determine an individual's social class?

CULTURE AND SUBCULTURE

Culture refers to the set of values, ideas, and attitudes that are accepted by a homogeneous group of people and are transmitted to the next generation. Subgroups within the larger, national culture, who share unique values, ideas, and attitudes are referred to as subcultures. An ethnic subculture is a segment of a larger society whose members are thought, by themselves and/or by others, to have a common origin and to participate in shared activities felt to be culturally significant. Three ethnic subcultures are referred to in the text, which ones?

CAN YOU PASS THE TEST?

OVERVIEW OF CHAPTER 6: TERMS AND DEFINITIONS (multiple choice)

1. The relatively permanent and homogeneous divisions in a society of people or families sharing similar values, life styles, interests, and behaviour are known as _____.
    - a. reference group
    - b. opinion leaders
    - c. subcultures
    - d. national character
    - e. social class

2. A situation's effect, or _____, on the nature and scope of the decision process. These include (1) the purchase task, (2) social surroundings, (3) physical surroundings, (4) temporal effects, and (5) antecedent states.
    - a. brand loyalty
    - b. evoked set
    - c. evaluative criteria
    - d. cognitive dissonance
    - e. situational influences

3. The _____ involves the steps or stages a buyer passes through in making choices about which products to buy.
    - a. purchase decision process
    - b. learning
    - c. consumer behaviour
    - d. family life cycle
    - e. consumer socialization

4. People to whom an individual turns as a standard of self appraisal or source of personal standards are known as _____.
    - a. reference group
    - b. opinion leaders
    - c. subcultures
    - d. national character
    - e. social class

5. The anxieties, or _____, felt because the consumer cannot anticipate the outcomes of a purchase but believes that there may be negative consequences.
    - a. brand loyalty
    - b. evoked set
    - c. evaluative criteria
    - d. cognitive dissonance
    - e. perceived risk

6. The _____ is the concept that each family progresses through a number of distinct phases, and each of which is associated with identifiable purchasing behaviours.
    - a. purchase decision process
    - b. learning
    - c. consumer behaviour
    - d. family life cycle
    - e. consumer socialization

7. The process by which an individual selects, organizes, and interprets information to create a meaningful picture of the world is known as _____.
     a. purchase decision process
     b. learning
     c. consumer behaviour
     d. family life cycle
     e. perception

8. A person's _____ is their enduring or consistent psychological traits, such as extroversion, aggression, or compliance.
     a. motivation
     b. perceived risk
     c. subliminal perception
     d. perception
     e. personality

9. _____ are subgroups within the larger or national culture with unique values, ideas, and attitudes.
     a. reference group
     b. opinion leaders
     c. subcultures
     d. national character
     e. social class

10. _____ is those behaviours that result from repeated experience and thinking.
     a. purchase decision process
     b. learning
     c. consumer behaviour
     d. family life cycle
     e. consumer socialization

11. A consumer's subjective perception of how well a product or brand performs on different attributes are known as _____, are based on personal experience, advertising, and discussions with other people.
     a. attitudes
     b. beliefs
     c. self-concept
     d. lifestyle
     e. involvement

12. The _____ is made up of a group of brands that a consumer would consider acceptable out of the set of brands in the product class of which he or she is aware.
     a. brand loyalty
     b. evoked set
     c. evaluative criteria
     d. cognitive dissonance
     e. situational influences

13. The _____ process by which people acquire the skills, knowledge, and attitudes necessary to function as consumers.
     a. purchase decision process
     b. learning
     c. consumer behaviour
     d. family life cycle
     e. consumer socialization

14. _____ is a favourable attitude toward and a consistent purchase of a single brand over time.
    a. brand loyalty
    b. evoked set
    c. evaluative criteria
    d. cognitive dissonance
    e. situational influences

15. _____ is the feeling of postpurchase psychological tension or anxiety.
    a. cognitive dissonance
    b. perceived risk
    c. subliminal perception
    d. perception
    e. word-of-mouth

16. A mode of living, or _____ is identified by how people spend their time and resources (activities), what they consider important in their environment (interests), and what they think of themselves and the world around them (opinions).
    a. attitudes
    b. beliefs
    c. self-concept
    d. lifestyle
    e. involvement

17. Both the objective and subjective attributes of a brand important to consumers when evaluating different brands or products constitute _____.
    a. brand loyalty
    b. evoked set
    c. evaluative criteria
    d. cognitive dissonance
    e. situational influences

18. _____ are a learned predisposition to respond to an object or class of objects in a consistent manner.
    a. attitudes
    b. beliefs
    c. self-concept
    d. lifestyle
    e. involvement

19. The _____ are a set of actions of a person to purchase and use products and services, including the mental and social processes that precede and follow these actions .
    a. purchase decision process
    b. learning
    c. consumer behaviour
    d. family life cycle
    e. consumer socialization

20. _____ are the personal, social, and economic significance of the purchase to the consumer.
    a. attitudes
    b. beliefs
    c. self-concept
    d. lifestyle
    e. involvement

21. _____ is the energizing force that causes behaviour that satisfies a need.
    a. motivation
    b. perceived risk
    c. subliminal perception
    d. perception
    e. word-of-mouth

22. Individuals who exert direct or indirect social influence over others make up the _____.
    a. reference group
    b. opinion leaders
    c. subcultures
    d. national character
    e. social class

23. The way people see themselves and the way they believe others see them is a person's _____.
    a. attitudes
    b. beliefs
    c. self-concept
    d. lifestyle
    e. involvement

24. _____ is a distinct set of personality characteristics common among people of a country or society.
    a. reference group
    b. opinion leaders
    c. subcultures
    d. national character
    e. social class

25. _____ is the act of people influencing each other during their face-to-face conversations.
    a. motivation
    b. perceived risk
    c. subliminal perception
    d. perception
    e. word of mouth

26. _____ means that a person sees or hears messages without being aware of them.
    a. motivation
    b. perceived risk
    c. subliminal perception
    d. perception
    e. word-of-mouth

For questions 27-31, match the following statements to the correct step in the purchase decision process:

27. I'm glad I didn't buy the scented tissues; they would have exacerbated my allergies.
    a. Problem recognition
    b. Information search
    c. Alternative evaluation
    d. Purchase decision
    e. Postpurchase behaviour

28. I'm tired of washing handkerchiefs; I need something more convenient.
    a. Problem recognition
    b. Information search
    c. Alternative evaluation
    d. Purchase decision
    e. Postpurchase behaviour

29. I can't decide between a designer box, convenience pack, or scented or unscented tissues.
    a. Problem recognition
    b. Information search
    c. Alternative evaluation
    d. Purchase decision
    e. Postpurchase behaviour

30. Can you tell me which kind of tissue you like best?
    a. Problem recognition
    b. Information search
    c. Alternative evaluation
    d. Purchase decision
    e. Postpurchase behaviour

31. I'm going to buy these, thank you.
    a. Problem recognition
    b. Information search
    c. Alternative evaluation
    d. Purchase decision
    e. Postpurchase behaviour

For questions 32-35, match the following statements to the correct source of information:

32. I guess I'll stick with this; I've been using the same brand of paint for years and have been very satisfied.
        a. internal source (internal)
        b. personal source (external)
        c. public source (external)
        d. marketer-dominated source
        e. all of the above

33. According to the instructions on the package, everything I need is included, and it guarantees professional results.
        a. internal source (internal)
        b. personal source (external)
        c. public source (external)
        d. marketer-dominated source
        e. all of the above

34. Before doing business with a new firm, I like to check with the Better Business Bureau.
        a. internal source (internal)
        b. personal source (external)
        c. public source (external)
        d. marketer-dominated source
        e. all of the above

35. Sam, can you tell me which dress you think looks better?
        a. internal source (internal)
        b. personal source (external)
        c. public source (external)
        d. marketer-dominated source
        e. all of the above

For questions 36-41, match the following statements to the correct level of problem solving:

36. Limited external information search is conducted to identify alternatives and important attributes.
        a. routine response behaviour
        b. limited problem solving
        c. extended problem solving
        d. both limited and routine problem solving
        e. both routine and extended problem solving

37. This is used with widely available products of low unit value and high familiarity .
        a. routine problem solving
        b. limited problem solving
        c. extended problem solving
        d. both limited and routine problem solving
        e. both routine and extended problem solving

38. This process would most likely be used with items such as toothpaste or chewing gum.
        a. routine problem solving
        b. limited problem solving
        c. extended problem solving
        d. both limited and routine problem solving
        e. both routine and extended problem solving

39. This involves each stage of the consumer purchase decision process.
    a. routine problem solving
    b. limited problem solving
    c. extended problem solving
    d. both limited and routine problem solving
    e. both routine and extended problem solving

40. This process would most likely be used for clothing, popcorn poppers, and/or electric can openers.
    a. routine problem solving
    b. limited problem solving
    c. extended problem solving
    d. both limited and routine problem solving
    e. both routine and extended problem solving

41. This process would most likely be used for real estate, automobiles, and/or personal computers.
    a. routine problem solving
    b. limited problem solving
    c. extended problem solving
    d. both limited and routine problem solving
    e. both routine and extended problem solving

For questions 42-46, match the following statements to the correct environmental situation:

42. I hate it when the aisles are cluttered and crowded.
    a. purchase task
    b. physical surroundings
    c. antecedent states
    d. social surroundings
    e. temporal effects

43. This is for my mother-in-law so it had better be good.
    a. purchase task
    b. physical surroundings
    c. antecedent states
    d. social surroundings
    e. temporal effects

44. "You're kidding, you don't accept credit cards?"
    a. purchase task
    b. physical surroundings
    c. antecedent states
    d. social surroundings
    e. temporal effects

45. The store is closing; we had better make up our mind.
    a. purchase task
    b. physical surroundings
    c. antecedent states
    d. social surroundings
    e. temporal effects

46. "Honey, what do you think?"
    a. purchase task
    b. physical surroundings
    c. antecedent states
    d. social surroundings
    e. temporal effects

For questions 47-51, match the following statements to the correct level of Maslow's Hierarchy of Needs:

47. Bananas, the almost perfect food.
    a. Physiological
    b. Safety
    c. Social
    d. Personal
    e. Self-actualization

48. "You're in good hands with Allstate."
    a. Physiological
    b. Safety
    c. Social
    d. Personal
    e. Self-actualization

49. "Hallmark, when you care enough to give the very best."
    a. Physiological
    b. Safety
    c. Social
    d. Personal
    e. Self-actualization

50. "You're the Pepsi generation."
    a. Physiological
    b. Safety
    c. Social
    d. Personal
    e. Self-actualization

For questions 51-54, which factor of perceived risk is being addressed in the following statements?

51. A Black & Decker circular saw displays the CSA seal.
    a. Financial outlay
    b. Performance of the product
    c. Physical harm
    d. Psychosocial factors
    e. all of the above

52. Free trial offers and/or small-sized packages of a new conditioning shampoo are sent through the mail.
    a. Financial outlay
    b. Performance of the product
    c. Physical harm
    d. Psychosocial factors
    e. all of the above

53. Only the finest students are enrolled in this school.
    a. Financial outlay
    b. Performance of the product
    c. Physical harm
    d. Psychosocial factors
    e. all of the above

54. When your boss says the package has to be in Toronto tomorrow, Purolator Courier says, ". We guarantee it!"
    a. Financial outlay
    b. Performance of the product
    c. Physical harm
    d. Psychosocial factors
    e. all of the above

Chapter 6--Answers

Discussion Questions

Problem Recognition

Example:
1. gasoline--gas gauge in car or the car sputtering and rolling to a stop

Information Search

Example:
1. Montreal--internal--memory, experience; external--brochures, travel agents, friends

Alternative Selection

Example:
1. coffee--criteria--strong and dark
   --brands--Starbucks, Gevalia
   --where and when to buy--now, Starbucks
   -- evaluation--outstanding
   --cognitive dissonance--add value by including frequent buyer incentives

Post Purchase Behaviour

Example:
1. automobile dealer--follow-up; good service; communication

Motivation

1. personal
2. social
3. safety
4. physiological
5. self-actualization

Perception

1. selective retention
2. selective exposure
3. selective retention
4. selective comprehension
5. selective comprehension
6. selective exposure

Learning

1. response
2. drive
3. reinforcement
4. stimulus generalization
5. stimulus discrimination

Values, Beliefs, and Attitudes

1. belief
2. value
3. attitude

Lifestyle

1. discontented
2. caring
3. assured
4. structured
5. fearful
6. resentful

Personal Influence

1. opinion leadership
2. opinion leadership
3. word of mouth
4. word of mouth
5. word of mouth

Reference Groups

1. aspiration group
2. membership group
3. disassociative group

Family Influence

Mrs. Nelson--information gather; influencer
Mr. Nelson--purchaser; influencer; decision maker
John--influencer
Kimberly--influencer

all are users

Sample Tests

1. e	28. a
2. e	29. c
3. a	30. b
4. a	31. d
5. e	32. a
6. d	33. d
7. e	34. c
8. e	35. b
9. c	36. b
10. b	37. a
11. b	38. a
12. b	39. c
13. e	40. b
14. a	41. c
15. a	42. b
16. d	43. a
17. c	44. c
18. a	45. e
19. c	46. d
20. e	47. a
21. a	48. b
22. b	49. d
23. c	50. c
24. d	51. b
25. e	52. c
26. c	53. d
27. e	54. a

CHAPTER 7

Organizational Markets and Buyer Behaviour

<u>Why is Chapter 7 important</u>? Just like the consumer market, the business-to-business market has a buying process that marketers must know and utilize. This chapter illustrates how that process works and the differences between it and the consumer buying process. It shows the participants and what influences their behaviour.

Business Marketing: The marketing of goods and services to commercial enterprises, governments, and other profit and nonprofit organizations for use in the creation of goods and services that they then produce and market to other business customers, as well as individuals and ultimate consumers.

CHAPTER OUTLINE

I. NATURE AND SIZE OF ORGANIZATIONAL MARKETS

    A. Industrial Markets
          1. Manufacturers
          2. Mining
          3. Construction
          4. Farms, forestry and fisheries
          5. Services

    B. Reseller Markets
          1. Wholesalers
          2. Retailers

    C. Government Markets
          1. Federal
          2. Provincial
          3. Local

    D. Global Organizational Markets

II. MEASURING DOMESTIC AND GLOBAL INDUSTRIAL, RESELLER, AND GOVERNMENT MARKETS

    A. Standard Industrial Classification (SIC)

    B. North American Industry Classification System (NAICS)

III. CHARACTERISTICS OF ORGANIZATION BUYING

    A. Demand Characteristics (Derived Demand)

    B.   Size of the Order or Purchase

    C.   Number of Potential Buyers

D. Organizational Buying Objectives

E. Organizational Buying Criteria
1. Price
2. Ability to meet quality specifications
3. Ability to meet required delivery schedules
a. just-in-time inventory system
4. Technical capability
5. Warranties and claim policies
6. Past performances on previous contracts
7. Production facilities and capacity

F. Buyer-Seller Relationship and Supply Partnership
1. Complex and lengthy negotiations
2. Reciprocity
3. Long-term relationships
4. Supply partnerships

G. The Buying Centre
1. Roles
a. Users
b. Influences
c. Buyers
d. Deciders
e. Gatekeepers

H. Stages in an Organizational Buyers Decision
1. Problem recognition
2. Information search
3. Alternative evaluation
4. Purchase decision
5. Postpurchase behaviour

I. Types of Buying Situations
1. Straight rebuy
2. Modified rebuy
3. New buy

You should be able to place these key terms in the outline and be able to discuss them.

bidders list	government units	NAICS	resellers
business marketing	industrial firms	organizational buyers	reverse marketing
buying centre	make-buy decision	organizational buying behaviour	straight rebuy
buy classes	modified rebuy	organizational buying criteria	supply partnership
derived demand	new buy	reciprocity	value analysis

QUESTIONS & PROBLEMS

ORGANIZATIONAL BUYERS

Industrial markets
Reseller markets
Government markets

Match the correct organizational buyer market with the statements below:

reseller markets 1. Wholesalers and retailers who buy physical products and resell them again without any reprocessing.

gov't markets 2. Federal, provincial, and local agencies that buy goods and services for the constituents they serve.

ind markets 3. They in some way reprocess a product or service they buy before selling it again to the next buyer.

reseller 4. K-Mart purchases food dehydrators from Alternative Pioneer Systems.

gov't 5. The Department of National Defense places an order with Scott for over 100,000 rolls of toilet tissue.

ind. 6. A large international firm hires Grant Thornton to do its accounting.

DERIVED DEMAND CHARACTERISTICS

Explain how derived demand is a factor for the following and what product(s) from which the demand could be derived:

Intel's Pentium Chip _Dell comp demand increases significantly_

Hot dogs_____

Liquid Paper Correcting Fluid_____

Windows 98_____

Refrigerators, Stoves and Dishwashers_____

CHARACTERISTICS OF ORGANIZATIONAL BUYING BEHAVIOUR - BUYING CRITERIA

There are seven important buying criteria most organizations use. The criteria may change from situation to situation even with the same product.

Rank the following purchase criteria for Personal Computers for the three different buying situations listed below. Be able to explain your rationale:

<u>College student</u>	**Rank**
Price	1
Quality	3
Delivery	5
Technical capability	4
Warranties	2
Past performance	6
Production facilities and capacity	7

<u>Small Business (under 10 employees)</u>	**Rank**
Price	1
Quality	4
Delivery	6
Technical capability	2
Warranties	3
Past performance	5
Production facilities and capacity	7

<u>General Motors</u>	**Rank**
Price	6
Quality	2
Delivery	5
Technical capability	1
Warranties	4
Past performance	3
Production facilities and capacity	7

ROLES IN THE BUYING CENTRE

John Wilson, a salesman for the Greater Copier Company, has just finished a successful sales call on Acme Structural Corporation. He had tried to make an appointment with the company president, Bob Miller, but was put off by Ms. Browne, his executive assistant. When he tried to leave material, Ms. Browne said she would look at it and forward it on to the appropriate people. After several weeks of hearing nothing and still unable to see Mr. Miller, he called on the office manager, Tom Watson. Mr. Watson said they were dissatisfied with their present copier and were in the market for a new one. As he left his brochures with Mr. Watson, he was surprised to see Rebecca Nelson, an old customer form Giant Steel, Inc. walk in. "I am now the purchasing manager for Acme," she said. "I will put in a good word for you because you gave us the best product with the best service we ever had." Later that day, Ms. Browne called and said Mr. Miller wanted a full presentation. At the end of the presentation, Mr. Miller signed a contract for a new high-speed copier and Ms. Nelson issued a purchase order. What roles did each of the people above play in the buying process?

STAGES IN AN ORGANIZATIONAL BUYING DECISION
There are five stages in an organizational buying decision:

Problem recognition
Information search
Alternative evaluation
Purchase decision
Postpurchase behaviour

Use common sense and your text to answer the following questions:

1. What situations are likely to make an organization recognize a problem? _breakdown_

2. What sources might an organization use to seek out information? _brochure_

3. What forms of alternative evaluation do organizational buyers use? _reference supply by manufacture_

4. What are likely differences between the purchase decision of an ultimate consumer and an organizational buyer? _less emotional_

5. What are likely differences between the postpurchase behaviour of an ultimate consumer and an organizational buyer? _formal evaluation_

BUY CLASSES
There are three buy classes:

Straight rebuy
Modified rebuy
New buy

Match the correct buy classes with the statements below:

Straight rebuy 1. The buyer or purchasing manager reorders a replacement ball bearing from the organization's list of ten acceptable suppliers on the bidders list.

new buy 2. Kmart and Wal-mart are considering a line of food dehydrators and is approached by Alternative Pioneering Systems. Neither has not carried this type of product before.

modified rebuy 3. Engineering has come up with a new design for the motor's cooling system that can save $20 per unit in assembly costs. I wonder if our current supplier can meet the tolerances for the new design.

CAN YOU PASS THE TEST?

OVERVIEW OF CHAPTER: TERMS AND DEFINITIONS (multiple choice)

1. The reordering of an existing product or service from the list of acceptable suppliers, generally without checking with the various users or influencers is considered a _____.
      a. Buy classes
      b. Make-buy decision
      c. Straight rebuy
      d. Modified rebuy
      e. New buy

2. _____ is a systematic appraisal of the design, quality, and performance requirements of a product to reduce purchasing costs.
      a. Reciprocity
      b. Derived demand
      c. North American Industry Classification System (NAICS)
      d. Value analysis
      e. Buy classes

3. An organizational buyer that in some way reprocesses a good or service before selling it again is called a(n) _____ .
      a. Organizational buyers
      b. Business marketing
      c. Reseller
      d. Government units
      e. Industrial firm

4. A buying situation in which the users, influencers, or deciders change the product specifications, price, delivery schedule, or supplier is a _____.
      a. Buy classes
      b. Make-buy decision
      c. Straight rebuy
      d. Modified rebuy
      e. New buy

5. The _____ is the group of persons within an organization who participate in the buying process and share common goals, risks, and knowledge important to that purchase.
      a. Organizational buying behaviour
      b. Reverse marketing
      c. Organizational buying criteria
      d. Buying centre
      e. Bidder's list

6. An evaluation of whether a product or its parts will be purchased from outside suppliers or built by the firm is called the _____.
      a. Buy classes
      b. Make-buy decision
      c. Straight rebuy
      d. Modified rebuy
      e. New buy

7. Units such as manufacturers, retailers, and government agencies that buy goods and services for their own use or for resale are _____.
   a. Organizational buyers
   b. Business marketing
   c. Resellers
   d. Government units
   e. Industrial firms

8. The _____ are the three specific buying situations organizations face: new buy, straight rebuy, and modified rebuy.
   a. Buy classes
   b. Make-buy decision
   c. Straight rebuy
   d. Modified rebuy
   e. New buy

9. A list of firms believed to be qualified to supply a given item is a _____.
   a. Organizational buying behaviour
   b. Reverse marketing
   c. Organizational buying criteria
   d. Buying centre
   e. Bidders list

10. The federal, provincial, and local agencies or _____, buy goods and services for the constituents they serve.
   a. Organizational buyers
   b. Business marketing
   c. Reseller
   d. Government units
   e. Industrial firm

11. The first-time purchase of a product or service by a firm is a _____.
   a. Buy classes
   b. Make-buy decision
   c. Straight rebuy
   d. Modified rebuy
   e. New buy

12. A wholesaler or retailer who buys physical products and resells them again without any processing is a
   _____.
   a. Organizational buyers
   b. Business marketing
   c. Reseller
   d. Government units
   e. Industrial firm

13. The federal government's system of classifying organizations, called the _____, classifies firms on the basis of major activity or the major good or service provided.
   a. Reciprocity
   b. Derived demand
   c. North American Industry Classification System (NAICS)
   d. Value analysis
   e. Buy classes

14. _____ is the decision-making process that organizations use to establish the need for products and identify, evaluate, and choose among alternative brands and suppliers.
    a. Organizational buying behaviour
    b. Reverse marketing
    c. Organizational buying criteria
    d. Buying centre
    e. Bidders list

15. The objective attributes of the supplier's products and services and the capabilities of the supplier itself make up the _____.
    a. Organizational buying behaviour
    b. Reverse marketing
    c. Organizational buying criteria
    d. Buying centre
    e. Bidders list

16. An industrial buying practice in which two organizations agree to purchase products and services from each other is called _____.
    a. Reciprocity
    b. Derived demand
    c. North American Industry Classification System (NAICS)
    d. Value analysis
    e. Buy classes

17. When sales of a product (typically industrial) which result from the sales of another item (often consumer), it is an example of _____.
    a. Reciprocity
    b. Derived demand
    c. North American Industry Classification System (NAICS)
    d. Value analysis
    e. Buy classes

18. _____ is the marketing of goods and services to commercial enterprises, governments, and other profit and nonprofit organizations for use in the creation of goods and services that they then produce and market to other business customers as well as individuals and ultimate consumers.
    a. Organizational buyers
    b. Business marketing
    c. Reseller
    d. Government units
    e. Industrial firm

19. _____ is the effort by organizational buyers to build relationships that shape suppliers' products, services, and capabilities to fit a buyer's needs and those of its customers.
    a. Organizational buying behaviour
    b. Reverse marketing
    c. Organizational buying criteria
    d. Buying centre
    e. Bidders list

20. _____ are individuals who have the formal authority and responsibility to select the supplier and negotiate the terms of the contract.
    a. Users
    b. Influencers
    c. Buyers
    d. Deciders
    e. Gatekeepers

21. _____ control the flow of information to other members of the buying centre.
    a. Users
    b. Influencers
    c. Buyers
    d. Deciders
    e. Gatekeepers

22. _____ have the formal or informal power to select or approve the supplier that receives the contract.
    a. Users
    b. Influencers
    c. Buyers
    d. Deciders
    e. Gatekeepers

23. _____ affect the buying decision usually by helping define the specifications for what is bought.
    a. Users
    b. Influencers
    c. Buyers
    d. Deciders
    e. Gatekeepers

24. The people in the organization actually use the product or service are called _____.
    a. Users
    b. Influencers
    c. Buyers
    d. Deciders
    e. Gatekeepers

Chapter 7--Answers

Discussion Questions

Organizational Buyers

1. reseller markets
2. government markets
3. industrial markets
4. reseller markets
5. government markets
6. industrial markets

Derived Demand Characteristics

Example: Intel Pentium Chip--Dell Computers demand increases significantly

Characteristics of Organizational Buying Behaviour--Buying Criteria

Suggested ranking:

	College Student	Small Business	General Motors
Price	1	1	6
Quality	3	4	2
Delivery	5	6	5
Technical capability	4	2	1
Warranties	2	3	4
Past performance	6	5	3
Production facilities	7	7	7

Roles in the Buying Centre

Bob Miller--decider
Ms. Browne--gatekeeper
Rebecca Nelson--influencer, purchaser
Tom Watson--user

Stages in an Organizational Buying Decision

Example:

1. breakdown
2. brochures
3. references supplied by manufacturer
4. less emotional
5. formal evaluation

Buy Classes

1. straight rebuy
2. new buy
3. modified rebuy

Sample Tests

1. c
2. d
3. e
4. d
5. d
6. b
7. a
8. a
9. e
10. d
11. e
12. c
13. c
14. a
15. c
16. a
17. b
18. b
19. b
20. c
21. e
22. d
23. b
24. a

CHAPTER 8

Interactive Marketing and Electronic Commerce

<u>Why is Chapter 8 important</u>? With the growth of Internet comes the need to understand how to utilize all forms of electronic marketing. This chapter illustrates who is using the Internet and how to identify them. In addition, it shows how to recognize those products that are most likely to be successfully marketed on the Internet.

Interactive Marketing: Involves buyer-seller electronic communications in a computer-mediated environment in which the buyer controls the kind and amount of information received from the seller.

CHAPTER OUTLINE

THE NEW MARKETSPACE AND ELECTRONIC COMMERCE

    A. Nature and Scope of Electronic Commerce
        1. Business-to-Customer
            a. Internet
            b. World Wide Web
            c. commercial online services
        2. Business Support Functions
            a. Intranet
        3. Business-to-Business
            a. electronic data interchanges
            b. Extranet

    B. Marketing.com: Electronic Commerce and Customer Value Creation

II. ONLINE CONSUMERS AND BUYING BEHAVIOUR IN THE NEW MARKETPLACE

    A. The Online Consumer
        1. Online consumer profile
        2. Online consumer psychographics

    B. Online Consumer Purchasing Behaviour
        1. What online consumers buy
        2. Why consumers buy online: The six C's
            a. convenient
            b. cost
            c. choice
            d. customization
            e. communication
            f. control

III. INTERACTIVE MARKETING IN THE NEW MARKETSPACE

    A. Creating a Presence in the New Marketspace
        1. Corporate and marketing Web sites
            a. corporate Web sites
            b. marketing Web sites
                i. transactional
               ii. promotional

2. Online advertising
    a. banner ads
    b. key word ads
    c. interstitials or intermercials
    d. Webcasting

B. How Companies Benefit from Electronic Commerce and Interactive Marketing

You should be able to place these key terms in the outline and be able to discuss them.

bots	Extranet	marketspace
commercial online services	interactive marketing	portals
cookies	Internet	Webcasting
corporate Web site	Intranet	Web communities
electronic commerce	marketing Web site	World Wide Web
electronic data interchange (EDI)		

QUESTIONS & PROBLEMS

The Nature and Scope of Electronic Commerce

Electronic commerce is made up of a family of three electronic networks:

Business-to-consumer electronic commerce
Business support functions
Business-to-business electronic commerce

Identify the type of electronic commerce in the examples below:

1. Dell Computer Corporation sells PCs and servers from its Web site to companies nationwide.
   _____

2. National Bank offers its customers Internet banking including balance inquiry, transfers between accounts, and bill payment. _____

3. Bank of Montreal offers job postings, financial news, and company announcements on its Intranet.
   _____

Online Consumers and Buying Behaviour

SRI International has developed iVALS, a psychographic profile of Internet users. They are divided along the line of (1) how heavily and enthusiastically they use the Internet and (2) the reason for usage. The 10 user segments are:

Wizards
Pioneers
Surfers
Socialites
Sociables
Workers
Seekers
Upstreamers
Mainstreamers
Immigrants

Profile yourself and interview one other classmate to see in which categories you fall.

What and Why Consumers Buy Online

Consumers prefer to buy online for six reasons. These are identified as the "Six Cs" They are:

Convenience
Choice
Cost
Customization
Communication
Control

Identify the reason behind each of the following consumer actions:

1. Amazon.com gives consumers the availability of millions of book titles, including textbooks.
   choice

2. The Toronto Maple Leafs Web site offers fans the ability to ask questions to players and management and talk baseball with other Leaf fans. _communication._

3. Dell Computer Corporation will let you "build your own computer" at their Web site.
   Customization.

4. Canadian Airlines offers bonus miles and special ticket prices for booking flights online.
   cost

5. Travelocity.com allows consumers to compare fares, flights, and availability of all airlines.
   control

6. Banks offering Internet banking allow customers to manage their bank accounts 24 hours a day, 365 days a year. _convenience_

Interactive Marketing in the New Marketspace

Companies have found a need for creating a Web presence for marketing their products. This can be accomplished by utilizing two types of presence on the Internet: Web sites and Web advertising. There are two types of each of these.

Web Sites	Web Advertising
Corporate Web Site	Portals
Marketing Web Site	Web Communities

Find and print out the Home Page for each of the types of Web presence above.

CAN YOU PASS THE TEST?

OVERVIEW OF CHAPTER 8: TERMS AND DEFINITIONS (multiple choice)

1. _____ is a company utilizing interactive marketing involving the Internet, World Wide Web, or commercial online services to sell to consumers.
   - a. Business-to-business electronic commerce
   - b. Business-to-consumer electronic commerce
   - c. Business support functions
   - d. Internet marketing
   - e. Electronic commerce

2. _____ utilizes Internet-based technology internally to support the company's external electronic commerce initiatives.
   - a. Business-to-business electronic commerce
   - b. Business-to-consumer electronic commerce
   - c. Business support functions
   - d. Internet marketing
   - e. Electronic commerce

3. _____ is the largest application of electronic commerce and comes in two forms: Electronic data interchanges and Extranet.
   - a. Business-to-business electronic commerce
   - b. Business-to-consumer electronic commerce
   - c. Business support functions
   - d. Internet marketing
   - e. Electronic commerce

4. The _____ is an integrated global network of computers that gives users access to information and documents.
   - a. Internet
   - b. Extranet
   - c. Electronic Data Interchange (EDI)
   - d. Portals
   - e. World Wide Web

5. The _____ is a part of the Internet that supports a retrieval system that formats information and documents into Web pages.
   - a. Internet
   - b. Extranet
   - c. Electronic Data Interchange (EDI)
   - d. Portals
   - e. World Wide Web

6. The _____ is an Internet/Web-based network that permits private business-to-business communication between a company and its suppliers, distributors, and other partners.
   - a. Internet
   - b. Extranet
   - c. Electronic Data Interchange (EDI)
   - d. Portals
   - e. World Wide Web

7. _____ electronic gateways to the World Wide Web that supply a broad array of news and entertainment, information resources, and shopping services.
     a. Internet
     b. Extranet
     c. Electronic Data Interchange (EDI)
     d. Portals
     e. World Wide Web

8. Computer files that a marketer can download into the computer of an online shopper who visits the marketer's Web site are known as _____.
     a. Internet
     b. Cookies
     c. Electronic Data Interchange (EDI)
     d. Portals
     e. World Wide Web

9. Amazon.com, which sells books and music to online consumers, is an example of a _____.
     a. Corporate Web site
     b. Transactional marketing Web site
     c. Promotional marketing Web site
     d. Online advertising
     e. Webcasting

10. A _____ is designed to accommodate interactive communication initiated by a company's employees, investors, suppliers, and customers.
     a. Corporate Web site
     b. Transactional marketing Web site
     c. Promotional marketing Web site
     d. Online advertising
     e. Webcasting

11. Buying space on a portal such Yahoo! is an example of _____.
     a. Corporate Web site
     b. Transactional marketing Web site
     c. Promotional marketing Web site
     d. Online advertising
     e. Webcasting

12. General Motors' www.saturn.com is an example of a _____.
     a. Corporate Web site
     b. Transactional marketing Web site
     c. Promotional marketing Web site
     d. Online advertising
     e. Webcasting

13. Taking advantage of Canadian Airlines special online fares is an example of the _____ reason for consumers shopping online.
     a. Cost
     b. Convenience
     c. Choice
     d. Control
     e. Customization

14. _____ is the reason a consumer would utilize Flowers.com send flowers to a cross-country friend.

    a. Cost
    b. Convenience
    c. Choice
    d. Control
    e. Customization

15. Being able to design and order your own computer at Compaq's Web site is an example of the _____ reason for shopping the Internet.

    a. Cost
    b. Convenience
    c. Choice
    d. Control
    e. Customization

Chapter 8--Answers

Discussion Questions

Nature and Scope of Electronic Commerce

1. Business-to-business electronic commerce
2. Business-to-consumer electronic commerce
3. Business support functions

What and Why Consumers Buy Online

1. Choice
2. Communication
3. Customization
4. Cost
5. Control
6. Convenience

Sample Tests

1. b
2. c
3. a
4. a
5. e
6. b
7. d
8. b
9. b
10. a
11. d
12. c
13. a
14. b
15. e

CHAPTER 9

Turning Marketing Information Into Action

Why is Chapter 9 important? Information is the lifeblood of any marketing program. This chapter illustrates how a company determines its information needs; the sources of that information and the best way to collect it; and finally, how to interpret and utilize that information. Information contributes the success of the promotion, pricing, distribution, and ultimately, the product itself.

Marketing Research: The process of defining a marketing problem and opportunity, systematically collecting and analyzing information, and recommending actions to improve an organization's marketing activities.

CHAPTER OUTLINE

I. WHAT MARKETING RESEARCH IS AND DOES

    A. Types of Marketing Research
       1. Exploratory
       2. Descriptive
       3. Causal

II. THE MARKETING RESEARCH PROCESS

    A. Problem Definition
    B. Formal Research Design
    C. Data Collection and Analysis
    D. Conclusions and Report

III. PROBLEM DEFINITION

    A. Exploratory Research
       1. Secondary data
       2. Focus groups
       3. Depth interviews

IV. FORMAL RESEARCH DESIGN

    A. Survey
       1. mail
       2. telephone
       3. personal interview

    B. Experiment

    C. Observation

    D. Is there an Optimal Research Design?

E. Sampling
   1. probability sampling
   2. nonprobability sampling

V. DATA COLLECTION AND ANALYSIS

A.   Field Work
B.   Cross-tabulation

VI. CONCLUSIONS AND REPORT

A.   Interpretation
B.   Action

VII. ETHICAL ISSUES IN THE MARKETING RESEARCH PROCESS

A.   Ethical dimensions
B.   Unethical behaviour

VIII. INFORMATION TECHNOLOGY AND MARKETING ACTIONS

A. Key elements of an information system
B. Querying the information system
C. Peopleless marketing actions

IX. MARKET AND SALES FORECASTING

A. Forecasting Terms
   1. Market or industry potential
   2. Sales or company forecast

B. Approaches
   1. Top-down forecast
   2. Buildup forecast

C. Techniques
   1. Judgments of decision makers
      a. direct forecast
      b. "lost horse" forecast
   2. Survey of knowledgeable groups
      a. Survey of Buyers' Intentions
      b. salesforce survey
      c. jury of executive opinion
      d. survey of experts
   3. Statistical methods
      a. trend extrapolation

You should be able to place these key terms in the outline and be able to discuss them.

buildup forecast

– depth interviews

direct forecast

experiment

— focus groups

information technology

jury of executive opinion forecast

lost-horse forecast

market or industry potential

marketing research

nonprobability sampling

observation

primary data

probability sampling

sales or company forecast

salesforce survey forecast

— sampling

secondary data

— survey

survey of buyers' intentions forecast

survey of experts forecast

top-down forecast

trend extrapolation

QUESTIONS & PROBLEMS

TYPES OF MARKETING RESEARCH

Marketing research is often classified on the basis of technique or function. Categorizing research by function reveals that there are three types of research:

Exploratory
Descriptive
Causal

Match the correct type of research with the statements below:

Descriptive   1.   A major television network surveyed its viewers and prepared a detailed profile of its viewers and made it available to potential advertisers.

causal   2.   A potato chip manufacturer dropped its per bag price in one market by ten cents and by twenty cents in another market to evaluate the effect of the price change on consumption.

exploratory   3.   A small university wanted to discover the information sources students used to make a university selection so it conducted a series of focus groups involving about 40 students to discuss the issue.

THE MARKETING RESEARCH PROCESS

The marketing research process is always conducted based on the scientific method. Accordingly, marketing research must meet two basic principles of the scientific method, namely:

1. _____

2. _____

All marketing research consists of four basic stages:

(A) Defining the problem
(B) Determining the research design
(C) Collecting and analyzing data
(D) Drawing conclusions and preparing a report

Match the following statements to the correct stage of the marketing research process:

A   1.   A blueberry grower wants to know if people in Germany would be interested in buying fresh and/or frozen blueberries from Canada.

C   2.   The research firm hires and trains 20 people to carry out fieldwork.

D   3.   The marketing research and management in the firm sit down to interpret the research findings.

_____	4.	After conducting several depth interviews with experts, the research determines that survey research should be undertaken to collect information needed to solve the marketing problem.

SECONDARY VERSUS PRIMARY DATA

Secondary data are data previously collected and assembled for some project other than the one at hand. Primary data are data gathered and assembled specifically for the project on at hand.

Determine which of the following is secondary or primary data:

_____P_____	1.	A Ford Motor Company of Canada mail survey of new car buyers.

_____S_____	2.	An industry study used by Clearly Canadian Beverage to determine new market opportunities.

_____S_____	3.	Statistics Canada data on family expenditures

_____S_____	4.	Internal sales data for the past year

_____P_____	5.	Results from a focus group on choices of airlines

_____S_____	6.	Nielsen ratings used by an advertiser to place its advertising

_____S_____	7.	A J.D. Power report on new automobile quality

_____S_____	8.	A company's financial statements

_____S_____	9.	Scanner data from a grocery store

_____P_____	10.	A telephone survey

SURVEY

The most common research method of generating new or primary data is the use of surveys. A survey is a research technique used to generate data by asking people questions and recording their responses on a questionnaire. Surveys can be conducted by mail, telephone, or personal interview. Proper phrasing of a question is vital when using surveys.

Below are poorly constructed questions. Rewrite each question to obtain the most accurate data:

1. Do you exercise often? _How often do you exercise._____

2. Do you prefer the sadistic inhumane neutering of loving family pets or the benevolent construction of pet care shelters?_____

3. Whom do you live with? [] Parents [] Spouse_____

4. Do you read mysteries and science fiction? [] Yes, [] No_____

5. My weight is between: []100-120 lbs. []120-140 lbs. []140-160 lbs._____

6. How many students in your class ate breakfast last Monday?_____

EXPERIMENTS

An experiment involves the manipulation of an independent variable (cause) and the measurement of its effect on the dependent variable (effect) under controlled conditions.

Identify the following variable(s) in the experiment given below:

independent variable
dependent variable
extraneous variable

A grocery manager set up a display of canned green beans at the end of an aisle with a large sign that said "green beans 3/$1.25." Down the aisle in their normal location, the identical green beans were being sold for $.40 per can. The store manager wanted to see if people tended to buy items in quantity (assuming that the price must be lower), rather than buy items priced individually.

1. independent variable_____

2. dependent variable_____

3. extraneous variable_____

SAMPLING

Sampling is the process of gathering data from a proportion of the total population rather than from all members (census) of that particular population. There are two basic sampling techniques:

Probability
Nonprobability

Decide whether the following statements are examples of probability or nonprobability sampling:

_Non_____1. A junior high principal wants to study the use of alcohol by his students. He selects one hundred students by choosing every tenth name on his enrollment list.

_Prob_____2. A principal at the junior high across town wants to attempt the same study as the principal in the previous question, but he chooses the one hundred students with the lowest grade point average.

BASIC FORECASTING TERMS

Describe what is meant by:

1. Market or industry potential = _max total sales of a product_____

2. Sales or company forecast = _what is expected to sell under the_____
controllable / uncontrollable factors

TWO BASIC APPROACHES TO FORECASTING

The two basic approaches to sales forecasting are (1) subdividing the total sales forecast (top-down forecast) or (2) building the total sales forecast by summing the components buildup approach).

Use the Buying Power Index (BPI) to figure the sales percentage for the province of Ontario using the following information:

BPI = (0.2 x percent of population) + (0.5 x percent of effective buying power) + (0.3 x percent of retail sales)

Percent of population	= 37.7
Percent of national income	= 40.4
Percent of retail sales	= 36.2

BPI = _____

If an automobile manufacturer estimates total market potential for sport utility vehicles in 2000 to be 200,000 units, what would the sales potential be for this given region (using the BPI alone)?_____
_____

Use the buildup approach to forecast company sales based on the information given below:

	Units
East coast manager's regional forecast	28,000
Midwest manager's regional forecast	24,500
South manager's regional forecast	21,700
Southwest manager's regional forecast	19,700
West coast manager's regional forecast	29,900

Company forecast = _____units

SPECIFIC SALES FORECASTING TECHNIQUES

There are three specific sales forecasting techniques:

Judgments of decision maker
Surveys of knowledgeable groups
Statistical methods

Match the following methods to the correct sales forecasting technique:

1. Salesforce survey forecast_____
2. Lost horse forecast_____
3. Linear trend extrapolation_____
4. Direct forecast_____
5. Technological forecast_____
6. Trend extrapolation_____
7. Survey of experts forecast_____
8. Jury of executive opinion forecast_____

CAN YOU PASS THE TEST?

OVERVIEW OF CHAPTER: TERMS AND DEFINITIONS (multiple choice)

1. Marketing research is a means of
   - a. Spending money
   - b. Delaying a decision
   - c. Replacing executive judgment
   - d. Reducing risk and uncertainty
   - e. Eliminating all risk inherent in decision making

2. Preliminary research conducted to clarify the scope and nature of the marketing problem
   - a. Exploratory research
   - b. Causal research
   - c. Descriptive research
   - d. Survey
   - e. Experiment

3. Research designed to describe the basic characteristics of a given population or to profile particular marketing situations
   - a. Descriptive research
   - b. Extraneous research
   - c. Assumptive research
   - d. Experiment
   - e. Exploratory research

4. A type of sampling that uses arbitrary judgments to select the sample so that the chance of selecting a particular element may be unknown or zero.
   - a. Panel
   - b. Hypothesis
   - c. Marketing research
   - d. Probability sampling
   - e. Nonprobability sampling

5. Research designed to identify cause-and-effect relationships among variables.
   - a. Panel research
   - b. Descriptive research
   - c. Assumptive research
   - d. Causal research
   - e. Dependent variable

6. Precise rules are used to select the sample such that each element of the population has a specific known chance of being selected.
   - a. Panel
   - b. Hypothesis
   - c. Marketing research
   - d. Probability sampling
   - e. Nonprobability sampling

7. Data gathered and assembled specifically for the project at hand
   - a. Primary data
   - b. Raw data
   - c. Secondary data
   - d. Data
   - e. Decision factors

8. A research method that involves watching either mechanically or in person how people actually behave
   - a. Methodology
   - b. Survey
   - c. Experiments
   - d. Objectives
   - e. Observation

9. Informal interview sessions with 6 to 10 persons, relevant to the research project, brought together in a room with a moderator to discuss topics surrounding the marketing research problem
   - a. Secondary data
   - b. Focus groups
   - c. Depth interviews
   - d. Surveys
   - e. Decision factors

10. The process of defining a marketing problem and then systematically collecting and analyzing information to recommend actions to improve an organization's marketing activities.
    - a. Panel
    - b. Hypothesis
    - c. Marketing research
    - d. Probability sampling
    - e. Nonprobability sampling

11. Data previously collected and assembled for some other project other than the one at hand
    - a. Primary data
    - b. Questionnaire data
    - c. Secondary data
    - d. Data
    - e. Decision factors

12. The variable that is expected to cause a change in the dependent variable.
    - a. Methods
    - b. Statistical inferences
    - c. Independent variable
    - d. Extraneous variable
    - e. Uncertainties

13. A sample of consumers or stores from which researchers take a series of periodic measurements.
    - a. Panel
    - b. Hypothesis
    - c. Marketing research
    - d. Probability sampling
    - e. Nonprobability sampling

14. The causal condition that is the result of outside factors that the experimenter can't control
   - a. Alternatives
   - b. Extraneous independent variable
   - c. Assumptions
   - d. Constraints
   - e. Dependent variable

Match the type of question to the examples below:

15. Please indicate your gender. [] Male [] Female
   - a. Open-end
   - b. Fixed alternative
   - c. Dichotomous question
   - d. Semantic differential scale
   - e. Likert scale

16. What is your attitude toward sweetened cereals?
   - a. Open-end
   - b. Fixed alternative
   - c. Dichotomous question
   - d. Semantic differential scale
   - e. Likert scale

17. My professor's tests are: Too Easy - - - - - - - - - - - - - - - - - -Too Hard
   - a. Open-end
   - b. Fixed alternative
   - c. Dichotomous question
   - d. Semantic differential scale
   - e. Likert scale

18. Children should be seen and not heard. [] Strongly disagree [] Disagree [] Don't know [] Agree []
Strongly agree
   - a. Open-end
   - b. Fixed alternative
   - c. Dichotomous question
   - d. Semantic differential scale
   - e. Likert scale

19. The reason I took this course is . . .
   - a. Open-end
   - b. Fixed alternative
   - c. Dichotomous question
   - d. Semantic differential scale
   - e. Likert scale

20. The most widely used technique for organizing and analyzing marketing data

   - a. Survey
   - b. Panels
   - c. Cross-tabulation
   - d. Interpretation
   - e. Data drudging

21. Extending a pattern observed in past data into the future is an example of _____.
    a. Market potential/industry potential
    b. Top-down forecast
    c. Trend extrapolation
    d. Expert forecast
    e. Direct forecast

22. Asking the firm's salespeople to estimate sales during a coming period is an example of _____.
    a. Buildup forecast
    b. Company forecast/sales forecast
    c. Salesforce survey forecast
    d. Expert forecast
    e. Direct forecast

23. Asking experts on a topic to make a judgment about some future event is an example of _____.
    a. Survey of buyers' intentions forecast
    b. Jury of executive opinion forecast
    c. Survey of experts forecast
    d. Lost-horse forecast
    e. Technological forecast

24. Maximum total sales of a product by all firms to a segment under specified environmental conditions and marketing efforts of the firm is an example of _____.
    a. Market potential/industry potential
    b. Top-down forecast
    c. Trend extrapolation
    d. Delphi forecast
    e. Direct forecast

25. A method of forecasting sales that involves asking prospective customers whether they are likely to buy the product or service during some future time period is an example of _____.
    a. Survey of buyers' intentions forecast
    b. Jury of executive opinion forecast
    c. Survey of experts forecast
    d. Lost-horse forecast
    e. Technological forecast

26. Starting with the last known value of the item being forecast, listing the factors that could affect the forecast, assessing whether they have a positive or negative impact, and making the final forecast is an example of _____.
    a. Market potential/industry potential
    b. Lost-horse forecast
    c. Trend extrapolation
    d. Expert forecast
    e. Direct forecast

27. Summing the sales forecasts of each of the components to arrive at a total forecast is an example of _____.
    a. Buildup forecast
    b. Company forecast/sales forecast
    c. Salesforce survey forecast
    d. Expert forecast
    e. Direct forecast

Chapter 9-Answers

Discussion Questions

Types of Marketing Research

1. Descriptive
2. Causal
3. Exploratory

The Marketing Research Process

1. Reliability
2. Validity

Matching

1. Problem
2. Collecting data
3. Conclusions
4. Research design

Secondary versus Primary Data

1. primary
2. secondary
3. secondary
4. secondary
5. primary
6. secondary
7. secondary
8. secondary
9. secondary
10. primary

Survey

Example: How often do you exercise? [] daily [] 3-5 times per week [] weekly [] seldom [] never

Experiments

1. price/quantity
2. green bean sales
3. location

Sampling

1. Probability
2. nonprobability

Basic Forecasting Terms

Market potential--maximum total sales of a product by all firms
Sales forecast--what one firm expects to sell

Two Basic Approaches to Forecasting

BPI = 38.6

sales potential = 77,200

company forecast = 123,800

Specific Sales Forecasting Techniques

1. surveys of knowledgeable groups
2. judgments of decision maker
3. statistical methods
4. judgments of decision maker
5. surveys of knowledgeable groups
6. statistical methods
7. surveys of knowledgeable groups
8. surveys of knowledgeable groups

Sample Tests

1. d	21. c
2. a	22. c
3. a	23. c
4. e	24. a
5. d	25. a
6. d	26. b
7. a	27. a
8. e	
9. b	
10. c	
11. c	
12. c	
13. a	
14. b	
15. c	
16. a	
17. b	
18. e	
19. a	
20. c	

CHAPTER 10

Market Segmentation, Targeting, and Positioning

<u>Why is Chapter 10 important</u>? This chapter shows how the tools of consumer behaviour and environmental scanning can be used to classify and group consumers so that a company can more effectively reach them with the marketing mix. It also illustrates how to select which group or groups to pursue and how to appeal to each of them.

Market Segmentation: Aggregation of prospective buyers into groups that (1) have common needs and (2) will respond similarly to marketing actions.

CHAPTER OUTLINE

I. WHEN TO SEGMENT MARKETS

    A. One Product--Multiple Market Segments

    B. Multiple Products--Multiple Market Segments

II. STEPS IN SEGMENTING AND TARGETING MARKETS

    A. Form Prospective Buyers into Segments
       1. Criteria
          a. Potential for increased profit and ROI
          b. Similarity of needs of potential buyers within a segment
          c. Differences of buyers among segments
          d. Feasibility of marketing action to reach segments
          e. Simplicity and cost of assigning potential buyers to segments
       2. Ways to segment consumer markets
          a. Geographic
          b. Demographic
          c. Psychographic
          d. Behavioural
             i. benefits sought
             ii. usage
       3. Ways to segment organizational markets
          a. Geographic
          b. Demographic (e.g. NAICS)
          c. Behavioural

    B. Form Products to be Sold into Group

    C. Develop a Market-Product Grid and Estimate Size of Market

    D. Select Target Market(s)
       1. Criteria
          a. Size
          b. Expected growth

          c. Competitive position

          d. Cost of reaching segment

          e. Compatibility with the organization's objectives and resources

      2. Choose the segments

E. Take Marketing Actions to Reach Target Market(s)

      1. Head-to-head positioning

      2. Differentiation positioning

III. ANALYZING MARKET SEGMENTS USING CROSS TABULATIONS

A. Developing Cross Tabulations

      1. Pairing the questions

      2. Forming the cross tabulations

B. Interpreting the Cross Tabulations

C. Value of Cross Tabulations

      1. Advantages

          a. Direct interpretation

          b. Easy means of communication

          c. Flexible

          d. Can be used to summarize data

          e. Easily generated

      2. Disadvantages

You should be able to place these key terms in the outline and be able to discuss them.

80/20 rule	market segmentation	product differentiation	synergy
cross tabulation	market segments	product positioning	usage rate
market-product grid	perceptual map	repositioning	

QUESTIONS & PROBLEMS

WHAT MARKET SEGMENTATION MEANS

Market segmentation involves aggregating prospective buyers into groups that (1) have common needs, and (2) will respond similarly to a marketing action. Market segments are a relatively homogeneous collection of prospective buyers.

Identify at least three distinct market segments for:

1. Shampoo

   _____
   _____
   _____

2. Dry cleaners

   _____
   _____
   _____

3. Book stores

   _____
   _____
   _____

4. Personal computers

   _____
   _____
   _____

Product differentiation involves a firm's using different marketing activities, such as product features and advertising, to help consumers perceive the product as different and better than competing ones.

Describe each firm's attempt at product differentiation:

Product	**Product differentiation**
Mountain Dew	_____
Compaq computers	_____
Jeep	_____
Panasonic products	_____
Fox Network	_____

CRITERIA USED IN FORMING MARKET SEGMENTS

There are five principal criteria used when forming segments in a market:

        a. Potential for increased profit and return on investment
        b. Similarity of needs of potential buyers within a segment
        c. Difference of needs of buyers between segments
        d. Feasibility of a marketing action to reach a segment
        e. Simplicity and cost of assigning potential buyers to a segment

Using the Apple Computer example from your text, give a concrete illustration for each of the criteria listed above:

1._____

2._____

3._____

4._____

5._____

WAYS TO SEGMENT CONSUMER MARKETS

The main dimensions used to segment Canadian consumer markets include:

Geographic segmentation
Demographic segmentation
Psychographic segmentation
Behavioural segmentation

Which type of segmentation is being used in the following examples:

1.Colgate-Palmolive markets Arctic Power on a energy-saving dimension in Quebec, but as a clothes saver in Western Canada. _____

2. Cyanamid Canada produces vitamins for various age groups including children, and seniors.

_____

3. McCain markets frozen entrees to working parents who are starved for time but want healthy food to serve their families._____

4. Ault Foods discovered some consumers were seeking a fresher, longer lasting fluid milk and were prepared to pay a premium price for such a product._____

5. Clinique combines gender, income, and occupation in order to develop different lines of cosmetics.

_____

SELECT TARGETS ON WHICH TO FOCUS EFFORTS

There are five different criteria for selecting target market segments:

Size
Expected growth
Competitive position
Cost of reaching the segment
Compatibility with the organization's objectives and resources

Using the example of Wendy's in Chapter 10, make statements (true or hypothetical to illustrate each of the five criteria above):

1._____

2._____

3._____

4._____

5._____

ANALYZING MARKET SEGMENTS USING CROSS TABULATION

Cross tabulation or cross-tabs, is a method of presenting and relating information having two or more variables. It is used to analyze and discover relationships in the data.

Movie Preference

Age	Comedy	Action	Romance
Ages 5-10	50	40	10
Ages 11-16	40	40	20
Ages 17-22	40	30	30

Answer the following questions using the (Age/Movie Preference) cross tabulation:

1. As a person grows older their preference for romantic movies:_____

2. The largest single segment for a movie that combined action and comedy:_____

3. The largest single segment for a movie that was a "romantic-comedy":_____

4. The segment that offers the greatest "growth" potential as a person gets older is:_____

PRODUCT POSITIONING

There are two major approaches to product positioning:

Head-to-Head
Product differentiation

Using television, radio, or print advertisements, make a list of five current product campaigns using head-to-head positioning, and five current product campaigns using product differentiation.

Head-to-head

1. _____ vs. _____

2. _____ vs. _____

3. _____ vs. _____

4. _____ vs. _____

5. _____ vs. _____

Product Differentiation

1. _____

2. _____

3. _____

4. _____

5. _____

CAN YOU PASS THE TEST?

OVERVIEW OF CHAPTER 10: TERMS AND DEFINITIONS (multiple choice)

1. Aggregating prospective buyers into groups or segments that (1) have common needs and (2) will respond similarly to a marketing action is called _____.
    a. Cross tabulation
    b. Product differentiation
    c. Market segmentation
    d. Product positioning
    e. Market segments

2. _____ are the groups that result from the process of market segmentation: these groups ideally have (1) common needs, and (2) respond similarly to a marketing action.
    a. Cross tabulation
    b. Product differentiation
    c. Market segmentation
    d. Product positioning
    e. Market segments

3. _____ is the framework for relating market segments to products offered or potential marketing actions by a firm.
    a. Repositioning
    b. Market-product grid
    c. Usage rate
    d. Perceptual map
    e. 80/20 rule

4. _____ is a strategy having different but related meanings; it involves a firm's using different marketing mix activities such as product featuring and advertising, to help consumers perceive the product as being different and better than other products.
    a. Cross tabulation
    b. Product differentiation
    c. Market segmentation
    d. Product positioning
    e. Market segments

5. _____ refers to quantity consumed or patronage during a specific period which varies significantly among different customer groups.
    a. Repositioning
    b. Market-product grid
    c. Usage rate
    d. Perceptual map
    e. 80/20 rule

6. The _____ suggests that 80 percent of a firm's sales are obtained from 20 percent of its customers.
   a. Repositioning
   b. Market-product grid
   c. Usage rate
   d. Perceptual map
   e. 80/20 rule

7. _____ are the method of presenting and relating data on two or more variables to display summary data and discover relationships in the data.
   a. Cross tabulation
   b. Product differentiation
   c. Market segmentation
   d. Product positioning
   e. Market segments

8. _____ is the place an offering occupies in consumer's minds with regard to important attributes relative to competing offerings.
   a. Cross tabulation
   b. Product differentiation
   c. Market segmentation
   d. Product positioning
   e. Market segments

9. A graph displaying consumers' perceptions of product attributes across two or more dimensions is called _____.
   a. Repositioning
   b. Market-product grid
   c. Usage rate
   d. Perceptual map
   e. 80/20 rule

10. Changing the place, or _____, an offering occupies in a consumer's mind with regard to important attributes relative to competitive offerings.
   a. Repositioning
   b. Market-product grid
   c. Usage rate
   d. Perceptual map
   e. 80/20 rule

11. Packard Bell recognizing the "home" computer market as one with fast growth and a customer who wanted all the "bells & whistles," making production far more predictable and efficient, is an example of _____.
   a. Potential for increased profit and return on investment
   b. Similarity of needs of potential buyers within a segment
   c. Difference of needs of buyers between segments
   d. Feasibility of a marketing action to reach a segment
   e. Simplicity and cost of assigning potential buyers to a segment

12. Head & Shoulders has become the leading shampoo in China as the dark-haired population has become concerned about dandruff shows _____.
    a. Potential for increased profit and return on investment
    b. Similarity of needs of potential buyers within a segment
    c. Difference of needs of buyers between segments
    d. Feasibility of a marketing action to reach a segment
    e. Simplicity and cost of assigning potential buyers to a segment

13. When General Motors found that buyers of the Suburban were no longer primarily businesses but families, they added features such as power steering, air conditioning, and three seats, to enhance the appeal. They recognized a _____.
    a. Potential for increased profit and return on investment
    b. Similarity of needs of potential buyers within a segment
    c. Difference of needs of buyers between segments
    d. Feasibility of a marketing action to reach a segment
    e. Simplicity and cost of assigning potential buyers to a segment

14. The National Hockey League is caught in a dilemma of needing to attract young fans but needing the income of television which insists on night games which last beyond the bedtime of younger fans.
    a. Potential for increased profit and return on investment
    b. Similarity of needs of potential buyers within a segment
    c. Difference of needs of buyers between segments
    d. Feasibility of a marketing action to reach a segment
    e. Simplicity and cost of assigning potential buyers to a segment

15. Yamaha makes jet skis in warm climate areas and snowmobiles in cold climate areas.
    a. Potential for increased profit and return on investment
    b. Similarity of needs of potential buyers within a segment
    c. Difference of needs of buyers between segments
    d. Feasibility of a marketing action to reach a segment
    e. Simplicity and cost of assigning potential buyers to a segment

Chapter 10--Answers

Discussion Questions

What Market Segmentation Means

Example:

1. Dry hair (need conditioners)
   styled hair
   dandruff suffers

Mountain Dew--flavor
Compaq computers--quality
Jeep--offroad vehicles
Panasonic products--technology
Fox Network--younger, more "hip"

Ways to segment Consumer Markets

1. geographic
2. demographic
3. psychographic
4. behavioural
5. demographic

Analyzing Market Segments Using Cross Tabulation

1. increases
2. 5-10
3. 17-22
4. romance

Product Positioning

Example:

Head-to-head--Tylenol, Advil

Product differentiation--Chrysler minivan

Sample Tests

1. c
2. e
3. b
4. b
5. c
6. e
7. a
8. d
9. d
10. a
11. a
12. b
13. e
14. d
15. c

CHAPTER 11

Developing New Products And Services

<u>Why is Chapter 11 important</u>? This chapter explains the first element of the marketing mix—the product and how products are classified. It illustrates the process of introducing a new product and how each step is vital to that product's success. It also shows some of the major reasons why a majority of all new products fail.

Product: A good, service, or idea consisting of a bundle of tangible and intangible attributes that satisfies consumers and is received in exchange for money or some other unit of value.

CHAPTER OUTLINE

I. VARIATIONS OF PRODUCTS

    A. Product Line
    B. Product Item
    C. Product Mix
    D. Classifying Products
        1. Tangibility
            a. nondurable good
            b. durable good
        2. Type of user
            a. consumer good
            b. industrial good

II. CLASSIFYING CONSUMER AND INDUSTRIAL GOODS

    A. Consumer Goods
        1. Convenience goods
        2. Shopping goods
        3. Specialty goods
        4. Unsought goods

    B. Industrial Goods
        1. Production goods
            a. raw materials
            b. component parts
        2. Support goods
            a. installations
                 i. buildings
                ii. fixed equipment
            b. accessory equipment
            c. supplies
            d. services

III. NEW PRODUCTS

    A. Newness
        1. Compared with existing products

    2. In legal terms
    3. From company's prospective
    4. From consumer's prospective
        a. continuous innovation
        b. dynamically continuous innovation
        c. discontinuous innovation

B. Marketing Reasons for Failure
    1. Insignificant "point of difference"
    2. Incomplete market and product definition
    3. Too little market attractiveness
    4. Poor executive of the marketing mix
    5. Poor product quality on critical factors
    6. Bad timing
    7. No economical access to buyers

C. New Product Process
    1. Strategy development
        a. identify markets
        b. identify strategic roles
    2. Idea generation
        a. customer suggestions
        b. employee and co-worker suggestions
        c. research and development breakthrough
            i. create cultures where new ideas thrive
            ii. have systems to move those ideas through development
                and get them to market quickly
        d. competitive products
    3. Screening and evaluation
        a. internal approach
        b. external approach
    4. Business analysis
    5. Development
    6. Market testing
        a. test marketing
        b. simulated test markets
    7. Commercialization

You should be able to place these key terms in the outline and be able to discuss them.

business analysis	idea generation	product line	slotting fee
commercialization	industrial goods	product mix	specialty goods
consumer goods	market testing	production goods	support goods
convenience goods	new-product process	protocol	unsought goods
development	new-product strategy development	screening & evaluation	
failure fee	product	shopping goods	

QUESTIONS & PROBLEMS

CLASSIFYING PRODUCTS

Two major ways to classify products are by degree of tangibility and by the type of user.

Degree of tangibility

Classification by tangibility divides products into three groups:

Nondurable goods
Durable goods
Services

Classify the following products listed below by their degree of tangibility:

1. ketchup___*non*___
2. paper plates___*non*___
3. lawn care___*service*___
4. day care___*service*___
5. bath towels___*durable*___
6. carpeting___*durable*___

Many students mistake the term "durable good" for something that is physically strong. A fine delicate crystal vase is a durable good because it can be used again and again whereas though a fireplace log might be heavy and strong, once it is burned it is gone! (The vase is durable, the log is nondurable)

Type of user

The second major type of product classification is based on the user.

Consumer goods
Industrial goods

Classify the following products according to user:

1. nails___*both*___
2. cake mix___*cons*___
3. ball bearings___*ind*___
4. farm machinery___*ind*___
5. printing press___*ind.*___
6. suitcase___*consumer*___

CONSUMER GOODS CLASSIFICATION

Consumer goods can be further classified by considering three characteristics: (1) the effort the consumer spends on the decision, (2) the attributes used in purchase, and (3) the frequency of purchase.

Convenience goods
Shopping goods
Specialty goods
Unsought goods

Classify the following products by the type of consumer goods:

1. breath mints_____*Conv*_____
2. personal computer_____*Shop*_____
3. pianos_____*Specialty*_____
4. burial plots_____*unsought*_____
5. life insurance_____*unsought*_____

It is important to remember that there is no "master list" of what is a convenience good and what is a specialty good; the classification depends on the characteristics of the purchase decision in terms of time, importance, risk, etc. A pair of running shoes could be a shopping good to one person and a specialty good to another.

INDUSTRIAL GOODS CLASSIFICATION

Industrial goods are classified not only on the attribute the consumer uses but also on how the item is to be used.

Production goods
Support goods

Classify the following industrial goods:

1. legal services for contracts_____*support*_____
2. wood glue for fastening veneer_____*production*_____
3. tomatoes for ketchup_____*production*_____
4. coal for heating plant furnaces_____*support*_____

There are four types of support goods. These include:

Installations
Accessory equipment
Supplies
Services

Match the correct industrial support goods classification with the examples listed below:

1. custodial work_____*Services*_____
2. stock warehouses_____*Inst*_____
3. advertising agency_____*services*_____
4. office chairs_____*accessory*_____

Newness from the consumer's perspective

Newness from the consumer's perspective classifies new products according to the degree of learning required by the consumer.

Discontinuous innovation
Dynamically continuous innovation
Continuous innovation

Match the correct term to the statements or examples listed below:

1. Although this product can be somewhat disruptive, totally new behaviour by the consumer is not required for its use._____

2. No new behaviours must be learned._____

3. Often a significant amount of time must be spent initially educating the consumer on how to use the product._____

4. An example of this type of product newness is the advent of automatic transmissions .
_____

5. An example of this type of product newness is the microwave oven._____

6. An example of this type of product newness is the disposable straight razor._____

NEW PRODUCTS AND WHY THEY FAIL

The greatest differences between those products that succeed and those that don't are in having a real product advantage and having a precise protocol - a statement that identifies a well-defined target market before product development begins; specifies customers' needs, wants, and preferences; and carefully states what the product would be and do.

DEVELOPING NEW PRODUCTS

Idea Generation

What are the sources of ideas for new products? Which are likely to be most successful?_____
_____

Screening and Evaluation

Who should participate in the screening of new product proposals? Why? (consider New Coke)_____
_____

Business Analysis

Check which of the following are performed at the business analysis stage of the new product process?

1. A determination is made as to whether the new product will help or hurt sales of existing products._____
_____

2. An assessment is made as to whether current distribution channels can be used or whether new channels will have to be developed._____

3. Costs for research and development are determined._____

4. Costs for production are determined._____

5. Forecasts are made for future sales._____

6. Forecasts are made for potential market share._____

7. A break-even analysis is performed._____

8. Estimates are made for return-on-investment to assess future profitability._____

Development

What problems are likely to arise during development? How can these effect the product and its marketing? (consider the Intel Pentium chip)_____

_____

Market Testing

The market testing stage of the new product process involves exposing actual products to prospective consumers under realistic purchase conditions to see if they will buy. Test marketing involves offering a product for sale on limited basis in a defined area.

Commercialization:

How do you determine when to commercialize the product? The video CD was introduced by RCA in the late 1970's and was a tremendous failure. They are successful now with very little change in technology. Why?_____

_____

_____

_____

CAN YOU PASS THE TEST?

OVERVIEW OF CHAPTER 11: TERMS AND DEFINITIONS (multiple choice)

1. A good, service, or idea consisting of a bundle of tangible and intangible attributes that satisfies consumers and is received in exchange for money or another unit of value is known as _____.
  - a. Product
  - b. Product line
  - c. Consumer goods
  - d. Product mix
  - e. Industrial goods

2. _____ is the number of product lines offered by a company.
  - a. Product
  - b. Product line
  - c. Consumer goods
  - d. Product mix
  - e. Industrial goods

3. _____ are items that the consumer purchases frequently and with a minimum of shopping effort.
  - a. Convenience goods
  - b. Production goods
  - c. Specialty goods
  - d. Shopping goods
  - e. Unsought goods

4. A group of products, or _____, are closely related because they satisfy a class of needs, are used together, are sold to the same customer group, are distributed through the same type of outlets, or fall within a given price range.
  - a. Convenience goods
  - b. Product line
  - c. Specialty goods
  - d. Shopping goods
  - e. Unsought goods

5. Products purchased by the ultimate consumer are called _____.
  - a. Product
  - b. Product line
  - c. Consumer goods
  - d. Product mix
  - e. Industrial goods

6. The sequence of activities, called the _____, are used by a firm to identify business opportunities and convert them to a salable good or service. There are seven steps: new product strategy, idea generation, screening and evaluation, business analysis, development, market testing, and commercialization.
    a. Failure fee
    b. Slotting fee
    c. Market testing
    d. New product process
    e. New product strategy development

7. Products for which the consumer will compare several alternatives using various criteria are known as _____.
    a. Convenience goods
    b. Production goods
    c. Specialty goods
    d. Shopping goods
    e. Unsought goods

8. _____ is the phase of the new product process in which a firm defines the role of new products in terms of overall corporate objectives.
    a. Business analysis
    b. Commercialization
    c. New product strategy development
    d. Screening and evaluation
    e. Idea generation

9. A phase of the new product process, called _____, in which prospective consumers are exposed to actual products under realistic purchase conditions to see if they will buy.
    a. Failure fee
    b. Slotting fee
    c. Market testing
    d. New product process
    e. New product strategy development

10. Products used in the production of other items for ultimate consumers are _____.
    a. Product
    b. Product line
    c. Consumer goods
    d. Product mix
    e. Industrial goods

11. _____ are products used in the manufacturing of other items that become part of the final product.
    a. Convenience goods
    b. Production goods
    c. Specialty goods
    d. Shopping goods
    e. Unsought goods

12. _____ are products that a consumer will make a special effort to search out and buy.
    a. Convenience goods
    b. Production goods
    c. Specialty goods
    d. Shopping goods
    e. Unsought goods

13. _____ are items used to assist in the production of other goods.
    a. Convenience goods
    b. Production goods
    c. Specialty goods
    d. Shopping goods
    e. Support goods

14. A phase of the new product process, in which a firm develops a pool of concepts as candidates for new products is known as _____.
    a. Business analysis
    b. Commercialization
    c. Development
    d. Screening and evaluation
    e. Idea generation

15. Step four of the new product process, _____, involves specifying the product features and marketing strategy and making necessary financial projections to commercialize a product.
    a. Business analysis
    b. Commercialization
    c. Development
    d. Screening and evaluation
    e. Idea generation

16. _____ is phase of the new product process in which the idea on paper is turned into a prototype; includes manufacturing and laboratory and consumer tests.
    a. Business analysis
    b. Commercialization
    c. Development
    d. Screening and evaluation
    e. Idea generation

17. _____ is a phase of the new product process in which a firm uses internal and external evaluations to eliminate ideas that warrant no further development effort.
    a. Business analysis
    b. Commercialization
    c. Development
    d. Screening and evaluation
    e. Idea generation

18. The final phase of the new product process, _____, in which the product is positioned and launched into full-scale production and sale.
    a. Business analysis
    b. Commercialization
    c. Development
    d. Screening and evaluation
    e. Idea generation

19. _____ are products that the consumer does not know about or knows about and does not initially want.
    a. Convenience goods
    b. Production goods
    c. Specialty goods
    d. Shopping goods
    e. Unsought goods

20. A penalty payment, or _____, is made to retailers by manufacturers if a new product does not reach predetermined sales levels.
    a. Failure fee
    b. Slotting fee
    c. Market testing
    d. New product process
    e. New product strategy development

21. _____ is payment by a manufacturer to place a new product on a retailer's shelf.
    a. Failure fee
    b. Slotting fee
    c. Market testing
    d. New product process
    e. New product strategy development

22. The number of product lines offered by a company make up the _____.
    a. Product line
    b. Product item
    c. Stock keeping unit (SKU)
    d. Product mix
    e. Strategic Business Unit (SBU)

23. _____ are a group of products that are closely related because they satisfy a class of needs, are used together, are sold to the same customer group, are distributed through the same type of outlets, or fall within a given price range.
    a. Product line
    b. Product item
    c. Stock keeping unit (SKU)
    d. Product mix
    e. Strategic Business Unit (SBU)

24. A specific product, or _____, is noted by a unique brand, size, or price.
    a. Product line
    b. Product item
    c. Stock keeping unit (SKU)
    d. Product mix
    e. Strategic Business Unit (SBU)

25. _____ is a revised item or totally new innovation - example: automatic focus on 35mm cameras or cellular car telephones.
    a. Newness compared with existing products
    b. Newness in legal terms
    c. Newness from a company perspective
    d. Newness from the consumer perspective
    e. Newness from an industry standpoint

26. The term "new" can be used by any product for up to a twelve-month period after it enters regular distribution. This represents _____.
    a. Newness compared with existing products
    b. Newness in legal terms
    c. Newness from a company perspective
    d. Newness from the consumer perspective
    e. Newness from an industry standpoint

27. _____ represents a product is functionally different from existing offerings - example: the first Polaroid camera.
    a. Newness compared with existing products
    b. Newness in legal terms
    c. Newness from a company perspective
    d. Newness from the consumer perspective
    e. Newness from an industry standpoint

28. _____ is the newness is determined by the degree of learning required by the consumer. For example: learning to cook with a microwave.
    a. Newness compared with existing products
    b. Newness in legal terms
    c. Newness from a company perspective
    d. Newness from the consumer perspective
    e. Newness from an industry standpoint

29. Many pharmaceutical companies have facilities for research and development of new drugs for rare diseases. Unfortunately, since so few people have these diseases, it would be financially unsound to produce them. This represents _____.
    a. Target market too small
    b. Insignificant point of difference
    c. Poor product quality
    d. No access to market
    e. Bad timing

30. A young musician goes on tour to promote his new album. The concerts are a huge success, but due to a problem in distribution, the records do not arrive in the music stores until six weeks after the concert. This is an example of _____.
    a. Target market too small
    b. Insignificant point of difference
    c. Poor product quality
    d. Bad timing
    e. Poor execution of the marketing mix

31. Holly Farm's new roasted chicken was edible for 18 days, but it took nine days to get from the production plant to the supermarket. This is an example of _____.
    a. Target market too small
    b. Insignificant point of difference
    c. Poor execution
    d. No access to market
    e. Bad timing

32. Duractin, an aspirin that gave eight hours of relief, lasted somewhat longer than other brands. However, people with headaches were more concerned with immediate relief than long-lasting relief, creating a(n) _____.
    a. Target market too small
    b. Insignificant point of difference
    c. Poor product quality
    d. No access to market
    e. Bad timing

33. When General Foods introduced Post Cereals with freeze-dried fruits, people found that by the time the fruit had absorbed enough milk, the flakes were soggy. This was an example of _____.
    a. Target market too small
    b. Insignificant point of difference
    c. Poor product quality
    d. No access to market
    e. Bad timing

34. Some new products are actually superior to ones on the market but they may not have the budget to compete for available shelf space because _____.
    a. Target market too small
    b. Insignificant point of difference
    c. Poor product quality
    d. No access to market
    e. Bad timing

35. In 1984 AT&T introduced its model 7300 Unix personal computer in order to establish a foothold in networked microcomputers, and to take advantage of the company's expertise in communication networks. This would have been the _____ stage of the new product process.
    a. Market testing
    b. Commercialization
    c. Screening and evaluation
    d. Business analysis
    e. Development

36. In 1991 McDonald's introduced hot soups, such as clam chowder and cream of broccoli, to several selected franchises. Only one of the several McDonalds in a given metro area carried it. This would have been the _____ stage of the new product process.
    a. Market testing
    b. Commercialization
    c. Screening and evaluation
    d. Business analysis
    e. Development

37. If Goorman's evaluation of the black foil package was favourable, then nationwide introduction would be sometime late in 1995. This would have been the _____ stage of the new product process.
    a. New product strategy development
    b. Idea generation
    c. Screening and evaluation
    d. Business analysis
    e. Development

38. Many companies use their own checklist for quickly evaluating product ideas early in the development process. This would have been the _____ stage of the new product process.
    a. New product strategy development
    b. Idea generation
    c. Screening and evaluation
    d. Business analysis
    e. Development

39. Hallmark Cards regularly solicits product ideas from members of its sales force through the use of a mail questionnaire. This would have been the _____ stage of the new product process.
    a. New product strategy development
    b. Idea generation
    c. Screening and evaluation
    d. Business analysis
    e. Development

40. At this stage, a major hospital supply company considers factors such as total market dollars, market growth rate, gross profitability, and cash flow. This would have been the _____ stage of the new product process.
    a. New product strategy development
    b. Idea generation
    c. Screening and evaluation
    d. Business analysis
    e. Development

41. At Mattel, new product prototypes are "child tested" in special testing playgrounds during this stage. This would have been the _____ stage of the new product process.
    a. New product strategy development
    b. Idea generation
    c. Screening and evaluation
    d. Business analysis
    e. Development

Chapter 11--Answers

Discussion Questions

Classifying Products

1. nondurable
2. nondurable
3. services
4. services
5. durable
6. durable

Type of User

1. both
2. consumer goods
3. industrial goods
4. industrial goods
5. industrial goods
6. consumer goods

Consumer Goods Classification

1. convenience
2. shopping
3. specialty
4. unsought
5. unsought

Industrial Goods Classification

1. support goods
2. production goods
3. production goods
4. support goods

1. services
2. installations
3. services
4. accessory equipment

Newness from the Consumer's Perspective

1. dynamically continuous innovation
2. continuous innovation
3. discontinuous innovation
4. dynamically continuous innovation
5. discontinuous innovation
6. continuous innovation

Developing New Products--Business Analysis

1. yes
2. yes
3. yes
4. yes
5. yes
6. yes
7. yes
8. yes

Commercialization

Focus was on recording ability not quality of picture. Most VCR and CD players were used with older TV's rendering the "quality of picture" argument moot.

Sample Tests

1. a	22. d
2. d	23. a
3. a	24. b
4. b	25. c
5. c	26. b
6. d	27. a
7. d	28. d
8. c	29. a
9. c	30. d
10. e	31. c
11. b	32. b
12. c	33. c
13. e	34. d
14. e	35. b
15. a	36. a
16. c	37. a
17. d	38. c
18. b	39. b
19. e	40. d
20. a	41. e
21. b	

CHAPTER 12

Managing Products and Brands

<u>Why is Chapter 12 important?</u> This chapter illustrates the importance of the marketing mix throughout the life of a product. It shows how each stage of a product's can be enhanced by utilizing different strategies with the mix elements. In addition, it describes the important of branding and choosing a good brand name.

Product Life Cycle: Concept describing the stages a new product goes through in the marketplace: introduction, growth, maturity, and decline.

CHAPTER OUTLINE

I. PRODUCT LIFE CYCLE

    A. Introduction Stage
         1. Promotion
              a. primary demand
              b. selective demand
         2. Price
              a. skimming
              b. penetration

    B. Growth Stage
         1. Competitor's appear
         2. Profit peaks
         3. Sales grow at increasing rate
         4. Product differentiation
         5. Expanded distribution

    C. Maturity Stage
         1. Leveling off of industry sales or product class revenue
         2. Marginal competitors leave
         3. Sales increase at decreasing rate
         4. Profit declines through price competition
         5. Marketing expenses directed at holding share

    D. Decline Stage
         1. Deletion
         2. Harvesting

    E. Dimensions
         1. Length of Product Life Cycle
         2. Shape of their curve
               a. generalized
              b. high learning
              c. low learning
              d. fashion
              e. fad
         3. Product level

        a. class
        b. form
        c. brand
    4. Product Life Cycle and consumers
        a. diffusion of innovation
            i. innovators
            ii. early adopters
            iii. early majority
            iv. late majority
            v. laggards

II. MANAGING THE PRODUCT LIFE CYCLE

    A. Product Modification
    B. Market Modification
        1. Increasing use
        2. Creating new use situations
        3. Finding new users
    C. Repositioning the Product
        1. Reacting to a competitor's position
        2. Reaching a new market
        3. Catching a rising trend
        4. Changing value offered
            a. trading up
            b. trading down

III. BRANDING

    A. Brand Personality and Brand Equity

    B. Licensing

    C. Picking a Good Brand Name
        1. Suggests product benefits
        2. Memorable, distinctive position
        3. Fits company and product image
        4. No legal or regulatory restrictions
        5. Simple and emotional

    D. Strategies
        1. Manufacturer branding
            a. multiproduct (family) branding
            b. co-branding
            c. multibranding
            d. eurobranding
        2. Private branding
        3. Mixed branding
        4. Generic branding

III. PACKAGING

    A. Benefits
        1. Communication
        2. Functional
        3. Perceptual

B. Trends
    1. Environmental sensitivity
    2. Health and safety concerns

IV. PRODUCT WARRANTY

A. Variations
    1. Express warranties
    2. Limited coverage warranties
    3. Full coverage warranties
    4. Implied warranties

B. Importance
    1. Product liability
    2. Marketing advantage

You should be able to place these key terms in the outline and be able to discuss them.

branding	generic brand	multiproduct branding	product modification
brand equity	licensing	packaging	trade name
brand name	manufacturer branding	private branding	trademark
brand personality	market modification	product class	trading down
co-branding	mixed branding	product form	trading up
downsizing	multibranding	product life cycle	warranty
euro-branding			

Questions & Problems

PRODUCT LIFE CYCLE

There are four distinct stages in the product life cycle. Each stage suggests its own distinct marketing strategy.

Introduction stage
Growth stage
Maturity stage
Decline stage

INTRODUCTION STAGE

High-definition televisions (HDTV) are considered in its introduction stage.

Describe the HDTV in its introductory stage in terms of:

1. Marketing objective:_____

2. Competition:_____

3. Product:_____

4. Price:_____

5. Promotion:_____

6. Place:_____

Select the appropriate term for the statements below:

1. This pricing strategy is used to help recover research and development costs and to capitalize on price insensitivity of early buyers._____

2. This pricing strategy discourages competitors and helps build unit volume._____

GROWTH STAGE

Wireless telephones (cellular or digital) can be considered in its growth stage.

Describe wireless telephones in its growth stage in terms of:

1. Marketing objective:_____

2. Competition:_____

3. Product:_____

4. Price:_____

5. Promotion:_____

6. Place:_____

MATURITY STAGE

Hard Rock Cafe could be describe as in the mature stage of "theme" restaurants.

Describe Hard Rock Cafe in its maturity stage in terms of:

1. Marketing objective:_____

2. Competition:_____

3. Product:_____

4. Price:_____

5. Promotion:_____

6. Place:_____

DECLINE STAGE

Underwood Typewriter could be described as in the decline stage of the Product Life Cycle.

Describe Underwood Typewriter in its decline stage in terms of:

1. Marketing objective:_____

2. Competition:_____

3. Product:_____

4. Price:_____

5. Promotion:_____

6. Place:_____

MODIFYING THE PRODUCT

Decide whether the following statements are examples of:

Increasing use
Creating new use situations
Finding new users

1. Tums antacid is now being advertised as an excellent calcium supplement._____

2. For years the makers of Dentyne chewing gum have advised people to chew Dentyne if they can't brush after every meal. Now they suggest chewing gum in those situations where you "can't smoke."_____

3. Major car makers are offering buying incentives to newly graduated university and college students who traditionally have had little or no credit history._____

PRODUCT REPOSITIONING

Product repositioning is changing the place a product occupies in a consumer's mind relative to competitive products. A firm can reposition a product by changing one or more of the four marketing mix elements. There are several reasons for repositioning a product:

Reacting to a competitor's position
Reaching a new market
Catching a rising trend
Changing the value offered

Match the reason for repositioning with the following examples:

1. Snickers chocolate bar was repositioned from a chocolate bar to a snack food which has twice as large a market _____

2. Mercedes traded down its line with the introduction of the Mercedes 190 sedan.
_____

3. Coke was repositioned as a slightly sweeter, less filling soft drink because Coca-Cola discovered that its 1984 market share in supermarkets was 2 percent behind Pepsi-Cola's.
_____

4. To reposition its athletic shoes, New Balance offered a new range of widths tailored for the aging baby boomer market._____

BRANDING

Find an example of a brand name that best exemplifies each characteristic below:

1. The name should describe product benefits._____

2. The name should be memorable, positive, and distinctive._____

3. The name should fit the company or product image._____

4. The name should have no legal restrictions._____

5. The name should be simple and emotional._____

PACKAGING

The packaging component of a product refers to any container in which it is offered for sale and on which information is communicated. There are three main benefits of packaging:

Communication benefits
Functional benefits
Perceptual benefits

Two current trends in packaging deal with (1) environmental sensitivity (packaging materials, recycling, etc.), and (2) the health and safety aspects of the packages themselves.

Indicate the type of benefits or trend each package represents:

1. Cereal in resealable packages._____

2. Coca-Cola's new contoured bottle._____

3. Windex's refillable sprayer._____

4. Tylenol's sealed packages._____

5. A product with a CSA seal of approval stamped right on the package._____

WARRANTIES

A warranty is a statement indicating the liability of the manufacturer for product deficiencies. There are four major types of warranties:

Express warranty
Limited-coverage warranty
Full warranty
Implied warranty

Match the type of warranty with the statement listed below:

1. Written statements of a manufacturer's liabilities for product deficiencies._____

2. Warranties assigning responsibility for product deficiencies to a manufacturer even though the item was sold by a retailer._____

3. A statement of liability by a manufacturer that has no limits of noncoverage._____

4. A manufacturer's statement indicating the bounds of coverage and noncoverage for any product deficiencies._____

CAN YOU PASS THE TEST?

OVERVIEW OF CHAPTER 12: TERMS AND DEFINITIONS (multiple choice)

1. A concept which describes the stages a new product goes through in the marketplace: introduction, growth, maturity, and decline is known as _____.
    a. Market modification
    b. Product life cycle
    c. Product modification
    d. Product class
    e. Product form

2. _____ is a practice whereby a company tries to increase a product's use among existing customers, create new use situations, or find new customers.
    a. Market modification
    b. Product life cycle
    c. Product modification
    d. Product class
    e. Product form

3. The practice of reducing the content of package without changing package size and maintaining or increasing the package price is called _____.
    a. Brand equity
    b. Downsizing
    c. Packaging
    d. Trading down
    e. Trading up

4. An entire product category or industry is called _____.
    a. Market modification
    b. Product life cycle
    c. Product modification
    d. Product class
    e. Product form

5. _____ involves altering a product's characteristics, such as its quality, performance, or appearance, to try to increase and extend the product's sales.
    a. Marketing modification
    b. Product life cycle
    c. Product modification
    d. Product class
    e. Product form

6. _____ is adding value to a product by including more features or higher-quality materials.
    a. Brand equity
    b. Downsizing
    c. Packaging
    d. Trading down
    e. Trading up

7. The legal identification, or _____, of a company's exclusive rights to use a brand name or trade name.
    a. Brand name
    b. Trade name
    c. Trademark
    d. Generic brand
    e. Private branding

8. A manufacturer's branding strategy in which a distinct name is given to each of its products is called _____.
    a. Branding
    b. Mixed branding
    c. Multibranding
    d. Multiproduct branding
    e. Euro-branding

9. When a company manufactures products that are sold under the name of a wholesaler or retailer, it is called _____.
    a. Brand name
    b. Trade name
    c. Trademark
    d. Generic brand
    e. Private branding

10. _____ is reducing the number of features, quality, or price of a product.
    a. Brand equity
    b. Downsizing
    c. Packaging
    d. Trading down
    e. Trading up

11. _____ is variations of a product within a product class.
    a. Marketing modification
    b. Product life cycle
    c. Product modification
    d. Product class
    e. Product form

12. _____ is a branding strategy in which the brand name for a product is designated by the producer, using either a multiproduct or multibrand approach.
    a. Licensing
    b. Warranty
    c. Manufacturer branding
    d. Generic brand
    e. Private branding

13. A branding strategy in which a company uses one name for all products _____ is also referred to as blanket or family branding.
    a. Branding
    b. Mixed branding
    c. Multibranding
    d. Multiproduct branding
    e. Euro-branding

14. A branding strategy which lists no product name, only a description of contents is called _____.
    a. Brand name
    b. Trade name
    c. Trademark
    d. Generic brand
    e. Private branding

15. A _____ is a statement indicating the liability of a manufacturer for product deficiencies.
    a. Licensing
    b. Warranty
    c. Manufacturer branding
    d. Generic brand
    e. Private branding

16. The activity in which an organization uses a name, phrase, design, or symbol or a combination of these to identify its products and distinguish them from those of a competitor is called _____.
    a. Licensing
    b. Warranty
    c. Manufacturer branding
    d. Generic brand
    e. Branding

17. A _____ is the commercial, legal name under which a company does business.
    a. Brand name
    b. Trade name
    c. Trademark
    d. Generic brand
    e. Private branding

18. The container, or _____, that holds a product offered for sale and on which information is communicated.
    a. Brand equity
    b. Downsizing
    c. Packaging
    d. Trading down
    e. Trading up

19. _____ is a branding strategy in which the company may market products under their own name and that of a reseller.
    a. Branding
    b. Mixed branding
    c. Multibranding
    d. Multiproduct branding
    e. Euro-branding

20. A contractual agreement, called a _____, whereby a company allows another firm to use its brand name and usually requires the product be made to their specifications .
    a. Licensing
    b. Warranty
    c. Manufacturer branding
    d. Generic brand
    e. Private branding

21. The added value, or _____, gives brand name provides a product.
    a. Brand equity
    b. Downsizing
    c. Packaging
    d. Trading down
    e. Trading up

22. Any word or "device" (design, shape, sound, or colour) that is used to distinguish one company's products from a competitor's is known as a _____.
    a. Brand name
    b. Mixed branding
    c. Multibranding
    d. Multiproduct branding
    e. Euro-branding

23. The strategy of using the same brand name for the same product across all countries in the European Union is called _____.
    a. Branding
    b. Mixed branding
    c. Multibranding
    d. Multiproduct branding
    e. Euro-branding

24. _____ is the strategy by which a company retains the product but reduces the support costs.
    a. Deletion
    b. Harvesting
    c. Contracting
    d. Repositioning
    e. Renewal

25. A strategy by which a company drops a product from the line is known as _____.
    a. Deletion
    b. Harvesting
    c. Contracting
    d. Repositioning
    e. Renewal

26. A set of human characteristics associated with a brand name is called _____.
    a. Branding
    b. Brand attributes
    c. Brand personality
    d. Repositioning
    e. Renewal

27. To discourage competitive entry, a company can price low, referred to as penetration pricing, during the _____.
    a. Introduction stage
    b. Growth stage
    c. Maturity stage
    d. Decline stage
    e. Death stage

28. Heavy promotional expenditures are made to build primary demand during the _____.
    a. Introduction stage
    b. Growth stage
    c. Maturity stage
    d. Decline stage
    e. Death stage

29. Promotional expenses at the _____ are often directed towards contests or games to keep people using the product.
    a. Introduction stage
    b. Growth stage
    c. Maturity stage
    d. Decline stage
    e. Death stage

30. Sales and profits drop steadily during the _____.
    a. Introduction stage
    b. Growth stage
    c. Maturity stage
    d. Decline stage
    e. Death stage

31. Often the _____ is entered because of environmental or technological factors .
    a. Introduction stage
    b. Growth stage
    c. Maturity stage
    d. Decline stage
    e. Death stage

32. During the _____ sales grow slowly and there is little profit, often a result of large investment costs.
    a. Introduction stage
    b. Growth stage
    c. Maturity stage
    d. Decline stage
    e. Death stage

33. Emphasis of advertising shifts to selective demand during the _____.
    a. Introduction stage
    b. Growth stage
    c. Maturity stage
    d. Decline stage
    e. Death stage

34. Improved versions or new features may be added to the original design during the _____.
    a. Introduction stage
    b. Growth stage
    c. Maturity stage
    d. Decline stage
    e. Death stage

35. A high initial price may be used as part of a skimming strategy to help recover costs of development during the _____.
    a. Introduction stage
    b. Growth stage
    c. Maturity stage
    d. Decline stage
    e. Death stage

36. During the _____, companies are competing aggressively for shelf space.
    a. Introduction stage
    b. Growth stage
    c. Maturity stage
    d. Decline stage
    e. Death stage

37. Profit declines since the cost of gaining each new buyer at this stage is greater than the incremental revenue during the _____.
    a. Introduction stage
    b. Growth stage
    c. Maturity stage
    d. Decline stage
    e. Death stage

38. The company may follow the strategies of deletion, harvesting, or contracting in the _____.
    a. Introduction stage
    b. Growth stage
    c. Maturity stage
    d. Decline stage
    e. Death stage

39. During the _____, the emphasis of advertising shifts to selective demand, product changes are made to help differentiate the brand from its competitors, and emphasis is put on gaining as much distribution as possible. CD-ROM's are currently in this stage.
    a. Introduction stage
    b. Growth stage
    c. Maturity stage
    d. Decline stage
    e. Death stage

40. During the _____, a company wants to maintain its existing buyers because few new buyers are available to replace any who are lost. Colour television is in this stage.
    a. Introduction stage
    b. Growth stage
    c. Maturity stage
    d. Decline stage
    e. Death stage

41. A marketing objective for a company at the _____ is to promote consumer awareness. Pentium III technology for personal computers is at this stage.
    a. Introduction stage
    b. Growth stage
    c. Maturity stage
    d. Decline stage
    e. Death stage

42. At the _____ a company may either drop the product from the line, retain the product but reduce support costs, or contract with a smaller company to manufacture the product.   Long playing records (vinyl) are at this stage.
     a. Introduction stage
     b. Growth stage
     c. Maturity stage
     d. Decline stage
     e. Death stage

43. Sales begin immediately, the benefits are readily understood for a _____.
     a. High learning product
     b. Low learning product
     c. Fashion product
     d. Fad
     e. Trend

44. There is an extended introductory period during which significant education of the customer is required for a _____.
     a. High learning product
     b. Low learning product
     c. Fashion product
     d. Fad
     e. Trend

45. Consumers have to be taught the benefits of the new product for a _____.
     a. High learning product
     b. Low learning product
     c. Fashion product
     d. Fad
     e. Trend

46. The life cycles for _____ appear most frequently in women's and men's clothing styles and may vary in length from years to decades.
     a. High learning product
     b. Low learning product
     c. Fashion product
     d. Fad
     e. Trend

47. The _____ cycle has rapid sales upon introduction and usually equally rapid sales declines.
     a. High learning product
     b. Low learning product
     c. Fashion product
     d. Fad
     e. Trend

48. The marketing strategy is to gain a strong distribution network at the beginning for a _____.
     a. High learning product
     b. Low learning product
     c. Fashion product
     d. Fad
     e. Trend

49. Often this cycle rises, declines, then rises again for a _____.
    a. High learning product
    b. Low learning product
    c. Fashion product
    d. Fad
    e. Trend

50. A perfect example of a _____ was the Teenage Mutant Ninja Turtles.
    a. High learning product
    b. Low learning product
    c. Fashion product
    d. Fad
    e. Trend

Chapter 12--Answers

Discussion Questions

Product Life Cycle

Introduction Stage

Example:

1. Build primary demand for the televisions
2. existing, especially large-screen TVs
3. High quality picture and CD sound
4. high price, estimated at $5000
5. mass media, widespread advertising
6. specialty retail outlets

1. skimming
2. market penetration

Growth Stage

Example:

1. Become the alternative to wired phones
2. wired telephones
3. high quality, wireless communications
4. at or above cost of wired phone usage
5. advertising
6. all retail outlets

Maturity Stage

Example:

1. maintain #1 position
2. Planet Hollywood, All Star Cafe
3. theme restaurants
4. medium to high
5. logo apparel, word-of-mouth
6. major cities and tourist destinations

Decline Stage

Example:

1. survival
2. word processors, computers
3. manual and electric typewriters
4. low, under $100
5. none
6. some office supply companies, small retailers

Modifying the Product

1. finding new users
2. increasing use
3. creating new use situations

Product Repositioning

1. catching a rising trend
2. changing value offered
3. reacting to a competitor's position
4. reaching a new market

Branding

Example:

1. Easy-Off Oven Cleaner
2. Netscape
3. PowerMac
4. Esso
5. Slice

Packaging

1. functional benefits
2. perceptual benefits
3. functional benefits
4. functional benefits
5. communicative benefits

Warranties

1. express warranty
2. implied warranty
3. full warranty
4. limited-coverage warranty

Sample Tests

1. b	28. b
2. a	29. c
3. b	30. d
4. d	31. d
5. c	32. a
6. e	33. b
7. c	34. b
8. c	35. a
9. e	36. b
10. d	37. c
11. e	38. d
12. c	39. b
13. d	40. c
14. d	41. a
15. b	42. d
16. e	43. b
17. b	44. a
18. c	45. a
19. b	46. c
20. a	47. d
21. a	48. b
22. a	49. c
23. e	50. d
24. b	
25. a	
26. c	
27. a	

CHAPTER 13

Managing Services

Why is Chapter 13 important? Services marketing is the fastest growing area of marketing. Within this chapter you will see the differences in product management for services versus tangible products. The chapter illustrates the successful use of the marketing mix for a company offering a service product.

Services: activities, deeds, or other basic intangibles offered for sale to consumers in exchange for money or something else of value.

CHAPTER OUTLINE

I. UNIQUENESS OF SERVICES

    A. Four I's of Services
        1. Intangibility
        2. Inconsistency
        3. Inseparability
        4. Inventory

    B. Service Continuum

II. HOW CONSUMERS PURCHASE SERVICES

    A. Purchasing a Service
        1. Search properties
        2. Experience properties
        3. Credence properties

    B. Customer Contact Audit

    C. Postpurchase Evaluation

III. MANAGING THE MARKETING OF SERVICES

    A. Internal Marketing

    B. Marketing Mix
        1. Product
            a. exclusivity
            b. branding
            c. capacity management
        2. Pricing
            a. to affect consumer perceptions
            b. to be used in capacity management
        3. Place
        4. Promotion

You should be able to place these key terms in the outline and be able to discuss them.

capacity management	gap analysis	internal marketing	service continuum
customer contact audit	idle production capacity	off-peak pricing	service
four I's of services			

QUESTIONS & PROBLEMS

THE FOUR I's OF SERVICES

There are four unique elements to services: intangibility, inconsistency, inseparability, and inventory. These four elements are referred to as the four I's of services.

Intangibility
Inconsistency
Inseparability
Inventory

Assume you own a car detailing service or a housesitting service, give at least one example of how you would compensate for each "I" of service:

1. intangibility_____
2. inconsistency_____
3. inseparability_____
4. inventory_____

THE SERVICE CONTINUUM

As companies look at what they bring to the market, there is a range from tangible to intangible, or product-dominant to service-dominant organizations, referred to as the service continuum.

Arrange the following in order from (1) most product-dominant to (13) most service-dominant entities:

	Rank
Purina Puppy Chow	_____
Levi's Jeans	_____
Raisin Bran	_____
Maupintour Travel	_____
College professor	_____
Licensed practical nurse	_____
TCI Cablevision	_____
Burger King	_____
Broadway theatre	_____
Graphic's Advertising	_____
Custom bootmaker	_____
Condominium	_____
Toyota Dealer	_____

HOW CONSUMERS PURCHASE SERVICES

There are three important factors to be considered during the purchase process:

Search qualities
Experience qualities
Credence qualities

Match the correct quality to the statement or definition below:

1. Qualities which can only be discerned after purchase or during consumption._____

2. These qualities are common to medical diagnoses and legal services._____

3. Dualities which can be determined before purchase._____

4. Services such as restaurants and child care have these qualities._____

5. Qualities or characteristics which the consumer may find impossible to evaluate even after purchase and consumption._____

6. Tangible goods such as jewellery, clothing, and furniture._____

CUSTOMER CONTACT AUDIT

A customer contact audit is the flow chart of the points of interaction between a consumer and a service provider.

Trace the points of customer contact when using the drive-in window of a fast food restaurant:

SERVICE QUALITY

Differences between the consumer's expectations and experiences are identified through gap analysis .

Describe a situation where your expectations far exceeded the actual outcome. Explain which element of the marketing mix was poorly executed, or which "I" of service was not addressed:

_____
_____

MANAGING THE MARKETING OF SERVICES

There are three areas of importance which should be considered in the product/service element of the marketing mix:

Exclusivity
Branding
Capacity management

Describe how each of these service issues differs from production goods:

1. exclusivity_____
_____

2. branding_____
_____

3. capacity management_____
_____

PRICING

Pricing services plays two roles: (1) to affect consumer perceptions and (2) to be used in capacity management .

What type of business would be hurt by "low" prices in terms of consumer perceptions:_____

List four types of services that use off-peak pricing.

1._____

2._____

3._____

4._____

DISTRIBUTION

Distribution is a major factor in developing a service marketing strategy because of the inseparability of services from the provider.

Charles Schwab now lets his customers make stock trades at home on their personal computer. Many banks have adopted, not only ATM's (automatic teller machines), but in-home banking by personal computer. How has this distribution philosophy helped to make them more competitive? Can you think of any other examples?_____

PROMOTION

In the past, advertising has been viewed negatively by many nonprofit and professional service organizations. Although opposition to advertising remains strong in some professional groups, the barriers to promotion are being broken down. In service marketing, public relations can play a major role in promotional strategy.

Explain what promotional tools you would use for each of the following and why:

1. National Hockey League_____

2. A law firm_____

3. A new physician_____

4. Your college or university_____

5. An accounting firm_____

CAN YOU PASS THE TEST?

OVERVIEW OF CHAPTER 13: TERMS AND DEFINITIONS (multiple choice)

1. A marketing philosophy based on the notion that a service organization must focus on its employees before successful programs can be directed at consumers is known as _____.
   a. Capacity management
   b. Internal marketing
   c. Customer contact audit
   d. Off-peak pricing
   e. Four I's of Services

2. With regard to service, _____ refers to a situation where the service provider is available, but there is no demand.
   a. Capacity management
   b. Service continuum
   c. Gap analysis
   d. Services
   e. Idle production capacity

3. Activities, deeds, or other basic intangibles offered for sale to consumers in exchange for money or some other value:
   a. Capacity management
   b. Service continuum
   c. Gap analysis
   d. Services
   e. Idle production capacity

4. Charging different prices during different times of the day or days of the week to reflect variations in demand for service reflects _____.
   a. Capacity management
   b. Internal marketing
   c. Customer contact audit
   d. Off-peak pricing
   e. Four I's of Services

5. _____ is managing the demand for a service so that it is available to consumers .
   a. Capacity management
   b. Internal marketing
   c. Customer contact audit
   d. Off-peak pricing
   e. Four I's of Services

6. A flow chart of the points of interaction between a consumer and a service provider is called _____.
   a. Capacity management
   b. Service continuum
   c. Customer contact audit
   d. Services
   e. Idle production capacity

7. The elements, called _____, that make services unique in relation to products. They include intangibility, inconsistency, inseparability, and inventory.
    a. Capacity management
    b. Internal marketing
    c. Customer contact audit
    d. Off-peak pricing
    e. Four I's of Services

8. A range from the tangible to the intangible or good-dominant or service-dominant offerings available in the marketplace is called _____.
    a. Capacity management
    b. Service continuum
    c. Gap analysis
    d. Services
    e. Idle production capacity

9. An evaluation tool, known as _____, which compares expectations about a particular service to the actual experience a consumer has with the service.
    a. Capacity management
    b. Internal marketing
    c. Gap analysis
    d. Off-peak pricing
    e. Four I's of Services

10. The product cannot be held, touched, or seen before the purchase decision is an example of _____.
    a. Intangibility
    b. Inconsistency
    c. Inseparability
    d. Inventory
    e. Intelligence

11. The performance of one service provider in the firm may vary in quality from another service provider in the firm. This is known as _____.
    a. Intangibility
    b. Inconsistency
    c. Inseparability
    d. Inventory
    e. Intelligence

12. Often there is a need to deal with idle production capacity, when the service provider is available but there is no demand. The I represented by this example is _____.
    a. Intangibility
    b. Inconsistency
    c. Inseparability
    d. Inventory
    e. Intelligence

13. There is difficulty in separating the service from the service provider or from the setting in which the service is provided because of _____.
    a. Intangibility
    b. Inconsistency
    c. Inseparability
    d. Inventory
    e. Intelligence

Chapter 13--Answers

Discussion Questions

The Four I's of Services

Example:

1. name or servicemark
2. training
3. staffing
4. scheduling

The Service Continuum

Suggested ranking:

	Rank
Purina Puppy Chow	_2_
Levi's Jeans	_3_
Raisin Bran	_1_
Maupintour Travel	_9_
Junior college professor	_13_
Licensed practical nurse	_12_
TCI Cablevision	_8_
Burger King	_7_
Broadway theater	_11_
Graphic's Advertising	_10_
Custom bootmaker	_6_
Condominium	_4_
Toyota Dealer	_5_

How Consumers Purchase Services

1. experience qualities
2. credence qualities
3. search qualities
4. experience qualities
5. credence qualities
6. search qualities

Customer Contact Audit

Example:

Greeting--timeliness, friendliness
Order taking--correctness of order and price
Order delivery--speed, correctness

Managing the Marketing of Services

Example:

1. custom service--individualized
2. gives tangibility
3. load factors and timing

Pricing

Example: Professional service practices would be hurt by low prices (low price = perception of low quality)

1. airlines
2. movie theatres
3. theme parks
4. hotels

Distribution

Example:

Online accounting systems

Promotion

Example:

1. autograph signings, picture opportunities, family nights with group pricing.

Sample Tests

1. b	11. b
2. e	12. d
3. d	13. c
4. d	
5. a	
6. c	
7. e	
8. b	
9. c	
10. a	

CHAPTER 14

Pricing: Relating Objectives To Revenue And Costs

<u>Why is Chapter 14 important</u>? This chapter begins the process of pricing a product. Within is shown the pricing constraints, both internal and external, and the pricing objectives that motivate a compnany's pricing policy. In addition, there is a thorough discussion of the revenues and costs and their relationship to pricing policy and the market environment.

Price: The money or other considerations (including other goods and services) exchanged for the ownership or use of a good or services.

CHAPTER OUTLINE

I. PRICING IN THE MARKETING MIX

    A. Identify Pricing Constraints and Objectives
        1. Identifying pricing constraints
            a. demand for product class, product and brand
            b. newness of product (stage of Product Life Cycle)
            c. single product versus product line
            d. cost of producing and marketing product
            e. cost of changing price and time period they apply
            f. type of competitive market
                i. pure monopoly
                ii. oligopoly
                iii. monopolistic competition
                iv. pure competition
            g. competitor's prices
        2. Identifying pricing objectives
            a. profit
            b. sales
            c. market share
            d. unit volume
            e. survival
            f. social responsibility

    B. Estimating Demand and Revenue
        1. Estimating demand
            a. demand curve
            b. demand factors
                i. consumer tastes
                ii. price and availability of other products
                iii. consumer income
        2. Estimating revenue
            a. total revenue
            b. average revenue
            c. marginal revenue
            d. price elasticity of demand

    C. Estimating Cost, Volume, and Profit Relationships
        1. Cost
            a. total cost
            b. fixed cost
            c. variable cost
            d. marginal cost
        2. Marginal analysis and profit maximization
        3. Break-even analysis

You should be able to place these key terms in the outline and be able to discuss them.

average revenue	demand factors	price	total cost
barter	fixed cost	price elasticity	total revenue
break-even analysis	marginal analysis	pricing constraints	value
break-even chart	marginal cost	pricing objectives	value-pricing
break-even point	marginal revenue	profit equation	variable cost
demand curve			

QUESTIONS & PROBLEMS

PRICE

The basic profit equation is: Profit = Total revenue - Total cost. Sometimes we become so concerned with memorizing formulas that we forget to use common sense to figure out how those formulas were devised in the first place. Many other formulas in this chapter are simply expansions or variations of this basic price equation formula. **THINK**, don't just memorize.

For example:

Profit = (Total revenue)-(Total cost)

=[unit price x quantity sold]-[fixed cost + (unit variable cost x quantity sold)]

COMMON MARKETING ABBREVIATIONS

TR = TOTAL REVENUE
MR = MARGINAL REVENUE
AR = AVERAGE REVENUE
TC = TOTAL COST
FC = FIXED COST
VC = VARIABLE COST
MC = MARGINAL COST
Q = QUANTITY
P = PRICE
BEP = BREAK-EVEN POINT
UVC = UNIT VARIABLE COST
PLC = PRODUCT LIFE CYCLE
E = ELASTICITY

IDENTIFYING PRICING CONSTRAINTS

There are seven primary pricing constraints:

Demand for product class, product and brand
Newness of product (stage of Product Life Cycle)
Single product versus product line
Cost of producing and marketing product
Cost of changing price and time period they apply
Type of competitive market
Competitor's prices

Decide which constraint(s) affects the following products:

1. local telephone service_____

2. an electric car_____

3. typewriters_____

4. a word processing program_____

5. credit cards with "smart card" technology_____

IDENTIFYING PRICING OBJECTIVES

Expectations that specify the role of price in an organization's marketing and strategic plans are pricing objectives. There are six main pricing objectives:

profit
sales
market share
unit volume
survival
social responsibility

Match the correct pricing objectives to the examples below:

1. An airline in bankruptcy cuts its fares._____

2. BIC prices its pens at 1/3 the cost of its leading competitor._____

3. Ford gives yearend incentives on Taurus to make sure it beats the Honda Accord for the number one car in the market._____

4. Coca-Cola begins to use returnable bottles and charge a deposit on them._____

5. America On-Line gives its software away and lowers connect prices for new customers._____

6. Rolls Royce continues to price its cars at a substantial premium over the rest of the industry._____
_____

DEMAND CURVES

A demand curve shows a maximum number of products consumers will buy at a given price. Below is a demand schedule showing the relationship between unit price and demand.

	UNIT PRICE (in dollars)	DEMAND (in units)
A.	250	200
B.	200	400
C.	150	600
D.	100	800
E.	50	1000

Plot a demand curve using the information listed above:

Determine total revenue at each point:

    1. A = _____

    2. B = _____

    3. C = _____

    4. D = _____

    5. E = _____

Using the information in example "A", plot a total revenue curve:

Assuming a selling price of $50 per unit, fixed costs of $20,000, and a unit variable cost of $30, calculate the break-even point in dollars and units.

    1. BEP (Dollars)_____

    2. BEP (Units)_____

PRICE ELASTICITY

Price elasticity of demand (E) is defined as the percentage change in quantity demanded relative to a percentage change in price.

Elasticity(E)= $[(Q_1 - Q_0)$ (divided by) $Q_0]$ (divided by) $[(P_1 - P_0)$ (divided by) P_0

where
        Q_0 = Initial quantity demanded
        Q_1 = New quantity demanded
        P_0 = Initial price
        P_1 = New price

Price elasticity of demand is not the same over all possible prices of the product.
Price elasticity may be expressed three ways:

1. If elasticity is greater than one, total revenue will be higher after a price decrease. The product demand is called "price elastic."

2. If elasticity is less than one, total revenue will be lower after a price decrease. The product demand is called "price inelastic."

3. If elasticity is equal to one, total revenue is the same as before, and the product demand is called "unitary elastic."

Using the information below, (1) calculate elasticity, and (2) determine whether the type of product demand is:

        Elastic
        Inelastic
        Unitary Elasticity

1. Elasticity = _____

Type_____

Initial Quantity	10,000
New Quantity	12,000
Initial Price	$2,000
New Price	$1,000

2. Elasticity = _____

Type_____

Initial Quantity	10,000
New Quantity	15,000
Initial Price	$2,000
New Price	$1,000

3. Elasticity = _____

Type_____

Initial Quantity	10,000
New Quantity	30,000
Initial Price	$2,000
New Price	$1,000

COST CONCEPTS

Students almost always have problems deciding which items are fixed costs and which items are variable costs; there is no "master" list. Variable cost are always related directly to the amount of product produced or sold. Test yourself, if you have to incur any expense for the production of a single new unit, then the expense is a variable cost. If you sell hot dogs, hot dog buns will be a variable cost even though you have to buy them all the time. If you sell one more hot dog, you will have to buy one more hot dog bun, if you sell three hot dogs, you will have to incur the expense of three more buns. The cost incurred varies directly with the quantity produced or sold.

Many students don't think of utility bills as being fixed costs since they vary from month to month. This is not so! Regardless of the varying amounts, you will always have a utility bill and there is not a direct relationship to the quantity of product produced or sold. If you have a hot dog stand, you have to pay for the bun warmer electricity whether there are eight hot dog buns inside or 28. There is no direct correlation between the cost of electricity and whether you have sold one more hot dog or not. Therefore, the electricity is a fixed cost.

MARGINAL ANALYSIS AND PROFIT MAXIMIZATION

Marginal analysis means that as long as revenue received from the sale of an additional product (marginal revenue) is greater than the additional cost of producing and selling it (marginal cost), a firm will expand its output of that product.

Answer the following questions:

1. Marginal revenue follows a_____slope.

2. The essence of marginal revenue is to operate up to the output quantity at which:_____

BREAK-EVEN ANALYSIS

Use the following information to determine the break-even point in dollars and in units:

>   Fixed costs: $12,000
>   Variable costs: $8
>   Unit variable price: $14

BEP dollars = _____

BEP units = _____

Determine how many units need to be produced in order to obtain a profit of $75,000:

profit = (P x Q) - [FC + (UVC x Q)]

P = $25
UVC = $5
FC = $25,000

Units produced = _____

A common mistake in using the profit formula is failing to "change the sign" when removing the brackets from the second part of the equation. The " + " sign becomes a "-" sign between the FC and the (UVC x Q).

FORMULA REVIEW

Write out the formulas, definitions, or equations for the following:

1. Price = _____

2. Profit = _____

3. Total Revenue = _____

4. Average Revenue = _____

5. Marginal Revenue = _____

6. Elasticity = _____

7. Total cost = _____

8. Fixed cost = _____

9. Variable cost = _____

10. Marginal cost = _____

11. BEP = _____

CAN YOU PASS THE TEST?

OVERVIEW OF CHAPTER 14: TERMS AND DEFINITIONS (multiple choice)

1. Factors that limit a firm's latitude in the price it may set are called _____.
   a. Barter
   b. Price elasticity of demand
   c. Pricing constraints
   d. Pricing objectives
   e. Profit equations

2. The average amount of money received for selling one unit of a product is known as _____.
   a. Total revenue
   b. Marginal revenue
   c. Break-even analysis
   d. Average revenue
   e. Break-even point

3. _____ is the money or other considerations exchanged for the purchase or use of the product, idea, or service.
   a. Demand factors
   b. Value
   c. Marginal analysis
   d. Value pricing
   e. Price

4. The total amount of money received from the sale of a product is _____.
   a. Total revenue
   b. Marginal revenue
   c. Break-even analysis
   d. Break-even chart
   e. Break-even point

5. _____ are those that determine the strength of consumers' willingness and ability to pay for goods and services.
   a. Demand factors
   b. Price elasticity of demand
   c. Pricing constraints
   d. Pricing objectives
   e. Profit equations

6. _____ are those objectives that specify the role of price in an organization's marketing and strategic plans.
   a. Barter
   b. Price elasticity of demand
   c. Pricing constraints
   d. Pricing objectives
   e. Profit equations

7. The change in total revenue obtained by selling one additional unit is called _____.
   a. Total revenue
   b. Marginal revenue
   c. Break-even analysis
   d. Break-even chart
   e. Break-even point

8. The graphic summation of points representing the maximum quantity of a product consumers will buy at different price levels is known as the _____.
   a. Demand curve
   b. Total cost
   c. Fixed cost
   d. Marginal cost
   e. Variable cost

9. _____ is the principle of allocation of resources that balances incremental revenues of an action against incremental costs.
   a. Total revenue
   b. Marginal analysis
   c. Break-even analysis
   d. Break-even chart
   e. Break-even point

10. An expense of the firm that is stable and does not change with the quantity of product that is produced and sold is called _____.
   a. Demand curve
   b. Total cost
   c. Fixed cost
   d. Marginal cost
   e. Variable cost

11. _____ is the percentage change in quantity demanded relative to a percentage change in price.
   a. Barter
   b. Price elasticity of demand
   c. Pricing constraints
   d. Pricing objectives
   e. Profit equations

12. An expense of the firm, or _____, is one that varies directly with the quantity of product produced and sold.
   a. Demand curve
   b. Total cost
   c. Fixed cost
   d. Marginal cost
   e. Variable cost

13. _____ is the change in total cost that results from producing and marketing one additional unit.
   a. Total revenue
   b. Marginal costs
   c. Break-even analysis
   d. Break-even chart
   e. Break-even point

14. Profit = Total revenue- Total cost is the equation for _____.
   a. Barter
   b. Price elasticity of demand
   c. Pricing constraints
   d. Pricing objectives
   e. Profit equations

15. The total expense a firm incurs in producing and marketing a product, which includes fixed cost and variable cost is known as _____.
   a. Demand curve
   b. Total cost
   c. Fixed cost
   d. Marginal cost
   e. Variable cost

16. _____ is an analysis of the relationship between total revenue and total cost to determine profitability at various levels of output.
   a. Total revenue
   b. Marginal analysis
   c. Break-even analysis
   d. Break-even chart
   e. Break-even point

17. _____ shows the quantity at which total revenue and total cost are equal and beyond which profit occurs.
   a. Total revenue
   b. Marginal revenue
   c. Break-even analysis
   d. Break-even chart
   e. Break-even point

18. _____ is a graphic presentation of a break-even analysis.
   a. Total revenue
   b. Marginal revenue
   c. Break-even analysis
   d. Break-even chart
   e. Break-even point

19. _____ is the ratio of perceived quality to price.
   a. Demand factors
   b. Value
   c. Marginal analysis
   d. Value pricing
   e. Price

20. The practice of simultaneously increasing service and product benefits and maintaining or decreasing price is called _____.
   a. Demand factors
   b. Value
   c. Marginal analysis
   d. Value pricing
   e. Price

21. _____ is the practice of exchanging goods and services for other goods and services rather than for money.
   a. Barter
   b. Price elasticity of demand
   c. Pricing constraints
   d. Pricing objectives
   e. Profit equations

22. _____ represents the total expenses incurred in producing and marketing the product.
   a. Total cost
   b. Fixed cost
   c. Variable cost
   d. Marginal cost
   e. Average cost

23. _____ is the change in total cost by producing and marketing one more unit
   a. Total cost
   b. Fixed cost
   c. Variable cost
   d. Marginal cost
   e. Average cost

24. Expenses, or _____, are those that are static regardless of the number of units marketed or produced
   a. Total cost
   b. Fixed cost
   c. Variable cost
   d. Marginal cost
   e. Average cost

25. _____ represents expenses vary directly with quantity of product produced and sold
   a. Total cost
   b. Fixed cost
   c. Variable cost
   d. Marginal cost
   e. Average cost

26. A cereal manufacturer prices all its oatmeal-based breakfast cereals within ten cents of each other. This represents _____
   a. Demand for the product class, product, or brand
   b. Competitor's prices
   c. Newness of product in the product life cycle
   d. Cost of changing prices and the time period
   e. Single product vs. product line to which they apply

27. A recent survey in Mademoiselle magazine stated that 61 percent of the working women they surveyed are willing to spend more money for snack foods with fewer calories. This represents _____.
   a. Demand for the product class, product, or brand
   b. Competitor's prices
   c. Cost of producing and marketing the product
   d. Cost of changing prices and the time period
   e. Type of competitive market

28. Colour inserts for supermarket price promotions appear each Wednesday. The deadline for proof copy is the preceding Saturday. This represents _____
   a. Demand for the product class, product, or brand
   b. Competitor's prices
   c. Cost of producing and marketing the product
   d. Cost of changing prices and the time period
   e. Type of competitive market

29. A product manager notices that 40 percent of his sales are coming from customers he classifies as laggards in the adoption process. He lowers his prices significantly to lure even more of them. This represents _____.
   a. Demand for the product class, product, or brand
   b. Competitor's prices
   c. Newness of product in the product life cycle
   d. Cost of changing prices and the time period
   e. Single product vs. product line to which they apply

30. Most public utilities must petition regulatory commissions in order to obtain a rate increase. This represents _____.
   a. Demand for the product class, product, or brand
   b. Competitor's prices
   c. Cost of producing and marketing the product
   d. Cost of changing prices and the time period
   e. Type of competitive market

31. It costs a consumer products company $700,000 to develop, test market, and introduce a new instant coffee. This represents _____.
   a. Demand for the product class, product, or brand
   b. Competitor's prices
   c. Newness of product in the product life cycle
   d. Cost of producing and marketing the product
   e. Single product vs. product line to which they apply

32. Texas Instruments was left with millions of dollars in lost revenue when it became involved in a price war and ended up selling units for $49, which originally sold for $1,100. This represents _____.
   a. Demand for the product class, product, or brand
   b. Competitor's prices
   c. Newness of product in the product life cycle
   d. Cost of changing prices and the time period
   e. Single product vs. product line to which they apply

33. Few sellers who are sensitive to each other's price in a(n) _____.
   a. Pure monopoly
   b. Monopolistic competition
   c. Oligopoly
   d. Pure competition
   e. Market economy

34. One seller who sets the price for a unique product in a(n) _____.
   a. Pure monopoly
   b. Monopolistic competition
   c. Oligopoly
   d. Pure competition
   e. Market economy

35. Many sellers following market price of identical, commodity products in a(n) _____.
    a. Pure monopoly
    b. Monopolistic competition
    c. Oligopoly
    d. Pure competition
    e. Market economy

36. Many sellers who compete on non-price factors in a(n) _____.
    a. Pure monopoly
    b. Monopolistic competition
    c. Oligopoly
    d. Pure competition
    e. Market economy

37. In the early 1980s Chrysler's president, Lee Iacocca, offered large cash rebates in order to maintain the firm's cash flow when unit sales were slumping. This represents a _____ pricing strategy.
    a. Profit
    b. Sales
    c. Market share
    d. Survival
    e. Social responsibility

38. Medtronics, makers of the first heart pacemakers, placed its priorities on recipients over profits. This represents a _____ pricing strategy.
    a. Profit
    b. Sales
    c. Market share
    d. Survival
    e. Social responsibility

39. In the rental car business, Hertz and Avis resorted to tie-in promotions with airlines in order to maintain their market position against National and Budget car rental companies. This represents a _____ pricing strategy.
    a. Profit
    b. Sales
    c. Market share
    d. Survival
    e. Social responsibility

40. Prior to the introduction of Datril, an identical and lower-priced acetaminophen product, Tylenol, was priced high in order to reap the highest possible revenue. This represents a _____ pricing strategy.
    a. Profit
    b. Sales
    c. Market share
    d. Survival
    e. Social responsibility

41. A supermarket prices Yoplait yogourt at a point that produces the largest margin between cost and selling price. This represents a _____ pricing strategy.
    a. Profit
    b. Sales
    c. Market share
    d. Survival
    e. Social responsibility

42. General Motors sought to reduce its car inventories through low interest car loans and rebates. This represents a _____ pricing strategy.
    a. Profit
    b. Sales
    c. Market share
    d. Survival
    e. Unit volume

Chapter 14--Answers

Discussion Questions

Identifying Pricing Constraints

1. type of competitive market
2. cost of production and marketing product
3. demand for product, class, or brand
4. competitors' prices
5. newness of product

Identifying Pricing Objectives

1. survival
2. sales
3. unit volume
4. social responsibility
5. market share
6. profit

Demand Curves

1. A = 50,000
2. B = 80,000
3. C = 90,000
4. D = 80,000
5. E = 50,000

1. BEP $ = 50,000
2. BEP units = 1000

Price Elasticity

1. Elasticity = .4--inelastic

2. Elasticity = 1--unitary elasticity

3. Elasticity = 4--elastic

Marginal Analysis and Profit Maximization

1. declining
2. MR = MC

Break-Even Analysis

$ = 28,000
units = 2000

units produced = 5000

Formula Review

1. Price = list price - discount allowances + extra fees

2. Profit = $(P \times Q) - [FC + (UVC \times Q)]$

3. Total Revenue = $P \times Q$

4. Average Revenue = TR/Q

5. Marginal Revenue = change in TR \ change in Q

6. Elasticity = % change in Q / % change in P

7. Total Cost = TVC + FC

8. Fixed Cost = the sum of all stable company expenses which do not vary directly with quantity produced and sold.

9. Variable Cost = the sum of the company expenses that vary directly with quantity produced and sold.

10. Marginal Cost = the change in TC / the change in Q

11. BEP = FC/(P - UVC)

Sample Tests

1. c	27. a
2. d	28. d
3. e	29. c
4. a	30. e
5. a	31. d
6. d	32. b
7. b	33. c
8. a	34. a
9. b	35. d
10. c	36. b
11. b	37. d
12. e	38. e
13. b	39. c
14. e	40. b
15. b	41. a
16. c	42. e
17. e	
18. d	
19. b	
20. d	
21. a	
22. a	
23. d	
24. b	
25. c	
26. e	

CHAPTER 15

Pricing: Arriving At The Final Price

Why is Chapter 15 important? This chapter continues the pricing process examining the selection of the appropriate price for a product. It discusses the strategy for pricing products and the types of pricing incentives that are utilized in both consumer and business-to-business marketing.

Price: The money or other considerations (including other goods and services) exchanged for the ownership or use of a good or service.

CHAPTER OUTLINE

I. SELECT AN APPROXIMATE PRICE LEVEL

    A. Demand-Oriented
        1. Skimming
            a. enough prospective customers are willing to by the product immediately at the high initial price to make these sales profitable
            b. the high initial price will not attract competition
            c. lowering the price has only a minor affect on increasing the sales volume and reducing the unit costs
            d. customers interpret the high price as signifying high quality
        2. Penetration pricing
            a. many segments of the market are price sensitive
            b. a low initial price discourages competitors from entering the market
            c. unit production and marketing costs fall dramatically as production volumes increase
        3. Prestige pricing
        4. Price lining
        5. Odd-even pricing
        6. Target pricing
        7. Bundle pricing
        8. Yield management pricing

    B. Cost-Oriented Approaches
        1. Standard markup pricing
        2. Cost-plus pricing
            a. cost-plus percentage-of-cost pricing
            b. cost-plus fixed-fee pricing
         3. Experience curve pricing

    C. Profit-Oriented Approaches
        1. Target profit pricing
        2. Target return-on-sales pricing
        3. Target return-on-investment pricing

    D. Competition-Oriented Approaches
        1. customary pricing
        2. above-, at-, or below-market pricing
        3. loss-leader pricing

II. SET UP THE LIST OR QUOTED PRICE

    A. One-Price Policy

    B. Flexible-Price Policy

    C. Company, Customer, and Competitive Effects
        1. Company effects
        2. Customer effects
        3. Competitive effects

    D. Balancing Incremental Costs and Revenues

III. MAKE SPECIAL ADJUSTMENTS TO THE LIST OR QUOTED PRICE

    A. Discounts
        1. Quantity discounts
            a. noncumulative
            b. cumulative
        2. Seasonal discounts
        3. Trade (functional) discounts
        4. Cash discounts

    B. Allowances
        1. Trade-in allowances
        2. Promotional allowances

    C. Geographic Adjustments
        1. FOB origin pricing
        2. Uniform delivered pricing
            a. single-zone pricing
            b. multiple-zone pricing
            c. FOB with freight allowed pricing
            d. basing point pricing

    D. Legal and Regulatory Aspects of Pricing
        1. Price fixing
        2. Price discrimination
        3. Deceptive pricing
        4. Predatory pricing
        5. Delivered pricing

You should be able to place these key terms in the outline and be able to discuss them.

above-, at-, or below-market pricing
basing-point pricing
bundle pricing
cost-plus pricing
customary pricing
everyday low pricing
experience curve policy
flexible-price policy
FOB origin pricing
loss-leader pricing

odd-even pricing
one-price policy
penetration pricing
predatory pricing
prestige pricing
price discrimination
price fixing
price lining
product-line pricing
promotional allowances

quantity discounts
skimming pricing
standard markup pricing
target pricing
target-profit pricing
target return-on-investment
target return-on-sales
uniform delivered pricing
yield management pricing

QUESTIONS & PROBLEMS

DEMAND-ORIENTED PRICING

1. RC has been testing Royal Crown Premium Draft Cola, targeting the high end of the market. This new soft drink is priced significantly higher than regular RC, Coca-Cola, and Pepsi. What type of pricing does this represent? Is this the type of product which can utilize this type of pricing?_____

2. General Motors original strategy was to have a starter car, the Chevrolet, for the new car owner at an entry level price; then the consumer would be "moved up" to the Pontiac at a slightly high price, then on to the Oldsmobile and Buick, and finally to the Cadillac. Each line of cars had it own identity (in fact, the Buick was once known as the doctor's car) and appealed to a certain market in their price range. The ultimate, the Cadillac was almost three times the cost of the Chevrolet. What type of pricing does this represent? Do you think it would work today?

3. The Saturn introduced its new "entry level" car priced at $10,495. What type of pricing does this represent? What is wrong with this price?_____

4. The new "all-in-one " account at the local bank includes no-service charge chequing, free cheques, a safe deposit box, free travellers cheques, and a reduced rate on a Visa card. What type of pricing is this? Why do companies use this type of pricing?_____

5. When the original BIC pen was introduced, it was priced at 19 cents. The most popular pen at the time cost 99 cents. What two types of pricing are represented here? What is the goal of each?_____ .

COST-ORIENTED PRICING

1. What type of product would indicate the use of a cost-plus percentage-of-cost pricing policy?_____

2. Under what conditions would you choose a cost plus fixed fee over a cost-plus percentage-of-cost pricing strategy?_____

PROFIT-ORIENTED APPROACHES

Assume you wish to establish a price for custom made computer covers using target profit pricing:

Variable cost is constant at $25 per unit
Fixed cost is constant at $1,200.
Demand is insensitive up to $45 per unit
A target profit of $2,500 is sought at an annual volume of 500 units.

Suggested Price:_____

Using the information above, but seeking a 20 percent return on sales, determine your price using target return on sales pricing.

Suggested Price:_____

COMPETITION-ORIENTED APPROACHES

1. List at least three specific products or product types that use customary pricing (other than those cited in the text):

_____

_____

_____

2. On many weekends you will find Coca-Cola priced at $1.99 per six-pack, while 7UP is priced at $3.29 per six-pack and Pepsi and Slice are priced at $2.29 per six-pack. Identify each as an example of the levels of the above, at-, or below market pricing strategy._____

_____

3. Wal-Mart runs a sale on Randy Travis CDs for $6.99. What type of pricing does this represent?_____

_____

SPECIAL ADJUSTMENTS TO LIST OR QUOTED PRICE

There are three special adjustments to the list or quoted price:

Discounts
Allowances
Geographical adjustments

Match the correct term to the statements below:

_____1. A bathing suit manufacturer offered a 20 percent reduction in price to retailers placing their orders by December 4th.

_____2. A pizza parlor issued special lunch cards. Every time a patron had lunch at the parlor, his card was stamped. Whenever a card had twelve stamps, the patron received a free pizza for lunch.

_____3. A manufacturer of garden tools using wholesalers and retailers quoted his price as list price less /30/15/net.

_____4. A supermarket manager agrees to promote a new line of sugarfree gum by sponsoring a "bubble-blowing contest." In appreciation, the manufacturer sends one free case of gum for every three purchases.

_____5. A gas station chain offers its customers a lower price on gas if they pay cash instead of using credit cards.

_____6. A supermarket offered a special price on new brooms to customers who brought their old brooms to the store. The old brooms were displayed by the door next to a barrel of new brooms.

_____7. A telephone company offered a special rate of $10 an hour for phone calls anywhere in Canada.

_____8. A company that sells materials for "build-it-yourself" homes charges a different fee depending upon how far you live from their warehouses.

LEGAL AND REGULATORY ASPECTS OF PRICING

1. A local store advertises a VCR at $89.95, but only has one of that model in the store. When customers come in and inquire, the sales personnel guide the customer to a model priced at $159.95. If asked about the advertised model the store simply says they are "all out" of those. Is this a type of illegal pricing? Why?_____
_____
_____

2. Wal-Mart has been accused of pricing prescriptions below cost in order to drive local pharmacies out of business. What type of pricing is this? What law would this come under?_____
_____

3. Giant Corporation sells office supplies to local office supply stores. For companies who have been long time customers, Giant discounts on all orders. For new customers, no discounts are given even though quantities and locations are virtually the same. Is this a violation under the Competition Act? Why?
_____
_____

CAN YOU PASS THE TEST?

OVERVIEW OF CHAPTER 15: TERMS AND DEFINITIONS (multiple choice)

1. _____ is the practice of replacing promotional allowances with lower manufacturer list prices.
   a. Customary pricing
   b. Price discrimination
   c. Pricing
   d. Everyday low pricing
   e. Price fixing

2. Deliberately pricing a product below its customary price to attract attention to it is known as _____.
   a. Above-, at-, or below-market pricing
   b. Flexible pricing policy
   c. Basing-point pricing
   d. Bundle pricing
   e. Loss-leader pricing

3. Setting the same price for similar customers who buy the same product and quantities under the same conditions is called _____.
   a. One-price policy
   b. Target return-on-sales pricing
   c. Cost plus percentage-of-cost pricing
   d. Predatory pricing
   e. Target return-on-investment

4. _____ is a method of pricing where price often falls following the reduction of costs associated with the firm's experience in producing or selling a product.
   a. Target return-on-sales pricing
   b. Experience curve pricing
   c. Promotional allowances
   d. Uniform delivered pricing
   e. Loss-leader pricing

5. The reduction in unit costs for a large order quantity is known as _____.
   a. Standard markup pricing
   b. FOB origin pricing
   c. Competitive pricing
   d. Quantity discounts
   e. Cost plus fixed-fee pricing

6. A method of pricing, known as _____, is where the title of goods passes to the buyer at the point of loading.
   a. Standard markup pricing
   b. FOB origin pricing
   c. Competitive pricing
   d. Quantity discounts
   e. Cost plus fixed-fee pricing

7. Setting a price to achieve a profit that is a specified percentage of the sales volume is known as
_____.
        a. One-price policy
        b. Target return-on-sales pricing
        c. Cost plus percentage-of-cost pricing
        d. Predatory pricing
        e. Target return-on-investment

8. _____ is the setting a price based on an annual specific-dollar-target volume of profit.
        a. Target profit pricing
        b. Experience curve pricing
        c. Promotional allowances
        d. Uniform delivered pricing
        e. Loss-leader pricing

9. _____ is the offering the same product and quantities to similar customers, but at different prices.
        a. Above-, at-, or below-market pricing
        b. Flexible pricing policy
        c. Basing-point pricing
        d. Bundle pricing
        e. Loss-leader pricing

10. Setting prices by adding a fixed percentage to the cost of all items in a specific product class is known as _____.
        a. Standard markup pricing
        b. FOB origin pricing
        c. Competitive pricing
        d. Quantity discounts
        e. Cost plus fixed-fee pricing

11. A method of pricing based on a product's tradition, standardized channel of distribution, or other competitive factors is called _____.
        a. Customary pricing
        b. Price discrimination
        c. pricing
        d. Everyday low pricing
        e. Price fixing

12. A pricing method, known as _____, is where a supplier is reimbursed for all costs, regardless of what they may be, plus a fixed percentage of the production or construction costs.
        a. Standard markup pricing
        b. FOB origin pricing
        c. Competitive pricing
        d. Quantity discounts
        e. Cost plus fixed-fee pricing

13. _____ is the pricing method based on what the "market price" is.
        a. Above-, at-, or below-market pricing
        b. Flexible pricing policy
        c. Basing-point pricing
        d. Bundle pricing
        e. Loss-leader pricing

14. _____ is the cash payment or extra amount of "free goods" awarded sellers in the channel of distribution for undertaking certain advertising or selling activities to promote a product.
    a. Target return-on-sales pricing
    b. Experience curve pricing
    c. Promotional allowances
    d. Uniform delivered pricing
    e. Loss-leader pricing

15. A geographical pricing practice, known as _____, is where the price the seller quotes includes all transportation costs.
    a. Target return-on-sales pricing
    b. Experience curve pricing
    c. Promotional allowances
    d. Uniform delivered pricing
    e. Loss-leader pricing

16. A method of setting prices to achieve a specific return-on-investment target is known as _____.
    a. One-price policy
    b. Target profit pricing
    c. Cost plus percentage-of-cost pricing
    d. Predatory pricing
    e. Target return-on-investment

17. _____ is the setting the price of a product or service by adding a fixed percentage to the production or construction cost.
    a. One-price policy
    b. Target return-on-sales pricing
    c. Cost plus percentage-of-cost pricing
    d. Predatory pricing
    e. Target return-on-investment

18. The marketing of two or more products in a single "package," is known as _____.
    a. Above-, at-, or below-market pricing
    b. Flexible pricing policy
    c. Basing-point pricing
    d. Bundle pricing
    e. Loss-leader pricing

19. _____ is a conspiracy among firms to set prices for a product.
    a. One-price policy
    b. Target profit pricing
    c. Cost plus percentage-of-cost pricing
    d. Price fixing
    e. Target return-on-investment

20. The practice of charging different prices to different buyers for goods of like trade and quality; is called _____ and can be illegal under the Competition Act.
    a. Customary pricing
    b. Price discrimination
    c. Predatory pricing
    d. Everyday low pricing
    e. Price fixing

21. Selling products at a low price to injure or eliminate a competitor is called _____.
    a. One-price policy
    b. Target profit pricing
    c. Cost plus percentage-of-cost pricing
    d. Predatory pricing
    e. Target return-on-investment

22. Selecting one or more geographical locations (basing points) from which the list price for products plus freight expenses are charged to the buyers is called _____.
    a. Above-, at-, or below-market pricing
    b. Flexible pricing policy
    c. Basing-point pricing
    d. Bundle pricing
    e. Loss-leader pricing

23. Texas Instruments intentionally priced its hand-held calculators and digital watches extremely low in order to make them immediately appealing to the mass market. This is a _____ strategy.
    a. Skimming pricing
    b. Penetration pricing
    c. Prestige pricing
    d. Price-lining pricing
    e. Odd-even pricing

24. A large discount shoe company carries numerous brands of shoes. In order to make it easier for retailers and consumers, shoe prices are limited to only four pricing points. This is a _____ strategy.
    a. Skimming pricing
    b. Penetration pricing
    c. Prestige pricing
    d. Price-lining pricing
    e. Odd-even pricing

25. A famous chocolatier charged an extremely high price for a chocolate chip cookie that had excellent taste and texture but only ten calories. The next best cookie by a competitor had 35 calories. This is a _____ strategy.
    a. Skimming pricing
    b. Penetration pricing
    c. Prestige pricing
    d. Price-lining pricing
    e. Odd-even pricing

26. Two shirts of identical quality and construction have a price discrepancy of $10 because one of them has a small appliqué near the pocket. This is a _____ strategy.
    a. Skimming pricing
    b. Penetration pricing
    c. Prestige pricing
    d. Price-lining pricing
    e. Odd-even pricing

27. Alternative Pioneering Systems decided that consumers would willingly pay $99.95 for a food dehydrator. Based on this price, they determined margins that would have to be paid to wholesalers and retailers. This is a _____ strategy.
    a. Skimming pricing
    b. Penetration pricing
    c. Prestige pricing
    d. Demand-backward pricing
    e. Bundle pricing

28. Several major hotel chains have offered a weekend getaway for only $49.95. This is a _____ strategy.
    a. Skimming pricing
    b. Penetration pricing
    c. Prestige pricing
    d. Price-lining pricing
    e. Odd-even pricing

29. Some cake mixes are sold with the baking pan and icing included. This is a _____ strategy.
    a. Skimming pricing
    b. Penetration pricing
    c. Prestige pricing
    d. Demand-backward pricing
    e. Bundle pricing

30. A convenience store carries hundreds of items. Rather than computing price differences for each item, a fixed percentage of 15 percent is added to the cost of staple items and 40 percent is added to the cost of discretionary items. This is a _____ strategy.
    a. Standard markup pricing
    b. Cost plus percentage-of-cost pricing
    c. Cost plus fixed-fee pricing
    d. Experience curve pricing
    e. Target return-on-investment

31. An eccentric millionaire custom orders a luxury sedan equipped with a foam and water waterbed and genuine chinchilla fur seat covers. The car manufacturer charges him for all costs (including procuring the chinchilla fur), regardless of what those costs may be, plus an additional fee of $8,000. This is a _____ strategy.
    a. Standard markup pricing
    b. Cost plus percentage-of-cost pricing
    c. Cost plus fixed-fee pricing
    d. Experience curve pricing
    e. Target return-on-investment

32. Digital watches once selling for $2,000.00 now sell for as little as $10.00. As demand has increased and production has doubled again and again, production, advertising, and selling costs have declined. This is a _____ strategy.
    a. Standard markup pricing
    b. Cost plus percentage-of-cost pricing
    c. Cost plus fixed-fee pricing
    d. Experience curve pricing
    e. Target return-on-investment

33. A construction firm is anxious to bid on a tract of homes that will cost approximately $150,000 to build. After including the construction firm's fee of 15 percent, the final homes will sell for $172,500 each. This is a _____ strategy.
    a. Standard markup pricing
    b. Cost plus percentage-of-cost pricing
    c. Cost plus fixed-fee pricing
    d. Experience curve pricing
    e. Target return-on-investment

34. The owner of a store specializing in gourmet cookware wants to be sure she realizes a profit of 25 percent on all goods shipped from France. She applies the formula 25 percent = (TR-TC)/TR to determine his prices. This is a _____ strategy.
    a. Target profit pricing
    b. Target return-on-sales pricing
    c. Target return-on-investment pricing
    d. Market penetration pricing
    e. Skimming

35. A craftsman makes wooden hobby horses in his spare time. In order to quit his full-time job he has to be able to make $12,000 profit per year. By inserting the amount $12,000 into the formula P=TR-TC he concludes he must sell 200 units at $140 apiece. This is a _____ strategy.
    a. Target profit pricing
    b. Target return-on-sales pricing
    c. Target return-on-investment pricing
    d. Market penetration pricing
    e. Skimming

36. Because of an oil shortage a plastic products manufacturer will have to pay twice as much this year as she did last year for petroleum-based production materials. In order to stay in business her prices and sales must reflect this change. She uses a computer spreadsheet to determine the best method of ensuring an 18 percent ROI before taxes. This is a _____ strategy.
    a. Target profit pricing
    b. Target return-on-sales pricing
    c. Target return-on-investment pricing
    d. Market penetration pricing
    e. Skimming

37. Rolex takes pride in emphasizing that it makes one of the most expensive watches you can buy. This is a _____ strategy.
    a. Customary pricing
    b. Above-, at-, or below-market pricing
    c. Loss-leader pricing
    d. Sealed-bid pricing
    e. Market penetration pricing

38. An independent grocer sold canned soft drinks at 12 for $1 during the Labour Day Weekend in hopes that customers would buy other higher-priced barbecue and picnic items as well. This is a _____ strategy.
    a. Customary pricing
    b. Above-, at-, or below-market pricing
    c. Loss-leader pricing
    d. Sealed-bid pricing
    e. Market penetration pricing

39. A candy manufacturer had to decide whether to make larger gumballs and charge a nickel, make smaller gumballs and keep the price at a penny, or switch to a different confection altogether that could be adapted to dispensers already found in groceries, etc. This is a _____ strategy.
   a. Customary pricing
   b. Above-, at-, or below-market pricing
   c. Loss-leader pricing
   d. Sealed-bid pricing
   e. Market penetration pricing

For questions 40-55, decide whether the following methods are:

40. Standard markup
   a. Demand based
   b. Cost based
   c. Profit based
   d. Competition based
   e. Market based

41. Skimming
   a. Demand based
   b. Cost based
   c. Profit based
   d. Competition based
   e. Market based

42. Target-profit
   a. Demand based
   b. Cost based
   c. Profit based
   d. Competition based
   e. Market based

43. Experience curve
   a. Demand based
   b. Cost based
   c. Profit based
   d. Competition based
   e. Market based

44. Target return on sales
   a. Demand based
   b. Cost based
   c. Profit based
   d. Competition based
   e. Market based

45. Penetration
   a. Demand based
   b. Cost based
   c. Profit based
   d. Competition based
   e. Market based

46. Prestige
    a. Demand based
    b. Cost based
    c. Profit based
    d. Competition based
    e. Market based

47. Customary
    a. Demand based
    b. Cost based
    c. Profit based
    d. Competition based
    e. Market based

48. Cost plus fixed percentage of cost
    a. Demand based
    b. Cost based
    c. Profit based
    d. Competition based
    e. Market based

49. Loss leader
    a. Demand based
    b. Cost based
    c. Profit based
    d. Competition based
    e. Market based

50. Odd-even pricing
    a. Demand based
    b. Cost based
    c. Profit based
    d. Competition based
    e. Market based

51. Above-, at-, or below-market
    a. Demand based
    b. Cost based
    c. Profit based
    d. Competition based
    e. Market based

52. Cost plus fixed fee
    a. Demand based
    b. Cost based
    c. Profit based
    d. Competition based
    e. Market based

53. Price lining
    a. Demand based
    b. Cost based
    c. Profit based
    d. Competition based
    e. Market based

54. Target return on investment
    a. Demand based
    b. Cost based
    c. Profit based
    d. Competition based
    e. Market based

55. Demand-backward pricing
    a. Demand based
    b. Cost based
    c. Profit based
    d. Competition based
    e. Market based

56. _____ is also called freight absorption pricing.
    a. Single-zone pricing
    b. Multiple zone pricing
    c. FOB with freight-allowed pricing
    d. Basing-point pricing
    e. Delivery price

57. A firm divides its selling territory into geographic areas, or zones. The delivered price to all buyers within a zone is the same, but prices across zones vary depending on the transportation to the zone and the level of competition and demand within the zone. This is a _____ strategy.
    a. Single-zone pricing
    b. Multiple zone pricing
    c. FOB with freight-allowed pricing
    d. Basing-point pricing
    e. Delivery price

58. In _____, all buyers pay the same delivered price for the products, regardless of their distance from the seller.
    a. Single-zone pricing
    b. Multiple zone pricing
    c. FOB with freight-allowed pricing
    d. Basing-point pricing
    e. Delivery price

59. _____ involves selecting one or more geographical locations from which the list price for products plus freight expenses is charged to the buyer.
    a. Single-zone pricing
    b. Multiple zone pricing
    c. FOB with freight-allowed pricing
    d. Basing-point pricing
    e. Delivery price

Chapter 15--Answers

Discussion Questions

Demand-Oriented Pricing

1. prestige, no, it is a convenience good
2. price lining
3. odd-even pricing, about $500 too high
4. bundle pricing, to sell slow moving goods sometimes.
5. market penetration and skimming. market share and profits

Cost-Oriented Pricing

1. one-of-a-kind or few-of-a-kind
2. buying highly technical, few-of-a-kind products

Profit-Oriented Pricing

1. $32.40
2. $34.25

Competition-Oriented Approaches

2. Coke--below; 7UP--above; Pepsi and Slice--at

3. loss leader

Special Adjustments to List or Quoted Price

1. discounts
2. discounts
3. discounts
4. allowances
5. discounts
6. allowances
7. geographic adjustments
8. geographic adjustments

Legal and Regulatory Aspects of Pricing

1. yes, bait and switch
2. predatory pricing
3. yes, price discrimination

Sample Tests

1. d	28. e	55. a
2. e	29. e	56. c
3. a	30. a	57. b
4. b	31. c	58. a
5. d	32. d	59. d
6. b	33. b	
7. b	34. b	
8. a	35. a	
9. b	36. c	
10. a	37. b	
11. a	38. c	
12. e	39. a	
13. a	40. b	
14. c	41. a	
15. d	42. c	
16. e	43. b	
17. c	44. c	
18. d	45. a	
19. d	46. a	
20. b	47. d	
21. d	48. b	
22. c	49. d	
23. b	50. a	
24. d	51. d	
25. a	52. b	
26. c	53. a	
27. d	54. c	

CHAPTER 16

Marketing Channels and Wholesaling

<u>Why is Chapter 16 important?</u> This chapter illustrates the types of intermediaries utilized in getting a product to the ultimate customer and importance of selecting the proper channels of distribution. It discusses the various types of distribution strategies available and how, once selected, to avoid conflict within those channels.

Marketing Channels: A system of distribution which consists of individuals and firms involved in the process of making a product or service available for use or consumption by consumers or individuals users.

CHAPTER OUTLINE

I. NATURE AND IMPORTANCE OF MARKETING CHANNELS

    A. Marketing Channels of Distribution
        1. Middleman
        2. Agent or broker
        3. Wholesalers
        4. Retailer
        5. Distributor
        6. Dealer

    B. Value Created by Intermediaries
        1. Functions
            a. Perform transactional function
            b. Perform logistical function
            c. Perform facilitating function
        2. Consumer benefits
            a. Time utility
            b. Place utility
            c. Form utility
            d. Possession utility

II. CHANNEL STRUCTURE AND ORGANIZATION

    A. Consumer Goods and Services
        1. Direct
        2. Indirect

    B. Industrial Goods and Services
        1. Direct
        2. Indirect

    C. Multiple Channels and Strategic Alliances

    D. Electronic Marketing Channels

    E. Direct Marketing Channels

      F. Channel Intermediaries
          1. Merchant wholesalers
               a. general merchandise wholesalers
               b. specialty merchandise wholesalers
               c. rack jobbers
               d. cash-and-carry wholesalers
               e. drop shippers
               f. truck jobbers
          2. Agents and brokers
               a. manufacturer's agents
               b. selling agents
               c. brokers
          3. Manufacturer's branches and offices

      G. Vertical Marketing Systems and Channel Partnerships
          1. Corporate systems
               a. forward integration
               b. backward integration
          2. Contractual systems
               a. wholesaler-sponsored voluntary chains
               b. retailer-sponsored cooperatives
               c. franchising
          3. Administered systems
          4. Channel partnerships

IV. CHANNEL CHOICE AND MANAGEMENT

      A. Factors
          1. Environmental factors
          2. Consumer factors
          3. Product factors
          4. Company factors

      B. Channel Design Considerations
          1. Target market coverage
               a. extensive distribution
               b. exclusive distribution
               c. selective distribution
          2. Satisfying buyer requirements
               a. information
               b. convenience
               c. variety
               d. attendant services
          3. Profitability

      C. Global Dimensions

      D. Channel Relationships: Conflict, Cooperation, and Law
          1. Conflict
               a. vertical
               b. horizontal
          2. Cooperation
          3. Legal considerations
               a. dual distribution
               b. vertical integration

c. exclusive dealing
d. tied selling
e. refusal to deal
f. resale or market restrictions

You should be able to place these key terms in the outline and be able to discuss them.

brokers   exclusive distribution   marketing channel
cash & carry wholesalers   franchising   rack jobbers
channel captain   general merchandise wholesalers selective distribution
channel partnership   indirect channels   selling agents
direct channel   industrial distributor   specialty merchandise wholesalers
direct marketing   intensive distribution   strategic channels alliances
disintermediation   electronic marketing channels truck jobbers
drop shippers   manufacturer's agents   vertical marketing systems
dual distribution

QUESTIONS & PROBLEMS

RATIONALE FOR INTERMEDIARIES

Intermediaries make possible the flow of products from producers to buyers by performing three basic functions. They are:

Transactional functions
Logistical functions
Facilitating functions

Decide whether the following functions are transactional, logistical, or facilitating functions:

1. marketing information and research_____

2. sorting_____

3. risk taking_____

4. buying_____

5. storing_____

6. financing_____

7. grading_____

8. transporting_____

9. assorting_____

10. selling_____

DIRECT MARKETING

Direct marketing includes mail-order selling, direct-mail sales, catalogue sales, telemarketing, video-text, and televised home shopping.

Tell how each of the following products uses direct marketing:

1. Music CDs and tapes_____

2. Clothing manufacturers_____

3. Book publishers_____

4. America On-Line_____

5. Sears_____

6. MCI_____

MERCHANT WHOLESALERS

There are two main types of merchant wholesalers: full-service wholesalers and limited-service wholesalers.

Indicate whether the following wholesalers are full-service wholesalers or limited-service wholesalers:

1. drop shipper_____

2. rack jobber_____

3. general merchandise wholesaler_____

4. cash and carry wholesaler_____

5. truck jobbers_____

6. specialty merchandise wholesaler_____

VERTICAL MARKETING SYSTEMS (VMS)

A corporate vertical marketing system is a combination of successive stages of production and distribution under a single ownership. A corporate vertical marketing system may use either forward or backward integration.

Match the correct term with the examples or statements listed below:

> Forward integration
> Backward integration

1. Sears owns a substantial share of Whirlpool, on whom it depends for its Kenmore appliances._____
_____

2. Sherwin Williams distributes its paint through a system of company-owned retail outlets._____
_____

3. Zales Corporation, a large jewellery retailer, owns its diamond cutting and polishing facility, as well as its own jewellery manufacturing plant._____

4. Hart, Shaffner, and Marx, which manufactures men's clothing, also owns over 200 retail outlets._____
_____

Under a contractual vertical marketing system, independent production and distribution firms integrate their efforts on a contractual basis to obtain greater functional economies and marketing impact than they could achieve alone. Three variations of contractual marketing systems exist:

Wholesaler-sponsored voluntary chains
Retailer-sponsored cooperatives
Franchising

Match the correct form of contractual marketing system with the statements below:

1. Ford Motor Corporation licenses dealers to sell its cars subject to various sales and service conditions.
_____

2. The Associated Grocers is a group of small independent retailers which formed an organization that operates a wholesale facility cooperatively. They concentrate their buying power through the wholesaler and plan collaborative promotional and pricing activities._____

3. Wholesalers who contract with smaller, independent retailers to standardize and coordinate buying practices, merchandising programs, and inventory management. I.G.A. is an example._____

4. H & R Block licenses individuals or firms to provide tax preparation services to the public._____
_____

CHANNEL DESIGN CONSIDERATIONS

There are three types of distribution density:

Intensive distribution
Selective distribution
Exclusive distribution

Match the type of distribution density to the statements below:

1. Only one retail outlet in a specified geographic area carries the firm's products._____

2. A firm tries to place its products or services in as many outlets as possible._____

3. A firm selects only a few retail outlets in a specific area to carry its products._____

4. BMW uses this approach in order to maintain product image and also to have more control over the selling effort of its dealers._____

5. Hallmark Cards is able to maintain good dealer relationships because it limits the number and maintains the quality of outlets it sells through._____

6. Convenience goods are typically distributed in this manner._____

There are three main considerations affecting channel design:

Target market coverage
Satisfying buyer requirements
Profitability

Match the consideration affecting channel design with the statements or examples listed below:

1. Major universities have begun to offer their "executive" programs off-campus at an industry site in order to reach the growing corporate market._____

2. Companies must decide the best way to satisfy needs for information, convenience, variety, and attendant services._____

3. A new company has to decide which marketing channel to use. They have to take into consideration costs of distribution, advertising, and selling expenses, relative to revenues generated._____

CHANNEL RELATIONSHIPS

Decide whether the following statements are examples of vertical conflict or horizontal conflict:

1. H.J. Heinz Company is embroiled in a conflict with its supermarkets in Great Britain because the supermarkets are promoting and displaying private brands at the expense of Helm brands._____

2. The owner of a downtown McDonald's complained vehemently to the franchiser when he learned that plans for the new enclosed mall included another McDonald's Restaurant._____

3. Friction emerged between Chrysler and its dealers when the company expected dealers to shoulder the burden of its $500 rebate program._____

4. K-Mart store managers complained to Kenner that Venture stores were getting faster delivery during the holiday rush period._____

CAN YOU PASS THE TEST?

OVERVIEW OF CHAPTER 16: TERMS AND DEFINITIONS (multiple choice)

1. A specific type of intermediary between producers and consumers that generally sells, stocks, and delivers a full product assortment is known as _____ .
> a. Brokers
> b. Industrial distributor
> c. Cash and carry wholesalers
> d. Manufacturer's agents
> e. Rack jobbers

2. _____ is a marketing channel where producers and ultimate consumers interact directly with each.
> a. Direct channel
> b. Marketing channel
> c. Direct marketing
> d. Drop shippers
> e. Selling agents

3. Individuals and firms involved in the process of making a product or service available for use or consumption by consumers or industrial users use a _____ .
> a. Direct channel
> b. Marketing channel
> c. Direct marketing
> d. Drop shippers
> e. Selling agents

4. _____ is a marketing channel where intermediaries are situated between producer and consumers.
> a. Intensive distribution
> b. Selective distribution
> c. Dual distribution
> d. Exclusive distribution
> e. Indirect channels

5. Small merchant wholesalers, known as _____, usually handle limited assortments of fast-moving or perishable items that are sold directly from trucks.
> a. Specialty merchandise wholesalers
> b. Franchising
> c. Strategic channel alliances
> d. General merchandise wholesalers
> e. Truck jobbers

6. _____ represent a single producer and are responsible for the entire marketing function of that producer.
> a. Channel captain
> b. Industrial distributor
> c. Cash and carry wholesalers
> d. Selling agents
> e. Vertical marketing systems (VMS)

7. A full service merchant wholesaler that carries a broad assortment of merchandise and performs all channel functions is known as _____.
     a. Specialty merchandise wholesalers
     b. Franchising
     c. Strategic channel alliances
     d. General merchandise wholesalers
     e. Truck jobbers

8. The contractual arrangement, called a _____, is between a parent company and an individual or firm that allows the franchise to operate a certain type of business under an established name and according to specific rules.
     a. Specialty merchandise wholesalers
     b. Franchising
     c. Strategic channel alliances
     d. General merchandise wholesalers
     e. Truck jobbers

9. Full-service merchant wholesalers, or _____, offer a relatively narrow range of products but carry extensive assortments within the product lines carried.
     a. Specialty merchandise wholesalers
     b. Franchising
     c. Strategic channel alliances
     d. General merchandise wholesalers
     e. Truck jobbers

10. An arrangement by which a firm reaches buyers by employing two or more different types of channels for the same basic product is known as _____.
     a. Intensive distribution
     b. Selective distribution
     c. Dual distribution
     d. Exclusive distribution
     e. Indirect channels

11. _____ is a distribution strategy whereby a producer sells its products or services in only one retail outlet in a specific geographic area.
     a. Intensive distribution
     b. Selective distribution
     c. Dual distribution
     d. Exclusive distribution
     e. Indirect channels

12. Individuals or firms that work for several producers and sell noncompetitive, complimentary merchandise in an exclusive territory are known as _____, and are also called manufacturer's representatives.
     a. Brokers
     b. Industrial distributor
     c. Cash and carry wholesalers
     d. Manufacturer's agents
     e. Rack jobbers

13. A distribution strategy, called _____, is where a producer sells his product in a few retail outlets in a specific geographic area.
- a. Intensive distribution
- b. Selective distribution
- c. Dual distribution
- d. Exclusive distribution
- e. Indirect channels

14. Channel intermediaries that do not take title to merchandise and make their profits from commissions and fees by negotiating contracts or deals between buyers and sellers are called _____.
- a. Brokers
- b. Industrial distributor
- c. Cash and carry wholesalers
- d. Manufacturer's agents
- e. Rack jobbers

15. _____ is a distribution strategy whereby a producer sells products or services in as many outlets as possible in a geographic area.
- a. Intensive distribution
- b. Selective distribution
- c. Dual distribution
- d. Exclusive distribution
- e. Indirect channels

16. A merchant wholesaler that owns the merchandise it sells but does not physically handle, stock, or deliver it is known as _____, and is also called a desk jobber.
- a. Direct channel
- b. Marketing channel
- c. Direct marketing
- d. Drop shippers
- e. Selling agents

17. _____ is a limited-service merchant wholesaler that takes title to merchandise but sells only to buyers who call on it and pay cash for and transport their own merchandise.
- a. Brokers
- b. Industrial distributor
- c. Cash and carry wholesalers
- d. Manufacturer's agents
- e. Rack jobbers

18. Professionally managed and centrally coordinated marketing channels designed to achieve channel function economies and maximum marketing impact are known as _____.
- a. Channel captain
- b. Industrial distributor
- c. Cash and carry wholesalers
- d. Manufacturer's agents
- e. Vertical marketing systems (VMS)

19. A merchant wholesaler that furnishes racks or shelves to display merchandise in retail stores, called a
_____ also performs all channel functions, and sells on consignment.
     a. Brokers
     b. Industrial distributor
     c. Cash and carry wholesalers
     d. Manufacturer's agents
     e. Rack jobbers

20. _____ is the selling products by having consumers interact with various advertising media
without a face-to-face meeting with a sales person.
     a. Direct channel
     b. Marketing channel
     c. Direct marketing
     d. Drop shippers
     e. Selling agents

21. _____ is a practice whereby one firm's marketing channel is used to sell another firm's products.
     a. Specialty merchandise wholesalers
     b. Franchising
     c. Strategic channel alliances
     d. General merchandise wholesalers
     e. Truck jobbers

22. A middleman who sells to consumers is a _____.
     a. Middleman
     b. Agent or Broker
     c. Wholesaler
     d. Retailer
     e. Distributor

23. _____ is a term that can mean the same as distributor, retailer, wholesaler, and so forth;
virtually synonymous with middleman.
     a. Middleman
     b. Agent or Broker
     c. Wholesaler
     d. Retailer
     e. Distributor

24. Any intermediary between manufacturer and ultimate user markets is called a _____.
     a. Middleman
     b. Agent or Broker
     c. Wholesaler
     d. Retailer
     e. Distributor

25. _____ is a middleman who sells to other middlemen, usually retailers and usually applies to
consumer markets.
     a. Middleman
     b. Agent or Broker
     c. Wholesaler
     d. Retailer
     e. Distributor

26. A middleman who performs a variety of distribution functions, including selling, maintaining inventories, extending credit, and so on; a more common term in industrial markets but may also be used to refer to wholesalers is known as _____.
    a. Middleman
    b. Agent or Broker
    c. Wholesaler
    d. Retailer
    e. Distributor

27. Any middleman with legal authority to act on behalf of the manufacturer could be called a _____.
    a. Middleman
    b. Agent or Broker
    c. Wholesaler
    d. Retailer
    e. Dealer

28. Mr. Green owns a wholesale hardware company. He carries a broad assortment of merchandise ranging from hand tools to kitchen supplies. However, he does not carry a great assortment within any single product line. He is most likely a _____.
    a. Drop shipper
    b. Rack jobber
    c. General merchandise wholesaler
    d. cash and carry wholesaler
    e. Truck jobber

29. Mrs. Sharp owns a wholesale company that specializes in cutlery. Although she sells only knives and scissors, she carries virtually every type of knife or scissors one could ask for. She is a _____.
    a. Drop shipper
    b. Rack jobber
    c. General merchandise wholesaler
    d. cash and carry wholesaler
    e. Specialty merchandise wholesaler

30. A company in the lumber business is located in an office in a high-rise building in Toronto. Although they neither stock, handle, nor deliver the lumber themselves, they solicit orders from retailers and wholesalers and have the merchandise shipped directly from producers to buyers. They are known as _____.
    a. Drop shipper
    b. Rack jobber
    c. General merchandise wholesaler
    d. cash and carry wholesaler
    e. Truck jobber

31. A seafood wholesaler purchases fresh fish from local fishermen. He in turn sells the fish to restaurants who call on him, pay cash for their purchases, and pick the fish or seafood up themselves. His business represents a _____.
    a. Drop shipper
    b. Rack jobber
    c. General merchandise wholesaler
    d. cash and carry wholesaler
    e. Truck jobber

32. John Smith distributes dairy items to small grocers in a metropolitan area. The drivers of his six trucks make deliveries once a day and all transactions are strictly cash. He is a _____.
   a. Drop shipper
   b. Rack jobber
   c. General merchandise wholesaler
   d. cash and carry wholesaler
   e. Truck jobber

33. A company distributes snack foods to business office cafeterias. The snacks are displayed in a free-standing cardboard rack. The offices are billed only for the snack foods used. They operate as a _____.
   a. Drop shipper
   b. Rack jobber
   c. General merchandise wholesaler
   d. cash and carry wholesaler
   e. Truck jobber

34. _____ design promotional plans, set prices, determine distribution policies, and make recommendations on product strategy .
   a. Manufacturer's agents
   b. Selling agents
   c. Brokers
   d. Rack jobbers
   e. Truck jobbers

35. _____ usually do not have a continuous relationship with the buyer or seller. Rather, they negotiate a contract or deal between two parties, then move on to another task.
   a. Manufacturer's agents
   b. Selling agents
   c. Brokers
   d. Rack jobbers
   e. Truck jobbers

36. _____ work for several producers and sell noncompetitive, complementary merchandise in an exclusive territory.
   a. Manufacturer's agents
   b. Selling agents
   c. Brokers
   d. Rack jobbers
   e. Truck jobbers

37. _____ are principally used in transactional channel functions, primarily selling.
   a. Manufacturer's agents
   b. Selling agents
   c. Brokers
   d. Rack jobbers
   e. Truck jobbers

38. _____ represent a single producer and are responsible for the entire marketing function of that producer.
   a. Manufacturer's agents
   b. Selling agents
   c. Brokers
   d. Rack jobbers
   e. Truck jobbers

39. _____ are independent firms or individuals whose principal function is to bring buyers and sellers together to make a sales transaction.
   a. Manufacturer's agents
   b. Selling agents
   c. Brokers
   d. Rack jobbers
   e. Truck jobbers

40. Ricoh Company, Ltd., studied information concerning the "serious" as opposed to the "recreational" camera user, and decided to change its marketing channel from a wholesaler to a manufacturer's agent. Sales volume tripled within 18 months. This change was initiated due to _____.
   a. Environmental factors
   b. Consumer factors
   c. Product factors
   d. Company factors
   e. Legal factors

41. When Ingersoll-Rand's pneumatic tools were first introduced, considerable buyer education and service were necessary to market these products, and a direct channel was used. As the products matured and buyers became more familiar with them, the company elected to use industrial distributors. This change was initiated due to _____.

   a. Environmental factors
   b. Consumer factors
   c. Product factors
   d. Company factors
   e. Legal factors

42. IBM distributes its correctable typewriter ribbons directly through its own sales force. Liquid Paper Corporation, partially because of more limited resources and a narrower product line, uses indirect channels. This difference is due to _____.

   a. Environmental factors
   b. Consumer factors
   c. Product factors
   d. Company factors
   e. Legal factors

43. Because of changes in economic factors, family structure, etc., companies such as Mary Kay and Tupperware are examining their current direct marketing channel strategies. This potential change was initiated due to _____.
   a. Environmental factors
   b. Consumer factors
   c. Product factors
   d. Company factors
   e. Legal factors

44. _____ is when a manufacturer distributes through its own vertically integrated channel in competition with independent wholesalers and retailers that also sell its products
    a. Vertical integration
    b. Tying arrangements
    c. Resale restrictions
    d. Refusal to deal
    e. Dual distribution

45. _____ is when a supplier requires channel members to sell only its products or restricts distributors from selling directly competitive products.
    a. Vertical integration
    b. Tied selling
    c. Resale restrictions
    d. Refusal to deal
    e. Exclusive dealing

46. _____ occurs when a supplier requires a distributor to purchase some products on the condition it buy others from the supplier.
    a. Vertical integration
    b. Tied selling
    c. Resale restrictions
    d. Refusal to deal
    e. Exclusive dealing

47. _____ refers to a supplier's attempt to stipulate to whom distributors may resell the supplier's products and in what specific geographical areas or territories they may be sold.
    a. Vertical integration
    b. Tying arrangements
    c. Resale restrictions
    d. Refusal to deal
    e. Exclusive dealing

Chapter 16--Answers

Discussion Questions

Rationale for Intermediaries

1. facilitating functions
2. logistical functions
3. transactional functions
4. transactional functions
5. logistical functions
6. facilitating functions
7. facilitating functions
8. logistical functions
9. logistical functions
10. transactional functions

Direct Marketing

1. direct mail, mail order
2. direct mail, catalogue, TV home shopping
3. direct mail, mail order
4. direct mail, catalogue
5. catalogue, TV home shopping
6. telemarketing, direct mail

Merchant Wholesalers

1. limited-service wholesalers
2. limited-service wholesalers
3. full-service wholesalers
4. limited-service wholesalers
5. limited-service wholesalers
6. full-service wholesalers

Vertical Marketing Systems

1. backward integration
2. forward integration
3. backward integration
4. forward integration

1. franchising
2. retailer-sponsored cooperatives
3. wholesaler sponsored voluntary chains
4. franchising

Channel Design Considerations

1. exclusive distribution
2. intensive distribution
3. selective distribution
4. exclusive distribution
5. selective distribution
6. intensive distribution

1. target market coverage
2. satisfying buyer requirements
3. profitability

Channel Relationships

1. vertical conflict
2. horizontal conflict
3. vertical conflict
4. horizontal conflict

Sample Tests

1. b	20. c	39. c
2. a	21. c	40. b
3. b	22. d	41. c
4. e	23. c	42. d
5. e	24. a	43. a
6. d	25. c	44. e
7. d	26. e	45. e
8. b	27. b	46. b
9. a	28. c	47. c
10. c	29. e	
11. d	30. a	
12. d	31. d	
13. b	32. e	
14. a	33. b	
15. a	34. b	
16. d	35. c	
17. c	36. a	
18. e	37. a	
19. e	38. b	

CHAPTER 17

Supply Chain and Logistics Management

<u>Why is Chapter 17 important</u>? This chapter examines the flow of products to the ultimate consumer and how to make that as efficient as possible. It shows how the proper selection of transportation, storage, and timing can reduce costs and lead to greater customer satisfaction.

Logistics Management: Organizing the cost-effective flow of raw materials, in-process inventory, finished goods, and related information from point-of-origin to point-of-consumption to satisfy customer requirements.

CHAPTER OUTLINE

I. SIGNIFICANCE OF SUPPLY CHAIN AND LOGISTICS MANAGEMENT

    A. Relating Marketing Channels, Logistics, and Supply Chain Management
        1. Supply Chain Management
        2. Logistics Management
            a. elements
                i. flow
                ii. cost-effective
                iii. customer service
            b. important factors
                i. number, weight, volume, and perishability
                ii. number of material supply points
                iii. number of material processing points
                iv. number of product consumption points

    B. Supply Chain Management and Marketing Strategy
        1. Product factors
        2. Pricing factors
        3. Promotional factors
        4. Place factors

II. OBJECTIVES OF THE LOGISTICS SYSTEM

    A. Total Logistics Cost Concept
        1. Traffic and transportation
        2. Warehousing and storage
        3. Packaging
        4. Materials handling
        5. Inventory control
        6. Order processing
        7. Customer service level
        8. Plant and warehouse site location
        9. Return goods handling

    B. Customer Service Concept
        1. Time
        2. Dependability

      3. Communication
      4. Convenience

III. LOGISTICS FUNCTIONS IN A SUPPLY CHAIN

    A. Transportation
         1. Railways
         2. Motor carriers
         3. Air carriers and express companies
         4. Freight forwarders

    B. Warehousing and Materials Handling
         1. Storage warehouses
         2. Distribution centres
         3. Materials handling

    C. Order Processing

    D. Inventory Management
         1. Reasons for inventory
             a. to offer buffer against variations in supply and demand
             b. to provide better service
             c. to promote production efficiencies
             d. to provide a hedge against price increases
             e. to promote purchasing and transportation discounts
             f. to protect the firm from contingencies
         2. Inventory costs
             a. capital costs
             b. inventory service costs
             c. storage costs
             d. risk costs
         3. Just-in-time (JIT) concept
         4. Vendor-managed inventory
         5. Reverse logistics

You should be able to place these key terms in the outline and be able to discuss them.

customer service	logistics	supply chain
efficient consumer response	logistics management	supply chain management
freight forwarders	materials handling	third-party logistics providers
intermodal transportation	quick response	total logistics cost
just-in-time (JIT) concept	reverse logistics	vendor-managed inventory
lead time		

QUESTIONS & PROBLEMS

RELATING MARKETING CHANNELS, LOGISTICS, AND SUPPLY CHAIN MANAGEMENT

Supply chain management is organizing the movement and storage of a finished product to the customer. Logistics management is organizing the cost-effective flow of raw materials, in-process inventory, finished goods, and related information from point-of-origin to point-of-consumption to satisfy customer requirements.

1. What factors account for the trend of increased emphasis on logistics systems?_____
_____

2. List four different factors that determine the relative importance of a firm's logistics system:

1. _____

2. _____

3. _____

4. _____

LOGISTICS SYSTEMS

Federal Express developed its own tracking systems and inventory control system and now works with company's needing a complete logistics system, especially those looking for Just-in-time inventory. Many of the companies contracting with Federal Express are high tech firms. Answer the following questions:

1. What is the key objective of the logistics system?_____
_____

2. What is the primary advantage of strategic alliances?_____
_____

3. What is the purpose of an electronic data interchange and what can it do?_____
_____

TOTAL LOGISTICS COST CONCEPT

List the key elements in total logistics cost:

1._____

2._____

3._____

4._____

5._____

6._____

7._____

8._____

9._____

CUSTOMER SERVICE CONCEPT

Customer service is the ability of a logistics system to satisfy users in terms of time, dependability, communications, and convenience. How would each of these facets of customer service be important to the following businesses?

1. Pizza Hut_____

2. Quick Lube_____

3. A 7-11 convenience store_____

4. Future Shops_____

5. A local florist_____

MAJOR LOGISTICAL FUNCTIONS

Transportation

There are five basic modes of transportation: railways, motor carriers, air carriers, pipelines, and water carriers. All can be evaluated on six basic service dimensions: cost, time, capability, dependability, accessibility, and frequency.

List the relative advantages and disadvantages for the modes of transportation listed below:

	Advantages	Disadvantages
Rail	_____	_____
Truck	_____	_____
Air	_____	_____
Pipeline	_____	_____
Water	_____	_____

To capitalize on the advantages and avoid the disadvantages, many firms use intermodal transportation. Make sure you know the meanings of the terms: TOFC, and piggyback transportation. Many times, smaller companies can't afford major transportation costs. These companies are able to make use of freight forwarders. Freight forwarders are firms that accumulate small shipments into larger lots and then hire a carrier to move them, usually at reduced rates. Air freight forwarders, or express companies, are firms that market air express services to the general public.

WAREHOUSING AND MATERIALS HANDLING

Warehouses may be classified in one of two ways: (1) storage warehouses and (2) distribution centres .

Answer the following questions:

What is the significant difference between storage warehouses and distribution centres?

_____

What are two major difficulties with materials handling?

1._____

2._____

INVENTORY MANAGEMENT

The major problem in managing inventory is maintaining the delicate balance between too little and too much of it.

List the six traditional reasons for carrying inventory:

1._____

2._____

3._____

4._____

5._____

6._____

Part of Wal-Mart's success has come from outstanding physical distribution and logistics management systems. They have made a science of cost control. Discuss how each of the six traditional reasons for carrying would affect a firm like Wal-Mart._____

_____

_____

INVENTORY STRATEGIES

The just-in-time (JIT) inventory supply system operates with very lean inventories to hold down costs and requires fast, on-time delivery.

List at least three relative advantages and disadvantages of the "JIT" inventory strategy for a company like Dell Computer:

Advantages	Disadvantages
_____	_____
_____	_____
_____	_____

CAN YOU PASS THE TEST?

OVERVIEW OF CHAPTER 17: TERMS AND DEFINITIONS (multiple choice)

1. _____ is the organizing the movement and storage of finished product to the customer .
   a. Supply chain management
   b. Freight forwarders
   c. Logistics management
   d. Replenishment time
   e. Intermodal transportation

2. Expenses associated with transportation, materials handling, and warehousing, inventory, stock outs, and order processing are known as _____.
   a. Materials handling
   b. Total logistics cost
   c. Logistics management
   d. Replenishment time
   e. Intermodal transportation

3. The ability of a logistics system to satisfy users in terms of time, dependability, communications, and convenience is known as _____.
   a. Customer service
   b. Just-in-time concept (JIT)
   c. Order cycle time
   d. Electronic data interchange (EDI)
   e. Lead time

4. _____ is the time required to transmit, process, prepare, and ship an order, from the seller's viewpoint.
   a. Customer service
   b. Just-in-time concept (JIT)
   c. Order cycle time
   d. Electronic data interchange (EDI)
   e. Lead time

5. Inventory-supply system, called _____, operates with very lean inventories to hold down costs and requires fast, on-time delivery.
   a. Customer service
   b. Just-in-time concept (JIT)
   c. Order cycle time
   d. Electronic data interchange (EDI)
   e. Lead time

6. Computers linked in two different firms to transmit documents such as purchase orders, bills of lading, and invoices is known as _____.
   a. Customer service
   b. Just-in-time concept (JIT)
   c. Order cycle time
   d. Electronic data interchange (EDI)
   e. Lead time

7. _____ is the moving goods over short distances into, within, and out of warehouses and manufacturing plants.
      a. Materials handling
      b. Freight forwarders
      c. Logistics management
      d. Replenishment time
      e. Intermodal transportation

8. Firms that accumulate small shipments into larger lots, then hire a carrier to move them, at reduced rates due to large shipment size are called _____.
      a. Supply chain management
      b. Freight forwarders
      c. Logistics management
      d. Replenishment time
      e. Intermodal transportation

9. _____ is the time required to transmit, process, prepare, and ship an order from the buyer's viewpoint.
      a. Customer service
      b. Just-in-time concept (JIT)
      c. Order cycle time
      d. Electronic data interchange (EDI)
      e. Replenishment time

10. Coordinating or combining different transportation modes to take advantage of the best features of each and minimizing the shortcomings is known as _____.
      a. Supply chain management
      b. Freight forwarders
      c. Logistics management
      d. Replenishment time
      e. Intermodal transportation

11. The lag from ordering an item until it is received in stock is called _____.
      a. Supply chain management
      b. Freight forwarders
      c. Logistics management
      d. Replenishment time
      e. lead time

12. _____ is the coordination of the movement and storage of raw materials, parts, and finished goods to achieve the given service level while minimizing the total cost of these activities.
      a. Supply chain management
      b. Freight forwarders
      c. Logistics management
      d. Replenishment time
      e. Intermodal transportation

13. Trade promotions and contests for the salesforce may create irregular demand. This is an example of the _____ factor.
      a. Product
      b. Pricing
      c. Promotion
      d. Place
      e. Positioning

14. Weight/bulk relationships, weight/value relationships, and associated buying risks are important aspects of this factor. This is an example of the _____ factor.
    a. Product
    b. Pricing
    c. Promotion
    d. Place
    e. Positioning

15. Special attention is placed on movement and storage. This is an example of the _____ factor.
    a. Product
    b. Pricing
    c. Promotion
    d. Place
    e. Positioning

16. The size of purchase can be affected both by quantity discount purchases as well as volume transportation discounts. This is an example of the _____ factor.
    a. Product
    b. Pricing
    c. Promotion
    d. Place
    e. Positioning

17. A two-way link between buyer and seller that helps in monitoring services. This represents _____ in customer service.
    a. Time
    b. Dependability
    c. Communication
    d. Convenience
    e. Cost

18. There should be a minimum of effort on the part of the buyer in doing business with the seller. This represents _____ in customer service.
    a. Time
    b. Dependability
    c. Communication
    d. Convenience
    e. Cost

19. This includes consistent lead time (the period from order placement to delivery), safe delivery, and correct delivery. This represents _____ in customer service.
    a. Time
    b. Dependability
    c. Communication
    d. Convenience
    e. Cost

20. Reduction of the order cycle time or replenishment time, depending on the viewpoint (seller or buyer). This includes recognition for the need to order, order transmittal, processing, documentation, and transportation. This represents _____ in customer service.
    a. Time
    b. Dependability
    c. Communication
    d. Convenience
    e. Cost

21. Warehousing space and materials handling are part of _____.
    a. Capital costs
    b. Inventory service costs
    c. Storage costs
    d. Risk costs
    e. Other costs

22. _____ are items such as insurance and taxes that are present in most states, sometimes at an expensive rate.
    a. Capital costs
    b. Inventory service costs
    c. Storage costs
    d. Risk costs
    e. Other costs

23. Possible loss, damage, pilferage, perishability, and obsolescence are part of _____.
    a. Capital costs
    b. Inventory service costs
    c. Storage costs
    d. Risk costs
    e. Other costs

24. The opportunity costs, called _____, result from tying up funds in inventory instead of using them in other more profitable investments.
    a. Capital costs
    b. Inventory service costs
    c. Storage costs
    d. Risk costs
    e. Other costs

Chapter 17--Answers

Discussion Questions

Relating Physical Supply, Physical Distribution, and Logistics

1. A large growth in the differentiation of products in order to respond to consumer demands and deregulation of transportation industries.

2. number, weight, volume, and perishability of raw materials and final products
   number of material supply points
   number of material processing points
   number of product consumption points

Logistics Systems

1. Minimize relevant logistics costs while delivering maximum customer service.

2. Better service through better information.

3. Links computers between manufacturer and transportation company to transmit all necessary documents for better service.

Total Logistics Cost Concept

1. traffic and transportation
2. warehousing and storage
3. packaging
4. materials handling
5. inventory control
6. order processing
7. customer service level
8. plant and warehouse site location
9. return goods handling

Customer Service Concept

Example:

Pizza Hut--quick service, dependability of product(consistent), communications of offer, and convenient

Major Logistical Functions

Example:

Rail--advantages--large loads, inexpensive; disadvantages--time, dependability, accessibility, and frequency

Warehousing and Materials Handling

Goods are intended to "rest" for some time in storage warehouses; distribution centres are designed for facilitating timely movement of goods.

1. high labour costs
2. high rates of loss and damage

Inventory Management

1. to offer a buffer against variations in supply and demand

2. to provide better service for those who wish to be served on demand

3. to promote production efficiencies

4. to provide a hedge against price increases by suppliers

5. to promote purchasing and transportation discounts

6. to protect the firm from contingencies such as strikes and shortages

Inventory Strategies

Example: Advantages--keeps inventory costs down
                Disadvantages--unanticipated large orders

Sample Tests

1. a
2. b
3. a
4. c
5. b
6. d
7. a
8. b
9. e
10. e
11. e
12. c
13. c
14. a
15. d
16. b
17. c
18. d
19. b
20. a
21. c
22. b
23. d
24. a

CHAPTER 18

Retailing

<u>Why is Chapter 18 important</u>? Retailing is the channel of distribution with which we are most familiar. This chapter illustrates the goods and services a retailer providers and the typers of retailers that are available in the marketplace. It shows how retailers are classified and how the selection of the retail outlet is keyed to the type of product offered.

Retailing: All activities involved in selling, renting, and providing goods and services to ultimate consumers for personal, family, or household use.

CHAPTER OUTLINE

I. VALUE OF RETAILING

    A. Utilities Provided to Consumers
        1. Time
        2. Place
        3. Possession
        4. Form

    B. Economic Value
        1. Employment
        2. Sales

II. CLASSIFYING RETAIL OUTLETS

    A. Form of Ownership
        1. Independent Retailer
        2. Corporate Chain
        3. Contractual System

    B. Level of Service
        1. Self Service
        2. Limited Service
        3. Full Service

    C. Merchandise Line
        1. Depth of Line
            a. Specialty outlets
                1. limited line
                2. single line
            b. Category "killers"
        2. Breadth of Line
            a. General merchandise store
            b. "Scrambled" merchandising
                1. hypermarkets
                2. supercentres

      D. Nonstore Retailing
          1. Automatic Vending
          2. Direct Marketing
              a. Direct mail and catalogues
              b. Television home shopping
              c. Online retailing
              d. Telemarketing
          3. Direct Selling

III. RETAILING STRATEGY

      A. Positioning
          1. Retail Positioning Matrix
              a. Breadth of product line
              b. Value added
          2. Keys to Positioning
              a. Identity with advantage
              b. Recognition of identity by customers

      B. Retailing Mix
          1. Goods and Services
              a. Pricing
                  1. markup
                  2. markdown
                  3. timing
                  4. off-price
                      a. warehouse club
                      b. factory outlet
                      c. single-price or extreme value
              b. Retail image and atmosphere
                  1. functional qualities
                  2. psychological attributes
          2. Physical Distribution (Store Location)
              a. Central business district
              b. Regional shopping centre
               c. Community shopping centre
              d. Strip shopping centre
              e. "Power" shopping centre

IV. CHANGING NATURE OF RETAILING

      A. Wheel of Retailing

      B. Retail Life Cycle

V. FUTURE CHANGES IN RETAILING

      A. Impact of Technology
      B. Changing Shopping Behaviour
      C. Importance of Brands

You should be able to place these key terms in the outline and be able to discuss them.

breadth of product line
central business district
community shopping centre
depth of product line
form of ownership
hypermarket
intertype competition

level of service
merchandise line
off-price retailing
power centre
regional shopping centres
retail positioning matrix
retail life cycle

retailing
retailing mix
scrambled merchandising
shrinkage
strip locations
telemarketing
wheel of retailing

QUESTIONS & PROBLEMS

VALUE OF RETAILING

Retailing is an important marketing activity. Not only do producers and consumers meet through retailing actions, but retailing also creates customer value and has a significant impact on the economy. To consumers, the value of retailing is in the form of utilities provided. Retailing's economic value is represented by the people employed in retailing, as well as by the total amount of money exchanged in retail sales.

Wal-Mart's innovation was to bring discount stores to small cities or towns. Dell Computer found that PC's had become "generic" and people wanted complete systems; PC Flowers knew that some consumers put off every until the last minute and yet still needed to buy gifts and remembrances; and Walt Disney company saw the need to make it easier for consumers to buy Disney "paraphernalia" leading to the Disney Stores and Catalogues. Discuss the utilities of each of these strategies.

CLASSIFYING RETAIL OUTLETS

Retail outlets can be classified by 1) Form of ownership; 2) Level of service; and 3) Merchandise line. These in turn can be classified as store or nonstore retailing. The form of ownership can be that of an independent retailer; a corporate chain; or a contractual system. Level of service ranges from self-service to limited service to full service; while the merchandise line is referred to by the breadth or the depth of the line carried.

Over the last decade, companies have expanded into nonstore retailing. IBM and Compaq, given the challenge of direct marketers such as Dell and Gateway, have started operations such as IBM Direct, to sell directly to consumers. Other companies, such as Sharper Image and Victoria's Secret, have gone the other direction from direct mail catalogues into retail outlets. A company in Vancouver, British Columbia, now offers a vending machine which accepts and processes credit cards. It has recently used this technology to sell both disposable cameras for Kodak and long distance phone cards for MCI. Discuss how each type of retailing can affect each classification category.

RETAILING STRATEGY

Using the 4 P's, product, price, promotion, and place, a retail store develops a strategy that will best position itself for the customers it seeks to attract. They develop a retailing mix utilizing such tools as the Retail Positioning Matrix. The Wheel of Retailing and the Retail Life Cycle help provide guidance for the retailer over the long run of the business.

The hardware industry has progressed from the general store, which carried everything for small communities; to the specialized hardware store, which was really a building and home supply store with tools and supplies; to hardware stores which sell everything from bicycles to hammers to gas fireplaces; to hardware departments of discount stores and major retailers like Sears; to large "category killers," like Home Depot, which are the old specialized hardware stores carried out to a mega-size. In addition, you have catalogue companies like Brookstone, which specialize in "hard to find tools," that have opened retail stores in large malls; not a normal place for hardware.

Discuss how each type of hardware outlet fits into the following concepts:

RETAIL POSITIONING MATRIX

The retail positioning matrix is a matrix developed by the MAC Group, Inc., a management consulting firm. This matrix positions retail outlets on two dimensions: breadth of product line and value added.

Using the Retail Positioning Matrix shown in Figure 18-8, position each type of hardware outlet on a retail matrix of two dimensions: Breadth of Product Line and Value Added.

	Breadth of Product Line	Value Added
General Store	_____	_____
Specialized Hardware	_____	_____
Household and Hardware	_____	_____
Hardware Departments	_____	_____
Hardware Mega-stores	_____	_____
Hardware Specialty Catalogues	_____	_____

RETAILING MIX

In developing retail strategy, managers work with the retailing mix which includes: (1) goods and services, (2) physical distribution, and (3) communications tactics. Decisions relating to the mix focus on the consumer.   There are three basic areas of importance: pricing, store location, image and atmosphere.

Identify each type of hardware outlet in relation to the focus of their retailing mix.

	Pricing	Store Location	Image & Atmosphere
General Store	_____	_____	_____
Specialized Hardware	_____	_____	_____
Household and Hardware	_____	_____	_____
Hardware Departments	_____	_____	_____
Hardware Mega-stores	_____	_____	_____
Hardware Specialty Catalogues	_____	_____	_____

RETAIL PRICING

A retailer purchased an order of brass candlesticks. The price paid was $30 per pair. The candlesticks were first offered for sale to customers at $60 per pair. Although before the holidays the candlesticks sold well, by February they were hardly selling at all. The price was then reduced to $45.

Using the information above, determine:

1. Original markup_____
2. Markdown_____
3. Maintained markup_____
4. Another name for maintained mark-up is:_____

Answer the following questions:

1. What is the difference between discount retailers and off-price retailers?

_____
_____
_____

2. What are two common types of off-price retailing?

_____
_____

WHEEL OF RETAILING

The Wheel of Retailing describes how new forms of retail outlets enter the market. Entering the market as low-status, low-margin stores, they gradually add services, fixtures and other amenities that increase their status. Eventually, they attract new competition in the low-status, low-margin area and the cycle begins again.

Using the Wheel of Retailing shown in Figure 18-10, discuss the evolution of the retail hardware industry using the Wheel of Retailing concept.

RETAIL LIFE CYCLE

The Retail Life Cycle describes the growth and decline of retail outlets. There are four stages in the retail life cycle: 1) Early Growth; 2) Accelerated Development; 3) Maturity Phase; & 4) Decline Stage.

Identify on the table below at what stage are each of the types of hardware retailing today.

	Early Growth	Accelerated Development	Maturity Phase	Decline Stage
General Store	_____	_____	_____	_____
Specialized Hardware	_____	_____	_____	_____
Household and Hardware	_____	_____	_____	_____
Hardware Departments	_____	_____	_____	_____
Hardware Mega-stores	_____	_____	_____	_____
Hardware Specialty Catalogues	_____	_____	_____	_____

FUTURE CHANGES IN RETAILING

Three trends in retailing--the increasing impact of technology, changing shopping behaviour, and the growing importance of brands--are likely to lead to many changes for retailers and consumers in the future. Technology has already had a tremendous affect on retailing, ranging from payment systems, the ordering process, promotional outlets, to distribution methods. Consumers are also changing the way they shop, becoming precision shoppers as well as demanding more convenience and value from retailers. Finally, brands have become almost "sacred" in some product categories such sports clothing; while store brands and other private labels have shown strength in other areas. Pick two retail products such as computers, pre-recorded music, or clothing, and describe how each has been affected by technology. Next pick a product where name-brands are very important and another area where national brands have seen an eroding of their market share.

CAN YOU PASS THE TEST?

OVERVIEW OF CHAPTER 18: TERMS AND DEFINITIONS (multiple choice)

1. _____ is a retail site location which typically has one primary store and a relatively large number of smaller outlets and serves a population base of about 100,000.
   a) Central business district
   b) Power centre
   c) Regional shopping centres
   d) Community shopping centre
   e) Strip location

2. The relative variety of different items a store, wholesaler, or manufacturer carries is known as _____.
   a) Breadth of product line
   b) Depth of product line
   c) Merchandise line
   d) Retailing mix
   e) Wheel of Retailing

3. Wendy's is an example of _____.
   a) Independent ownership
   b) Corporate chain ownership
   c) Cooperative chain
   d) Franchise
   e) Wheel of Retailing

4. Competition between dissimilar types of retail outlets brought about by scrambled merchandising is known as _____.
   a) Intertype competition
   b) Wheel of Retailing
   c) Retailing mix
   d) Hypermarket
   e) Merchandise line

5. _____ is the assortment of each item a store, wholesaler, or retailer carries.
   a) Breadth of product line
   b) Depth of product line
   c) Merchandise line
   d) Retailing mix
   e) Wheel of Retailing

6. _____ is how and where a retailer provides services; the alternative approaches are an in-store or a nonstore format (mail, vending etc.).
   a) Scrambled merchandising
   b) Retailing mix
   c) Method of operation
   d) Level of service
   e) Merchandise line

7. _____ is a framework for positioning retail outlets in terms of breadth of product line and value added.
   a) Scrambled merchandising
   b) Retailing mix
   c) Retail Positioning Matrix
   d) Retail Life Cycle
   e) Wheel of Retailing

8. A term used by retailers to describe theft of merchandise by customers and employees is _____.
   a) Scrambled merchandising
   b) Retailing mix
   c) Shrinkage
   d) Strip location
   e) Retail Life Cycle

9. Burger King has begun offering table service at selected locations during the evening hours. They have gone from _____.
   a) Self-service to limited service
   b) Limited service to full service
   c) Full service to limited service
   d) Full service to self-service
   e) Self-service to full service

10. _____ is the oldest retail setting; the community's downtown area.
    a) Central business district
    b) Power centre
    c) Regional shopping centres
    d) Community shopping centre
    e) Strip location

11. The number of different types of products and the assortment a store carries makes up the _____.
    a) Breadth of product line
    b) Depth of product line
    c) Merchandise line
    d) Retailing mix
    e) Wheel of Retailing

12. _____ is the concept that describes a retail operation over four stages: early growth, accelerated development, maturity, and decline.
    a) Scrambled merchandising
    b) Retailing mix
    c) Retail Positioning Matrix
    d) Retail Life Cycle
    e) Wheel of Retailing

13. Selling brand name merchandise at lower than regular price is called _____.
    a) Off-price retailing
    b) Scrambled merchandising
    c) Retailing
    d) Wheel of Retailing
    e) Retailing mix

14. Offering several unrelated product lines in a single retail store is known as _____.
    a) Breadth of product line
    b) Depth of product line
    c) Merchandise line
    d) Retailing mix
    e) Scrambled merchandising

15. _____ is a cluster of stores that serves people who live within a 5-10 minute drive in a population base of under 30,000.
    a) Central business district
    b) Power centre
    c) Regional shopping centres
    d) Community shopping centre
    e) Strip location

16. The strategy components that a retailer offers, including goods and services, physical distribution, and communications tactics is known as _____.
    a) Scrambled merchandising
    b) Retailing mix
    c) Retail Positioning Matrix
    d) Retail Life Cycle
    e) Promotional mix

17. Suburban mall with up to 100 stores that typically draws customers from a 5- to 10-mile radius, usually containing one or two anchor stores is called _____.
    a) Central business district
    b) Power centre
    c) Regional shopping centres
    d) Community shopping centre
    e) Strip location

18. All activities in the selling, renting, and providing of services to ultimate consumers for personal, non-household use are known as _____.
    a) Intertype competition
    b) Wheel of Retailing
    c) Retailing
    d) Hypermarket
    e) Promotional Mix

19. _____ is a concept that describes how new retail outlets enter the market and change gradually in terms of status and margin.
    a) Intertype competition
    b) Wheel of Retailing
    c) Retailing
    d) Hypermarket
    e) Retail Life Cycle

20. Large stores (over 100,000 square feet) which offer a mix of 40 percent food products and 60 percent general merchandise items are known as _____.
    a) Hypermarkets
    b) Power centre
    c) Regional shopping centres
    d) Community shopping centres
    e) Mall

21. Megasized strip malls with multiple anchor (or national) stores. Retailers that offer large selections in a narrow range of products at very competitive prices sometimes called category killers. These are predominately found in
_____.
     a) Hypermarkets
     b) Power centres
     c) Franchises
     d) Corporate chains
     e) Independent Stores

23. IGA (Independent Grocers' Alliance) grocery stores are an example of _____.
     a) independent ownership
     b) corporate chain ownership
     c) a cooperative chain
     d) a franchise
     e) Hypermarkets

23. Tupperware, one of the largest direct sales companies, gives product demonstrations in customers' homes and delivers the customer orders, sorted and bagged, directly to the party hostess and in some areas, directly to the guests. This is an example of _____.
     a) Time
     b) Place
     c) Possession
     d) Form
     e) All of the above.

24. A diner in a university town stays open 24 hours a day to cater to students who study late and factory workers who work second shift is focusing on the _____ utility.
     a) Time
     b) Place
     c) Possession
     d) Form
     e) All of the above.

25. A sewing machine retailer offers five free sewing lessons with the purchase of a new machine is offering an example of _____ utillity.
     a) Time
     b) Place
     c) Possession
     d) Form
     e) All of the above.

26. A car dealer guarantees a $1,000 trade-in on your old car, regardless of its condition, when applied towards the purchase of a new car. This is an example of the _____ utility.
     a) Time
     b) Place
     c) Possession
     d) Form
     e) All of the above.

27. _____ is a form of ownership consisting of multiple outlets under common ownership.
     a) Independent
     b) Corporate chain
     c) Contractual system
     d) Franchise
     e) Cooperative chain

28. _____ is a form of ownership consisting of independently owned stores banding together to act like a chain. They may be either retail-sponsored or wholesale-sponsored.
    a) Independent
    b) Corporate chain
    c) Contractual system
    d) Franchise
    e) Cooperative chain

29. One of the most common forms of retail ownership is ownership by an individual known as _____ ownership.
    a) Independent
    b) Corporate chain
    c) Contractual system
    d) Franchise
    e) Cooperative chain

30. The Food Barn grocery store offers a full line of grocery products. However, merchandise is displayed in its original shipping packages (cardboard boxes) rather than in fancy displays, and customers box, bag, and carry their own groceries. This is an example of _____.
    a) Self-service
    b) Limited-service
    c) Full-service
    d) Standard service
    e) VIP service

31. A furniture store carries a broad line of high quality furniture. They also provide personal financing, free delivery, and free interior decorating services when you make a purchase. This is an example of _____.
    a) Self-service
    b) Limited-service
    c) Full-service
    d) VIP service
    e) Standard service

32. A department store carries a broad selection of small kitchen appliances in their housewares department. They have an informed sales staff, and will gladly gift wrap your purchases. However, they do not have a shop for repairs should your appliance need work after a long period of regular use. This is an example of _____.
    a) Self-service
    b) Limited-service
    c) Full-service
    d) Standard service
    e) VIP service

33. Stores that carry a considerable assortment (depth) of a related line of items, or stores that carry extraordinary depth in one primary line of merchandise. This is an example of _____.
    a) General merchandise
    b) Limited line
    c) Scrambled merchandise
    d) Specialty line
    e) Single line merchandising

34. Stores that offer several unrelated product lines in a single store are _____ stores.
    a) General merchandise
    b) Limited line
    c) Scrambled merchandise
    d) Specialty line
    e) Single line merchandising

35. _____ are stores that carry a broad product line, with limited depth.
   a) General merchandise
   b) Limited line
   c) Scrambled merchandise
   d) Specialty line
   e) Single line merchandising

Chapter 18--Answers

Discussion Questions

Value of Retailing

All of these strategies target the place utility

Classifying Retail Outlets

Example:

General Store   single owner   personal service   broad line of merchandise

Retailing Positioning Mix

Example:

General Store   broad line of merchandise   personal service value added

Retailing Mix

Example:

General Store   full retail price   single location (town centre)   homey, cluttered

Retail Pricing

1. $30
2. $15
3. $15
4. gross margin

1. The off-price retailer buys excess inventory from the manufacturer at less than wholesale, while the discounter takes less of a markup on regular wholesale price.

2. warehouse club and factory outlet store

Retail Life Cycle

Example:

General Store--decline
Specialized Hardware--decline
Household and hardware--maturity
Hardware departments--maturity
Hardware mega-stores--accelerated growth
Hardware specialty catalogues--early growth

Sample Tests

1. d	14. e	27. b
2. a	15. e	28. c
3. d	16. b	29. a
4. a	17. c	30. a
5. b	18. c	31. c
6. c	19. b	32. b
7. c	20. a	33. b
8. c	21. b	34. c
9. b	22. c	35. a
10. a	23. b	
11. c	24. a	
12. d	25. d	
13. a	26. c	

CHAPTER 19

Integrated Marketing Communications And Direct Marketing

<u>Why is Chapter 19 important</u>? This chapter outlines the tools of communications used by a business to tell their markets about their products. It illustrates how the different elements of the promotional are used for different types of products, customers, and buying situations. It then outlines the designing of a successful promotional campaign.

Communication: The process of conveying a message to others requiring six elements: a source, a message, a channel of communication, a receiver, and the processes of encoding and decoding.

CHAPTER OUTLINE

I. THE COMMUNICATION PROCESS

      A. Encoding and Decoding

      B. Feedback

      C. Noise

II. THE PROMOTION ELEMENTS

      A. Advertising

      B. Personal Selling

      C. Public Relations

      D. Sales Promotion

      E. Direct Marketing

III. INTEGRATED MARKETING COMMUNICATION--DEVELOPING THE PROMOTIONAL MIX

      A. Target Audience

      B. Product Life Cycle
            1. Introduction stage
                  a. inform
            2. Growth stage
                  a. persuade
            3. Maturity stage
                  a. remind
            4. Decline stage

    C. Product Characteristics
       1. Complexity
       2. Risk
       3. Ancillary services

    D. Stages of the Buying Decision
       1. Prepurchase stage
       2. Purchase stage
       3. Postpurchase stage

    E. Channel Strategies
       1. Push strategy
       2. Pull strategy

    F. Integrated Marketing Communication

IV. DEVELOPING THE PROMOTIONAL PROGRAM

    A. Identifying the Target Audience

    B. Specifying Promotional Objectives
       1. Hierarchy of effects
          a. awareness
          b. interest
          c. evaluation
          d. trial
          e. adoption
       2. Qualities
          a. designed for a well-defined target audience
          b. be measurable
          c. cover a specified time period

    C. Setting the Promotional Budget
       1. Percentage of sales
       2. Competitive parity
       3. All you can afford
       4. Objective and task
          a. determine promotional objectives
          b. outline tasks to accomplish objective
          c. determine promotional costs of performing these tasks

    D. Selecting the Right Promotional Tools

    E. Designing the Promotion

    F. Scheduling the Promotion

    G. Executing and Evaluating the Promotional Program

V. DIRECT MARKETING

    A. Direct Marketing Growth

    B. Direct Marketing Value
        1. Direct ordering
        2. Lead generation
        3. Traffic generation

    C. Direct Marketing Issues
        1. Technological
        2. Global
        3. Ethical

You should be able to place these key terms in the outline and be able to discuss them.

advertising	hierarchy of effects	publicity
all-you-can-afford budgeting	integrated marketing communications	pull strategy
channel of communication	lead generation	push strategy
communication	message	receivers
competitive parity budgeting	noise	sales promotion
decoding	objective and task budgeting	source
direct marketing	percentage of sales budgeting	traffic generation
direct orders	personal selling	
encoding	promotion mix	
feedback	public relations	
field of experience		

QUESTIONS & PROBLEMS

THE COMMUNICATION PROCESS

List the six elements required for communication to occur:

1._____

2._____

3._____

4._____

5._____

6. _____

Encoding and Decoding are essential to communication. Encoding is the process of having the sender transform an abstract idea into a set of symbols. Decoding is the reverse, or the process of having the receiver take a set of symbols, the message, and transform them back to an abstract idea. For the message to be communicated effectively, the sender and receiver must have a mutually shared field of experience - similar understanding and knowledge. Feedback is the communication flow from receiver back to sender and indicates whether the message was decoded and understood as intended. Noise can adversely affect how the receiver decodes a message. Noise can include such things as printing mistakes, visual clutter, busy-looking photos, etc.

PROMOTIONAL MIX

A company can communicate with consumers by using one or more of five promotional alternatives:

Advertising
Personal selling
Public relations
Sales promotion
Direct marketing

Identify which method of promotion is being used:

1. Roger Ebert critiques current motion pictures. His evaluation of a movie can have a significant effect on box office sales._____

2. Tupperware dealers do product demonstrations in homes. They sell new products, replace broken products, and give personal advice on kitchen organization. Consumer feedback through dealers has resulted in many new and innovative product ideas._____

3. Toyota Motor Sales purchased a full-page color advertisement in MacLean's Magazine to promote its 2000 Family Camry._____

4. Colgate Palmolive mailed samples of its Ajax Dishwashing Liquid along with a $0.25 store coupon.
_____

5. To supplement their retail stores, Shaper Image maintains a Web page and sends out millions of catalogues on a regular basis. _____

List advantages and disadvantages for each of the five promotional elements:

	<u>Advantages</u>	<u>Disadvantages</u>
1. Advertising	_____	_____
2. Personal selling	_____	_____
3. Public relations	_____	_____
4. Sales promotion	_____	_____
5. Direct Marketing	_____	_____

PRODUCT LIFE CYCLE

The composition of the promotional mix changes over the four product life cycle stages.

Match the product life-cycle stage to the objectives below:

Introduction stage
Growth stage
Maturity stage
Decline stage

1. Gain brand preference and solidify distribution._____

2. Increase the level of consumer awareness._____

3. Maintain existing buyers, encourage brand loyalty._____

4. Few promotional objectives; little money is spent on the promotional mix._____

During which stage in the product life cycle would you expect the relative emphasis of the promotional mix elements to be as follows?

1. Sales promotion is less, publicity is not a factor, the major promotional element is advertising, which stresses brand differences, personal selling is used to solidify the channel of distribution._____

2. Usually a period of phaseout and little money is spent on any element of the promotional mix._____

3. Advertising's role is reduced to reminding buyers of the product's existence. Sales promotion in the form of discounts and coupons are offered to both ultimate consumers and intermediaries. Salesforce maintains satisfaction of intermediaries._____

4. All promotional elements are stressed, trial samples may be sent, salesforce approaches new intermediaries._____

PRODUCT CHARACTERISTICS

State whether the promotional emphasis would be towards (1) personal selling, or (2) advertising:

1. A relatively complex product like a VAX minicomputer._____

2. A product with little social, physical, or monetary risk, such as Bayer aspirin._____

3. A statistical software program featuring sales, technical, and service support._____

In designing the proper blend of elements in the promotional mix, companies consider three product characteristics: complexity, degree of risk, and ancillary service. Complexity, refers to the technical sophistication of the product; risk, refers to the risk to the consumer in terms of financial, social, and physical factors; and ancillary services refers to the degree of service or support required after the sale.

CUSTOMER'S STAGE OF DECISION MAKING

Knowing the customer's stage in decision making can also affect the promotional mix. There are three stages in a consumer's purchase decision:

Prepurchase stage
Purchase stage
Postpurchase stage

At which stage in the consumer purchase decision would the following statements hold true?

1. The importance of personal selling is highest and the impact of advertising is lowest; sales promotion in the form of price discounts can be very helpful._____

2. Advertising and personal selling help reduce the buyer's feelings of anxiety; sales promotion in the form of coupons can help encourage repeat purchases._____

3. Advertising is more helpful than personal selling; sales promotion in the form of free samples encourages low-risk trial._____

CHANNEL STRATEGIES

Find a current example of a push strategy and a pull strategy:

1. push:_____

2. pull:_____

SELECTING PROMOTIONAL TOOLS

In which of the following situations would you emphasize advertising and in which situations would you emphasize personal selling?

1. Pull channel strategy_____

2. Great geographic dispersion of customers_____

3. High level of ancillary services_____

4. Purchase stage of purchase decision_____

5. Product simple to understand_____

6. Small DMU (Decision-Making Unit)_____

7. Push channel strategy_____

8. Complex product_____

9. Large DMU (Decision-Making Unit)_____

10. Ultimate consumer is target market_____

11. Low risk purchase_____

12. Geographic concentration of customers_____

13. Target market of resellers and industrial buyers_____

14. High risk purchase_____

15. Prepurchase stage of purchase decision_____

16. Low level of ancillary services_____

SETTING THE ADVERTISING BUDGET

After setting the advertising objectives, a company must decide on how much to spend.
There are several methods used to set the advertising budget:

Percentage-of-sales budgeting
Competitive parity budgeting
All-you-can-afford budgeting
Objective-and-task budgeting

Match the method of advertising budget to the statements below:

1. Our chief competitor is placing three full-page colour ads in Good Housekeeping magazine. We must direct enough funds through advertising to cover at least three full-page colour ads, if not more._____
_____

2. Our gross sales last year were $300,000 and our anticipated sales for next year are $400,000. Let's budget our advertising based on five percent of the average of last year's sales and this year's anticipated sales, or $17,500._____

3. "How much money can we possibly allocate for advertising?" "Fine, then, that's what we need."_____
_____

4. We have to reach at least 75 percent of the commuters in a 50 km radius. To do that we'll have to advertise on local radio between 6-8 a.m. and 4-6 p.m. This will cost us $3,700. If we can't afford full coverage we can cut the evening ads to one hour.

_____

DIRECT MARKETING

There are three types of response goals that make direct marketing valuable and have contributed to its how level of growth as a marketing communications tool. They are:

Direct orders
Lead generation
Traffic generation

For the statements below, please indicate the response goal sought in each promotion.

1. IBM Canada places advertising in The Financial Post Magazine introducing a new laptop computer giving a toll-free number and Web address to get more information.
_____

2. Donny Osmond appears on a late night cable television commercial to sell a CD of his greatest hits. He accepts credit cards through his toll-free number and the album is not available in stores.
_____

3. A vacation community sends out letters to families within a 200 km radius offering a new colour television to any family who comes out and receives a guided tour of their facilities. _____

CAN YOU PASS THE TEST?

OVERVIEW OF CHAPTER 19: TERMS AND DEFINITIONS (multiple choice)

1. A _____ is a company or person who has information to convey.
    a. Receivers
    b. Field of experience
    c. Source
    d. Promotional mix
    e. Pull strategy

2. The _____ direct the promotional mix to channel members or intermediaries to gain their cooperation in ordering and stocking a product.
    a. Receivers
    b. Field of experience
    c. Source
    d. Promotional mix
    e. Push strategy

3. _____ is the two-way flow of communication between a buyer and seller, often in a face-to-face encounter, designed to influence a person's or group's purchase decision.
    a. Advertising
    b. Personal selling
    c. Direct marketing
    d. Publicity
    e. Sales promotion

4. The consumers who read, hear, or see the message sent by a source in the communication process are called _____.
    a. Receivers
    b. Field of experience
    c. Source
    d. Promotional mix
    e. Pull strategy

5. _____ is the process of having the sender transform an abstract idea into a set of symbols.
    a. Noise
    b. Decoding
    c. Encoding
    d. Feedback
    e. Message

6. This is a person's understanding and knowledge; to communicate effectively, a sender and a receiver must have a mutually shared _____.
    a. Receivers
    b. Field of experience
    c. Source
    d. Promotional mix
    e. Pull strategy

7. _____ is a sales tool to support a company's advertising and personal selling efforts directed to ultimate consumers; examples include coupons, sweepstakes, and rebates.
    a. Advertising
    b. Public relations
    c. Direct Marketing
    d. Personal selling
    e. Sales promotion

8. The information sent by a source to a receiver in the communication process is known as _____.
    a. Noise
    b. Decoding
    c. Encoding
    d. Feedback
    e. Message

9. _____ is any paid form of nonpersonal communication about an organization, good, service, or idea by an identified sponsor.
    a. Advertising
    b. Personal selling
    c. Direct marketing
    d. Publicity
    e. Sales promotion

10. The sharing of meaning. Six elements - a source, message, channel, receiver, and process of encoding and decoding are needed for _____.
    a. Advertising
    b. Personal selling
    c. Communication
    d. Publicity
    e. Sales promotion

11. The process of having the receiver take a set of symbols, the message, and transform them back to an abstract idea is known as _____.
    a. Noise
    b. Decoding
    c. Encoding
    d. Feedback
    e. Message

12. The communication flow from receiver back to sender; indicates whether the message was decoded and understood as intended is called _____.
    a. Noise
    b. Decoding
    c. Encoding
    d. Feedback
    e. Message

13. A _____ is the directing the promotional mix at ultimate consumers to encourage them to ask the retailer for the product.
    a. Receiver
    b. Field of experience
    c. Source
    d. Promotional mix
    e. Pull strategy

14. _____ is the combination of one or more of the promotional elements a firm uses to communicate with consumers. The promotional elements include: advertising, personal selling, sales promotion, public relations, and direct marketing.
   a. Receivers
   b. Field of experience
   c. Source
   d. Promotional mix
   e. Pull strategy

15. _____ is a nonpersonal, indirectly paid presentation of an organization, good, or service.
   a. Cooperative advertising
   b. Publicity
   c. Advertising
   d. Trade-oriented sales promotions
   e. Consumer-oriented sales promotions

16. _____ is a short-term inducement of value offered to arouse interest in buying a good or service.
   a. Receivers
   b. Field of experience
   c. Sales promotion
   d. Promotional mix
   e. Pull strategy

17. A form of communication management that seeks to influence the feelings, opinions, or beliefs held by customers, stockholders, suppliers, employees and others about a company is called _____.
   a. Advertising
   b. Personal selling
   c. Communication
   d. Public relations
   e. Sales promotion

18. _____ is extraneous factors that work against effective communication by distorting a message or the feedback received.
   a. Noise
   b. Decoding
   c. Encoding
   d. Feedback
   e. Message

19. Allocating funds to advertising as a percentage of past or anticipated sales, in terms of either dollars or units sold is known as _____.
   a. All-you-can-afford budgeting
   b. Competitive parity budgeting
   c. Objective-and-task budgeting
   d. Cost per thousand (CPM)
   e. Percentage-of-sales budgeting

20. _____ is a budgeting approach whereby the company (1) determines its advertising objectives, (2) outlines the tasks to accomplish these objectives, and (3) determines the advertising cost of performing these tasks.
    a. All-you-can-afford budgeting
    b. Competitive parity budgeting
    c. Objective-and-task budgeting
    d. Cost per thousand (CPM)
    e. Percentage-of-sales budgeting

21. Matching the competitors' absolute level of spending or the proportion per point of market share is known as _____.
    a. All-you-can-afford budgeting
    b. Competitive parity budgeting
    c. Objective-and-task budgeting
    d. Cost per thousand (CPM)
    e. Percentage-of-sales budgeting

22. _____ is when funds allocated to advertising only after all other budget items are covered.
    a. All-you-can-afford budgeting
    b. Competitive parity budgeting
    c. Objective-and-task budgeting
    d. Cost per thousand (CPM)
    e. Percentage-of-sales budgeting

23. _____ is the direct selling of a product to a customer without person-to-person contact.
    a. Advertising
    b. Personal selling
    c. Direct marketing
    d. Public relations
    e. Sales promotion

24. Direct orders, lead generation, and traffic generation are the goals of _____.
    a. Advertising
    b. Personal selling
    c. Direct marketing
    d. Public relations
    e. Sales promotion

Chapter 19--Answers

Discussion Questions

The Communications Process

1. source
2. message
3. channel of communication
4. receiver
5. encoding
6. decoding

Promotional Mix

1. public relations
2. personal selling
3. advertising
4. sales promotion
5. direct marketing

Example: Advertising, advantage--reaches broad audience; disadvantage--expensive

Product Life Cycle

1. growth
2. introduction
3. maturity
4. decline

1. growth
2. decline
3. maturity
4. introduction

Product Characteristics

1. personal selling
2. advertising
3. advertising

Customer's Stage of Decision Making

1. purchase stage
2. postpurchase stage
3. prepurchase stage

Direct Marketing

1. lead generation
2. direct orders
3. traffic generation

Sample Tests

1. c	14. d
2. e	15. b
3. b	16. c
4. a	17. d
5. c	18. a
6. b	19. e
7. e	20. c
8. e	21. b
9. a	22. a
10. c	23. c
11. b	24. c
12. d	
13. e	

CHAPTER 20

Advertising, Sales Promotion, And Public Relations

Why is Chapter 20 important? This chapter illustrates the types of advertising and sales promotional tools and how they can be used effectively. It goes through the steps to plan and execute a successful advertising program and looks at the effective use of public relations and publicity. In addition, it studies the different types of media and when they are best utilized.

Advertising: Any paid form of nonpersonal communication about an organization, good, service, or idea, by an identified sponsor.

CHAPTER OUTLINE

I. TYPES OF ADVERTISEMENTS

    A. Product
        1. Pioneering (informational)
        2. Competitive (persuasive)
        3. Reminder

    B. Institutional
        1. Advocacy
        2. Pioneering
        3. Competitive
        4. Reminder

II. DEVELOPING THE ADVERTISING PROGRAM

    A. Identifying the Target Audience

    B. Specifying Advertising Objectives

    C. Setting the Advertising Budget

    D. Designing the Advertisement
        1. Message content
            a. fear appeal
            b. sex appeal
            c. humorous appeal
        2. Creating the actual message

    E. Selecting the Right Media
        1. Goals
            a. maximizing exposure
            b. minimizing costs
        2. Basic terms
            a. reach
            b. rating
            c. frequency
            d. gross rating points (GRP)
            e. cost per thousand (CPM)

F. Different Media Alternatives
1. Television
2. Radio
3. Magazines
4. Newspapers
5. Direct mail
6. Internet
7. Outdoor
8. Other media

G. Scheduling the Advertising
1. Factors
   a. buyer turnover
   b. purchase frequency
   c. forgetting rate
2. Approaches
   a. continuous
   b. flighting
   c. pulse

III. EXECUTING THE ADVERTISING PROGRAM

A. Pretesting
1. Portfolio tests
2. Jury tests
3. Theatre tests

B. Carrying Out the Advertising Program
1. Full-service agencies
2. Limited-service agencies
3. In-house agencies

C. Evaluating the Advertising Program

D. Posttesting
1. Aided recall
2. Unaided recall
3. Attitude tests
4. Inquiry test
5. Sales tests

E. Making Needed Changes

IV. SALES PROMOTION

A. Importance

B. Consumer-oriented
1. coupons
2. deals
3. premiums
4. contests
5. sweepstakes
6. samples
7. continuity programs
8. point-of-purchase displays

        9. rebates
       10. product placement

   C. Trade-Oriented
      1. Allowances and discounts
      2. Cooperative advertising
      3. Training of distributors' salesforce

V. PUBLIC RELATIONS

   A. Public Relations Tools
      1. Publicity (news release, news conference, PSAs)
      2. Special Events
      3. Public service activities
      4. Collateral materials

You should be able to place these key terms in the outline and be able to discuss them.

advertising	infomercials	product advertisements
consumer-oriented sales promotions	in-house agencies	product placement
cooperative advertising	institutional advertisements	rating
cost per thousand	limited-service agencies	reach
frequency	post-tests	trade-oriented
full-service agencies	pretests	sales promotions
gross rating points		

QUESTIONS & PROBLEMS

PRODUCT ADVERTISING

Product advertising focuses on selling a product or service, and can take three forms:

Pioneering
Competitive
Reminder

Match the correct form of product advertising with the definitions or statements below:

1. Advertising that promotes a specific brand's features and benefits. One form shows one brand's strengths relative to another's._____

2. Advertising that tells what a product is, what it can do, and where it can be found. The key objective is to inform the target market._____

3. This form of advertisement is used to reinforce previous knowledge of a product or a service. A variation of this form of advertisement, reinforcement advertising, is used to reassure current users they made the right choice._____

INSTITUTIONAL ADVERTISING

There are four alternative forms of institutional advertising:

Advocacy advertisements
Pioneering institutional advertisements
Competitive institutional advertisements
Reminder institutional advertisements

Match the correct form of institutional advertising to the definitions or statements below:

1. These advertisements are used for a new announcement such as what a company is, what it can do, or where it is located._____

2. These advertisements promote the advantages of one product class over another.
_____

3. These advertisements state the position of a company on a given issue.
_____

4. These advertisements bring the name of the company to the attention of their target market._____
_____

DEVELOPING THE ADVERTISING PROGRAM

What are the six steps used in developing the advertising program?

1._____

2._____

3._____

4._____

5._____

6._____

MESSAGE CONTENT

Information and persuasive content can be combined in the form of an appeal to provide a basic reason for the consumer to act. There are three commonly used methods of appeal:

Fear appeal
Sex appeal
Humorous appeal

Find the best current example (in your opinion) of advertisements that incorporate each of the forms of appeal listed above:

Advertisement	Type of Appeal	Media
1._____	_____	_____
2._____	_____	_____
3._____	_____	_____

BASIC MEDIA TERMS

Media buyers speak a language of their own, so every advertiser involved in selecting the right media for their campaigns must be familiar with some common terms used in the advertising industry .

Define the following advertising terms:

1. Reach_____

2. Rating_____

3. Frequency_____

4. Gross rating points_____

5. Cost per thousand_____

6. Splitting 30s_____

7. Wasted coverage_____

DIFFERENT MEDIA ALTERNATIVES

List the advantages and disadvantages of the media alternatives:

	Advantages	Disadvantages
1. Television	_____	_____
2. Radio	_____	_____
3. Magazines	_____	_____
4. Newspapers	_____	_____
5. Direct mail	_____	_____
6. Outdoor	_____	_____
7. Internet	_____	_____

SCHEDULING THE ADVERTISING

There is no correct schedule to advertise a product, but three factors must be considered. These factors include:

Buyer turnover
Purchase frequency
Forgetting rate

Match the correct term to the statements listed below:

1. The speed with which buyers forget the brand if advertising is not seen._____

2. How often new buyers enter the market to buy the product._____

3. The more frequently the product is purchased, the less repetition is required._____

TIMING

Setting schedules requires an understanding of how the market behaves. Most companies tend to follow one of two basic approaches.

Steady "drip" schedule
Flighting "intermittent" schedule
Pulse "burst" schedule

Match the correct scheduling approach to the statements below:

1. Periods of advertising are scheduled between periods of no advertising to reflect seasonal demand.

_____

2. A flighting schedule is combined with a steady schedule because of increases in demand, heavy periods of promotions, or introduction of a new product.

_____

3. When seasonal factors are unimportant, advertising is run at a steady or regular schedule throughout the year._____

PRETESTING ADVERTISING

Pretesting is done to determine whether the advertisement communicates the intended message, or to select the best alternative version of an advertisement. There are three common forms of pretesting:

Portfolio tests
Jury tests
Theatre tests

Match the correct form of pretesting with the statements below:

1. This is used to test copy alternatives. The test ad is placed in a booklet with several other ads and stories. Subjects are asked to read through and give their impressions of the ad on several evaluative scales._____

2. The ad is shown to a panel of consumers: the panel rates how much they liked the ad, how much it drew their attention, how attractive it was, etc._____

3. This is the most sophisticated form of pretesting. Consumers are invited to view a new movie or television show. During the show, commercials are shown. Viewers register their feeling about the advertisements either on hand held electronic recording devices used during the viewing or on questionnaires afterwards._____

CARRYING OUT THE ADVERTISING PROGRAM

The responsibility for actually carrying out the advertising program can be handled in one of three ways.

Full-service agency
Limited-service agency
In-house agency
Match the correct term to the statements below:

1. The firm's own advertising staff may provide full services or a limited range of services.

_____

2. Specializes in one aspect of the advertising process such as providing creative services to develop the advertising copy or buying previously unpurchased media space.

_____

3. Provides the most complete range of services, including market research, media selection, copy development, art work, and production._____

POST-TESTING METHODS

There are several post-testing methods:

Aided recall
Unaided recall
Attitude tests
Inquiry tests
Sales tests

Match the correct posttesting method to the statements below:

1. This technique questions respondents without any prompting to determine whether they saw or heard advertising messages._____

2. This technique offers additional product information, samples, or premiums in response to consumer requests. Ads generating the most inquiries are presumed to be the most effective.

_____

3. After being shown an ad, respondents are asked whether their previous exposure to it was through reading, viewing, or listening._____

4. This technique involves studies such as controlled media comparison experiments and consumer purchase tests._____

5. Respondents are asked questions to measure changes in their dispositions towards a particular product following an advertising campaign._____

CONSUMER-ORIENTED SALES PROMOTION

There are numerous consumer-oriented sales promotion alternatives:

Coupons
Deals
Premiums
Contests
Sweepstakes
Samples
Continuity programs
Point-of-purchase displays
Rebates
Product placement

List an example of each of the sales promotion alternatives below:

1. Coupons_____

2. Deals_____

3. Premiums_____

4. Contests_____

5. Sweepstakes_____

6. Samples_____

7. Continuity programs_____

8. Point-of-purchase displays_____

9. Rebates_____

10. Product placement _____

TRADE-ORIENTED SALES PROMOTIONS

There are three major approaches to trade-oriented sales promotions:

Allowances and discounts (merchandise, case, and finance allowances)
Cooperative advertising
Training of distributors' salesforce

Match the type of trade-oriented sales promotion with the examples or statements below (be specific):

1. This reimburses a retailer for extra in-store support or special featuring of the brand._____

2. Manufacturers allow discounts on each case ordered during a specific time period._____

3. This may involve the production of educational pamphlets or manufacturer sponsored national sales meetings._____

4. Retailers are paid for financing costs or financial losses associated with consumer sales promotions.____
_____

5. Usually the manufacturer pays a percentage, often 50% of the cost of advertising, up to a certain dollar limit which is based on the amount of the purchases the retailer makes of the manufacturer's products._____
_____

PUBLIC RELATIONS

The most frequently used public relations tool is publicity. Publicity usually takes the form of a news releases, news conferences, and public service announcements (PSAs).

Find an example of each of the three types of publicity:

News releases_____

News conferences_____

PSAs_____

CAN YOU PASS THE TEST?

OVERVIEW OF CHAPTER 20: TERMS AND DEFINITIONS (multiple choice)

1. _____ are advertisements which focus on selling a product or service and take three forms: (1) pioneering, (2) competitive, and (3) reminder.
   a. Advertising
   b. Institutional advertisements
   c. Product advertisements
   d. Hierarchy of effects
   e. Rating

2. _____ is the number of different people exposed to the message.
   a. Frequency
   b. Post-tests
   c. Pretests
   d. Gross rating points
   e. Reach

3. _____ are tests conducted before an advertisement is placed to determine whether it communicates the intended message or to select between alternative versions of an advertisement.
   a. Frequency
   b. Post-tests
   c. Pretests
   d. Gross rating points
   e. Reach

4. _____ is an advertising agency which specializes in one aspect of the advertising process, such as providing creative services to develop the advertising copy or buying previously unpurchased media space.
   a. Limited-service agency
   b. Institutional advertisements
   c. Product advertisements
   d. Full-service agency
   e. In-house agency

5. _____ is the sequence of stages a prospective buyer goes through, from initial awareness of a product to achieve eventual action (either trial or adoption of a product). The stages include awareness, interest, evaluation, trial, and adoption.
   a. Advertising
   b. Institutional advertisements
   c. Product advertisements
   d. Hierarchy of effects
   e. Rating

6. _____ is a company's own advertising staff which may provide full services or a limited range of services.
    a. Limited-service agencies
    b. Institutional advertisements
    c. Product advertisements
    d. Full-service agency
    e. In-house agencies

7. _____ is an advertising agency providing a complete range of services, including market research, media selection, copy development, art work, and production.
    a. Limited-service agencies
    b. Institutional advertisements
    c. Product advertisements
    d. Full-service agency
    e. In-house agencies

8. Advertisements designed to build goodwill or an image for an organization, rather than promote a specific product or service _____.
    a. Advertising
    b. Institutional advertisements
    c. Product advertisements
    d. Hierarchy of effects
    e. Rating

9. The average number of times a person in the target audience is exposed to a message or advertisement is called _____.
    a. Frequency
    b. Post-tests
    c. Pretests
    d. Gross rating points
    e. Reach

10. _____ are tests conducted after an advertisement has been shown to the target audience to determine whether it has accomplished its intended purpose.
    a. Frequency
    b. Post-tests
    c. Pretests
    d. Gross rating points
    e. Reach

11. _____ is the percentage of households in a market watching or listening to a broadcast .
    a. Advertising
    b. Institutional advertisements
    c. Product advertisements
    d. Hierarchy of effects
    e. Rating

12. _____ is a reference number for advertisers, created by multiplying reach by frequency.
    a. Frequency
    b. Post-tests
    c. Pretests
    d. Gross rating points
    e. Rating

13. Any paid form of nonpersonal communication about an organization, good, service, or idea, by an identified sponsor is called _____.
    a. Advertising
    b. Institutional advertisements
    c. Product advertisements
    d. Hierarchy of effects
    e. Rating

14. Buy one dinner, get a second dinner of equal value, for half price is an example of _____.
    a. coupons
    b. deals
    c. premiums
    d. contests
    e. sweepstakes

15. Try your skill at creating a new recipe using our crisp new crackers, and you may win a beautiful fully equipped kitchen is an example of _____.
    a. coupons
    b. deals
    c. premiums
    d. contests
    e. sweepstakes

16. Just rub off the magic seal and see if you are an instant winner is an example of _____.
    a. coupons
    b. deals
    c. premiums
    d. contests
    e. sweepstakes

17. Send in five box tops and 50-cents postage and handling to receive your beautiful colour poster of Michael Jordan is an example of _____.
    a. samples
    b. continuity programs
    c. point of purchase displays
    d. rebates
    e. premiums

18. Earn free airline tickets by accumulating bonus points for every 500 km you fly is an example of _____.
    a. samples
    b. continuity programs
    c. point of purchase displays
    d. rebates
    e. deals

19. Please try these new local cookies with our compliments is an example of _____.
    a. samples
    b. continuity programs
    c. point of purchase displays
    d. rebates
    e. coupons

20. Retailers, these new lollipops come with their own attractive free-standing carousel that fits perfectly next to your cash register is an example of _____.
    a. samples
    b. continuity programs
    c. point of purchase displays
    d. rebates
    e. sweepstakes

21. Mail in three UPCs and cash register tapes with the price circled to receive a check for the full purchase price is an example of _____.
    a. coupons
    b. deals
    c. premiums
    d. rebates
    e. sweepstakes

22. Receive $0.25 off your next purchase of Green Giant frozen peas for redeeming this is an example of _____.
    a. coupons
    b. deals
    c. premiums
    d. contests
    e. sweepstakes

23. Advertising programs by which a manufacturer pays a percentage of the retailer's local advertising expense for advertising the manufacturer's products are called _____.
    a. Cooperative advertising
    b. Publicity tools
    c. Advertising
    d. Trade-oriented sales promotions
    e. Consumer-oriented sales promotions

24. _____ are sales tools used to support a company's advertising and personal selling efforts directed to wholesalers, distributors or retailers: three common approaches are the allowances, cooperative advertising, and sales force training.
    a. Cooperative advertising
    b. Publicity tools
    c. Advertising
    d. Trade-oriented sales promotions
    e. Consumer-oriented sales promotions

Chapter 20--Answers

Discussion Questions

Product Advertising

1. competitive
2. pioneering
3. reminder

Institutional Advertising

1. pioneering
2. competitive
3. advocacy
4. reminder

Developing the Advertising Program

1. Identifying the target audience
2. Specifying advertising objectives
3. Setting the advertising budget
4. Designing the advertisement
5. Selecting the right media
6. Scheduling the advertising

Basic Media Terms

1. Reach_____

2. Rating_____

3. Frequency_____

4. Gross rating points_____

5. Cost per thousand_____

6. Splitting 30s_____

7. Wasted coverage_____

Different Media Alternatives

Example: Television--advantages--reach; disadvantages--cost

Scheduling the Advertising

1. forgetting rate
2. buyer turnover
3. purchase frequency

Timing

1. intermittent
2. burst
3. drip

Pretesting Advertising

1. portfolio test
2. jury test
3. theatre test

Carrying Out the Advertising Program

1. in-house
2. limited-service
3. full-service

Post-testing Methods

1. unaided recall
2. inquiry test
3. aided recall
4. sales test
5. attitude test

Consumer-oriented Sales Promotion

Example: coupon - .50 cents off the purchase of Colgate Total

Trade-oriented Sales Promotion

1. allowances and discounts
2. allowances and discounts
3. training
4. allowances and discounts
5. cooperative advertising

Public Relations

Example: news release announcing new drug by Merck

Sample Tests

1. c	14. b
2. e	15. d
3. c	16. e
4. a	17. e
5. d	18. b
6. e	19. a
7. d	20. c
8. b	21. d
9. a	22. a
10. c	23. a
11. e	24. d
12. d	
13. a	

CHAPTER 21

Personal Selling and Sales Management

<u>Why is Chapter 21 important</u>? Personal selling is the lifeblood of much of the marketing function, especially the business-to-business segment. This chapter illustrates the participants in the personal selling process and their selection and management. It also outlines the personal selling process showing how to make it more effective.

Personal Selling: The two-way flow of communication between a buyer and seller, often in a face-to-face encounter, designed to influence a person's or group's purchase decision.

CHAPTER OUTLINE

I. SCOPE AND SIGNIFICANCE OF PERSONAL SELLING AND SALES MANAGEMENT

      A. Nature of Personal Selling and Sales Management

      B. Pervasiveness of Selling

      C. Personal Selling in Marketing

      D. Creating Customer Value through Salespeople: Relationship and Partnership Selling

II. FORMS OF PERSONAL SELLING

      A. Order Taking
          1. Outside order takers
          2. Inside order takers

      B. Order Getting

      C. Sales Support Personal
          1. Missionary salespeople
          2. Sales engineer
          3. Team selling
               a. conference selling
               b. seminar selling

III. PERSONAL SELLING PROCESS: BUILDING RELATIONSHIPS

      A. Prospecting
          1. Lead
          2. Prospect
          3. Qualified prospect

      B. Preapproach

      C. Approach

      D. Presentation

       1. Stimulus-response format
       2. Formula selling format
       3. Need-satisfaction format
           a. adaptive selling
           b. consultative selling
       4. Handling objections
           a. acknowledge and convert the objection
           b. postpone
           c. agree and neutralize
           d. accept the objection
           e. denial
           f. ignore the objection

E. Close
       1. Trial close
       2. Assumptive close
       3. Urgency close

F. Followup

IV. SALES MANAGEMENT PROCESS

A. Sales Plan Formulation
       1. Setting objectives
           a. output related
           b. input related
           c. behaviourally related
       2. Organizing the salesforce
           a. types of sales personnel
                i. own salesforce
                ii. independents agents
           b. structure
                i. geography
                ii. customer type
                iii. product or service
           c. salesforce size
                i. number of accounts
                ii. frequency of calls
                iii. length of calls
                iv. time devoted to selling
       3. Developing account management policies

B. Sales Plan Implementation
       1. Salesforce recruitment and selection
           a. job analysis
           b. job description
                i. to whom the salesperson reports
                ii. how a salesperson interacts with other company personnel
                iii. the customers to be called on
                iv. the specific activities to be carried out
                v. physical and mental demands of the job
                vi. types of products and services to be sold
           c. job qualifications
                i. imagination and problem-solving ability
                ii. honesty

        iii.   intimate product knowledge

        iv.   attentiveness reflected in responsiveness to buyer needs and customer loyalty and follow-up

        v.   emotional intelligence

2. Salesforce training
3. Salesforce motivation and compensation
   a. clear job description
   b. effective sales management practices
   c. a sense of achievement
   d. proper compensation, incentives, or rewards
      i. straight salary
      ii. straight commission
      iii. combination
4. Salesforce evaluation and control
   a. quantitative assessments
   b. behavioural evaluation
5. Salesforce automation
   a. computerization
   b. communication
   c. sales management in the age of automation

You should be able to place these key terms in the outline and be able to discuss them.

account management policies	need-satisfaction presentation	salesforce automation
adaptive selling	order getter	sales management
conference selling	order taker	sales plan
consultative selling	partnership selling	seminar selling
emotional intelligence	personal selling	stimulus-response presentation
formula selling presentation	personal selling process	team selling
major account management	relationship selling	workload method
missionary salespeople	sales engineer	

QUESTIONS & PROBLEMS

PERSONAL SELLING IN MARKETING

What three major roles does personal selling play in a firm's overall marketing efforts?

1._____

2._____

3._____

The practice of building ties based on a salesperson's attention and commitment to customer needs over time is called relationship selling. This involves mutual respect and trust among buyers and sellers.

THE MANY FORMS OF PERSONAL SELLING

Which of the following activities are performed by order takers, and which are performed by order getters?

1. Handles routine product orders and/or reorders_____

2. Generates new sales volume_____

3. Identifies new customers and sales opportunities_____

4. Maintains sales volume_____

5. Focuses on straight rebuy purchase situations_____

6. Requires significant clerical training_____

7. Performs order processing functions_____

8. Acts as a creative problem solver_____

9. Focuses on new buy and modified rebuy purchase situations_____

10. Represents complex products with many options_____

SALES SUPPORT PERSONNEL

Sales support personnel augment the selling effort of order getters by performing a variety of services.

Missionary salespeople
Sales engineer
Team selling

Match the correct type of sales support personnel to the examples below:

1. Ms. Pedrotti prepares promotions and information packets for hospitals. She promotes the purchase of new pharmaceutical products although she does not directly solicit orders._____

2. A computer firm sends out three people on sales calls: one to explain the product's technical capabilities, one to explain the software, and a third to arrange logistics such as price, delivery, and installation._____

3. Mr. Green, an electrical engineer works in the sales department. He does not solicit sales but provides any and all information concerning the electrical function of the product his company manufactures and sells._____

THE PERSONAL SELLING PROCESS

Prospecting

Personal selling begins with prospecting, the search for and qualification of potential customers. There are three types of prospects:

Lead
Prospect
Qualified prospect

Match the type of prospect to the definition below:

1. A customer who wants and needs a product_____

2. The name of a person who may be a possible customer_____

3. A person who wants a product, can afford the product, and has the decision power to buy the product

_____

List at least five ways to generate leads and prospects (use creativity):

1._____

2._____

3._____

4._____

5._____

PREAPPROACH AND APPROACH STAGE

One of the major competitive advantages IBM had over its mainframe computer competitor's was its sales personnel. When IBM came in to make a presentation, they were prepared. They knew the prospect's business and how a computer, an IBM computer would benefit that business. Consider the following situation. A company which prepared specialized reports for the financial services industry was in the market to upgrade their computer system. IBM and Unisys were the two companies making presentations. Both companies had made cold calls and supplied the company officers with literature and specifications. At the presentation, Unisys presented a prepackaged system directed toward someone in the "publishing" industry complete with canned programs for data entry on the computer. IBM, by doing the necessary preapproach preparation, knew the company wrote its own software and really needed high speed computing and high speed quality printers. Their presentation was geared to the company's needs. It doesn't take much imagination to guess who got the sale.

You are a salesperson for a major office furniture and equipment manufacturer. You have been invited in to present your products to several new tenants of a large office complex in Vancouver. What type of preapproach questions and preparations do you need? If these tenants are a law firm, advertising agency and real estate firm, what will you approach be?

The approach stage is very important in international settings. In many societies outside Canada, considerable time is devoted to nonbusiness talk designed to establish a rapport between buyers and sellers.

PRESENTATION

The presentation is at the core of the order getting selling process, and its objective is to convert a prospect into a consumer by creating a desire for the product or service.

There are three types of presentation format:

Stimulus-response format
Formula selling format
Need-satisfaction format

Match the type of selling presentation with the examples or statements below:

1. A popular version of this format is the canned sales presentation._____

2. After you select a new Gant dress shirt, the salesperson suggests a matching club tie._____

3. This format emphasizes probing and listening by the salesperson to identify needs and interests of prospective buyers._____

4. The salesperson tries many appeals, hoping to "hit the right button."_____

5. This approach is most consistent with the marketing concept._____

6. This format is commonly used in telephone and door-to-door selling and treats every prospect the same regardless of differences in needs or preferences._____

Answer the following questions:

1. Assume you are a salesperson at an upscale women's clothing store. Demonstrate how you would use suggestive selling:_____
_____
_____

2. Design a canned sales presentation for someone selling burial plots over the telephone (keep it to one paragraph)._____
_____
_____
_____

3. What is adaptive selling?_____

4. What is consultative selling?_____

4. What is consultative selling?_____

CLOSE

The closing stage in the selling process involves obtaining a purchase commitment from the prospect. There are three common closing methods:

Trial close
Assumptive close
Urgency close

Match the correct type of close to the statements below:

1. This technique involves asking the prospect to make a decision on some aspect of the purchase.

_____

2. This technique is used to commit the prospect quickly by making reference to the timeliness of the purchase._____

3. This technique entails asking the prospect to make choices concerning delivery, warranty, or financing terms._____

FOLLOW-UP

The selling process does not end with the closing of a sale.

List two reasons why follow-up is such an important policy (in your opinion):

THE SALES MANAGEMENT PROCESS

List the three interrelated functions of sales management:

1._____

2._____

3._____

What are the three tasks in sales plan formulation?

1._____

2._____

3._____

ORGANIZATIONAL STRUCTURE

If a company elects to employ its own salespeople, then it must choose an organizational structure based on (1) geography, (2) customer, or (3) product/service.
Which type of organizational structure is best described by the statements below:

1. This structure minimizes travel time, expenses, and duplication of selling effort._____

2. When specialized knowledge is required to sell certain types of products, this structure is suggested._____
_____

3. When different buyers have different needs, this structure is suggested._____

4. This structure often leads to higher administrative costs since two or more separate salesforces represent the same products._____

5. Reporting to the General Sales Manager are the Eastern and Western Regional Sales Managers._____
_____

6. At Magic Micros, John sells the company's line of six microcomputers to existing customers and prospects in his territory. About once a week John will meet his friend Jane (who also works for Magic) in a customer's waiting room. Jane sells the company's line of specialized software and consulting services.___
_____

The "workload method" is the most commonly used determinate of salesforce size.

$$NS = (NC \times CF \times CL)/ AST$$
where,

        NS = Number of salespeople
        NC = Number of customers
        CF = Call frequency
        CL = Average call length
        AST = Average selling time available per sales person per year

Apple Computer has 15,000 retail outlets and company policy mandates at least one call per month per store. An average sales call takes three hours. Each Apple salesperson spends 50% of each 2,000-hour work-year selling.

Use the workload method to determine the number of salespeople Apple needs to service these accounts:

NS = _____

SALES PLAN IMPLEMENTATION

The sales plan is a statement describing what is to be achieved and where and how the selling effort of salespeople is to be deployed. Formulating the sales plan is the most basic of the three sales management functions.

What are the three tasks in sales plan implementation?
1._____

2._____

3._____

Salespeople are paid by using one of three plans. Each method has special uses, advantages, and disadvantages.

      Straight salary compensation plan
      Straight commission compensation plan
      Combination compensation plan

Which methods of compensation are being described by the examples or statements below:

1. Provides little incentive, necessitates close supervision of salespersons_____

2. Especially useful when highly aggressive selling is required_____

3. Provides a certain amount of financial security while still providing some financial incentive_____
_____

SALESFORCE EVALUATION AND CONTROL

What are the two tasks in evaluation and control?

1._____

2._____

Sales force evaluation uses both quantitative and behavioural objectives. Quantitative evaluations can be either input- or output-related.

Identify whether the basis of salesforce evaluation is quantitative or behavioural:

1. Account management policies_____

2. Number of sales calls_____

3. Product knowledge_____

4. Communication skills_____

5. Appearance_____

6. Number of new accounts_____

7. Number of reports submitted to superiors_____

8. Accounts generated_____

SALESFORCE AUTOMATION

Discuss how automation has enhanced the salesforces' ability to use the marketing mix, i.e., 4 P's of marketing.

CAN YOU PASS THE TEST?

OVERVIEW OF CHAPTER 21: TERMS AND DEFINITIONS (multiple choice)

1. Using a group of professionals in selling to and servicing major customers is called _____.
   - a. Seminar selling
   - b. Missionary salespeople
   - c. Team selling
   - d. Order getter
   - e. Order taker

2. _____ is a statement describing what is to be achieved and where and how the selling effort of salespeople is to be deployed.
   - a. Account management policies
   - b. Sales engineer
   - c. Sales management
   - d. Job description
   - e. Sales plan

3. A salesperson who sells in a conventional sense and engages in identifying prospective customers, providing customers with information, persuading customers to buy, closing sales, and following up on customers' experience with a product or service is known as _____.
   - a. Seminar selling
   - b. Missionary salespeople
   - c. Team selling
   - d. Order getter
   - e. Order taker

4. Sales activities occurring before and after the sale itself consist of six stages: (1) prospecting, (2) preapproach, (3) approach, (4) presentation, (5) close, and (6) follow-up. This is called the _____.
   - a. personal selling process
   - b. Sales engineer
   - c. Sales management
   - d. Job description
   - e. Sales plan

5. Policies that specify whom salespeople should contact, what kinds of selling and customer service activities should be engaged in, and how these activities should be carried out is known as _____.
   - a. Account management policies
   - b. Sales engineer
   - c. Sales management
   - d. Job description
   - e. Sales plan

6. _____ is a written description of what a salesperson is expected to do.
   - a. Account management policies
   - b. Sales engineer
   - c. Sales management
   - d. Job description
   - e. Sales plan

7. _____ is a salesperson who processes routine orders and reorders for products that have already been sold by the company.
    a. Seminar selling
    b. Missionary salespeople
    c. Team selling
    d. Order getter
    e. Order taker

8. _____ is a selling formula that emphasizes probing and listening by salespeople to identify the needs and interests of prospective buyers.
    a. Stimulus-response presentation
    b. Need-satisfaction presentation
    c. Personal selling process
    d. Work-load method
    e. Formula selling presentation

9. _____ is a formula-based method that integrates the number of customers served, call frequency, call length, and available selling time to arrive at a sales force size figure.
    a. Stimulus-response presentation
    b. Need-satisfaction presentation
    c. Personal selling process
    d. Work-load method
    e. Formula selling presentation

10. _____ is a salesperson who specializes in identifying, analyzing, and solving customer problems and who brings technical expertise to the selling situation, but often does not actually sell goods and services.
    a. Account management policies
    b. Sales engineer
    c. Sales management
    d. Job description
    e. Sales plan

11. _____ is a selling format that assumes the prospects will buy if given the appropriate stimulus by the salesperson.
    a. Stimulus-response presentation
    b. Need-satisfaction presentation
    c. Personal selling process
    d. Work-load method
    e. Formula selling presentation

12. The planning, implementing, and controlling of the personal selling effort of the firm is known as _____.
    a. Account management policies
    b. Sales engineer
    c. Sales management
    d. Job description
    e. Sales plan

13. The two-way flow of communication between buyer and seller that often occurs in a face-to-face encounter, designed to influence a person's or group's purchase decision is called _____.
    a. Personal selling
    b. Adaptive selling
    c. Conference selling
    d. Relationship selling
    e. Consultative selling

14. The selling format that consists of providing information in an accurate, thorough, and step-by-step manner to persuade the prospect to buy is known as _____.
    a. Stimulus-response presentation
    b. Need-satisfaction presentation
    c. Personal selling process
    d. Work-load method
    e. Formula selling presentation

15. _____ are sales support personnel who do not directly solicit orders but rather concentrate on performing promotional activities and introducing new products.
    a. Seminar selling
    b. Missionary salespeople
    c. Team selling
    d. Order getter
    e. Order taker

16. _____ is a need-satisfaction sales presentation involving adjusting the sales presentation to fit the selling situation.
    a. Personal selling
    b. Adaptive selling
    c. Conference selling
    d. Relationship selling
    e. Consultative selling

17. _____ is a need-satisfaction sales presentation where the salesperson focuses on problem definition and serves as an expert on problem recognition and resolution.
    a. Personal selling
    b. Adaptive selling
    c. Conference selling
    d. Relationship selling
    e. Consultative selling

18. _____ is a form of team selling where a sales person and other company resource people meet with buyers to discuss problems and opportunities .
    a. Personal selling
    b. Adaptive selling
    c. Conference selling
    d. Relationship selling
    e. Consultative selling

19. _____ is a form of team selling where a company team conducts an educational program for a customer's technical staff describing state-of-the-art developments.
    a. Seminar selling
    b. Missionary salespeople
    c. Team selling
    d. Order getter
    e. Order taker

20. The practice of using team selling to focus on important customers to build mutually long-term, cooperative relationships is known as _____.
     a. Account management policies
     b. Sales engineer
     c. Sales management
     d. Job description
     e. Major account management plan

21. The practice of building ties based on a salesperson's attention and commitment to customer needs over time is called _____.
     a. Personal selling
     b. Adaptive selling
     c. Conference selling
     d. Relationship selling
     e. Consultative selling

For questions 22-27 select the stage of the Personal Selling Process involved.

22. Use the trial or assumptive approach to obtain a commitment of sale.
     a. Prospecting
     b. Preapproach
     c. Approach
     d. Presentation
     e. Close

23. Create a desire for the product by paying special attention to the customer's needs. Incorporate any of several methods to highlight the product, allay fears, and provide information.
     a. Prospecting
     b. Preapproach
     c. Approach
     d. Presentation
     e. Close

24. Gather information through personal observation, sales staff and/or other customers, to find the best way to introduce yourself and your product to a new customer.
     a. Prospecting
     b. Preapproach
     c. Approach
     d. Presentation
     e. Close

25. Resolve any unsolved problems, ensure customer satisfaction.
     a. Prospecting
     b. Preapproach
     c. Approach
     d. Presentation
     e. Follow-up

26. Use advertising, referrals, cold canvassing, etc. to search for and qualify potential customers.
     a. Prospecting
     b. Preapproach
     c. Approach
     d. Presentation
     e. Close

27. Gain the prospect's attention, stimulate interest, and build the foundation for the sales presentation.
    a. Prospecting
    b. Preapproach
    c. Approach
    d. Presentation
    e. Close

28. _____ is a technique where the salesperson lets the prospect express such views, probe for the reason behind them, and attempt to stimulate discussion on the objections.
    a. Acknowledge and convert the objection
    b. Postpone
    c. Agree and neutralize
    d. Accept the objection
    e. Denial

29. This technique, called _____, is used when it appears that the objection is a stalling mechanism or is clearly not important to the prospect.
    a. Acknowledge and convert the objection
    b. Postpone
    c. Agree and neutralize
    d. Accept the objection
    e. Ignore the objection

30. _____ is a technique used when the objection will be dealt with later in the presentation.
    a. Acknowledge and convert the objection
    b. Postpone
    c. Agree and neutralize
    d. Accept the objection
    e. Denial

31. This technique, known as _____, is used when a prospect's objection is clearly untrue and based on misinformation.
    a. Acknowledge and convert the objection
    b. Postpone
    c. Agree and neutralize
    d. Accept the objection
    e. Denial

32. This technique involves using the objection as a reason for buying. It is known as _____.
    a. Acknowledge and convert the objection
    b. Postpone
    c. Agree and neutralize
    d. Accept the objection
    e. Denial

33. _____ is the technique by which the salesperson agrees with the objection, then shows that it is unimportant.
    a. Acknowledge and convert the objection
    b. Postpone
    c. Agree and neutralize
    d. Accept the objection
    e. Denial

Chapter 21--Answers

Discussion Questions

Personal Selling in Marketing

1. Salespeople are critical links between the firm and its customers.

2. Salespeople are the company in the customer's eye.

3. It may play a dominant role in the firm's marketing program typically when a firm uses a push marketing strategy.

The Many Forms of Personal Selling

1. order taker
2. order getter
3. order getter
4. order taker
5. order taker
6. order taker
7. order taker
8. order getter
9. order getter
10. order getter

Sales Support Personnel

1. missionary salespeople
2. team selling
3. sales engineer

The Personal Selling Process

1. prospect
2. lead
3. qualified prospect

Example: D&B reports on new businesses

Preapproach and Approach Stage

Example: type of firm, workplace only or customer contact

Presentation

1. formula selling
2. stimulus-response
3. need-satisfaction
4. stimulus-response
5. need-satisfaction
6. formula selling

3. A need-satisfaction sales presentation involving adjusting the sales presentation to fit the selling situations.

4. A need-satisfaction sales presentation where the salesperson focuses on problem definition and serves as an expert on problem recognition and resolution.

Close

1. trial close
2. urgency close
3. assumptive close

Follow-Up

Example: to make further sales in the future.

The Sales Management Process

1. sales plan formulation
2. sales plan implementation
3. evaluation and control of salesforce

1. setting objectives
2. organizing the salesforce
3. developing account management policies

Organizational Structure

1. geography
2. product/service
3. customer
4. customer
5. geography
6. product/service

NS = (15000 x 12 x 3) / 1000 = 540

Sales Plan Implementation

1. salesforce recruitment and selection
2. salesforce training
3. salesforce motivation

1. straight salary
2. straight commission
3. combination

Salesforce Evaluation and Control

1. quantitative assessments
2. behavioural evaluation

1. quantitative
2. quantitative
3. behavioural
4. behavioural
5. behavioural
6. quantitative
7. quantitative
8. quantitative

Salesforce Automation

Example:

Product--better product knowledge

Price--up-to-the-minute quotes

Promotion--better and more current presentations

Place--in touch with headquarters for tracking orders

Sample Tests

1. c	14. e	27. c
2. e	15. b	28. d
3. d	16. b	29. e
4. a	17. e	30. b
5. a	18. c	31. e
6. d	19. a	32. a
7. e	20. e	33. c
8. b	21. d	
9. d	22. e	
10. b	23. d	
11. a	24. b	
12. c	25. e	
13. a	26. a	

CHAPTER 22

The Strategic Marketing Process

Why is Chapter 22 important? This chapter deals with the strategic marketing process and examines its use in successfully meeting a company's goals. This includes both planning and implementation as well as the control phases of the process.

Strategic Marketing Process: The activities whereby an organization allocates its marketing mix resources to reach its target markets.

CHAPTER OUTLINE

I. STRATEGIC MARKETING'S GOAL: EFFECTIVE RESOURCE ALLOCATION

    A. Allocating Marketing Resources Using Sales Response Functions
        1. Maximizing incremental revenue minus incremental cost
        2. Share points

    B. Allocating Marketing Resources in Practice

    C. Resource Allocation and the Strategic Marketing Process

II. THE PLANNING PHASE OF THE STRATEGIC MARKETING PROCESS

    A. Varieties of Marketing Plans
        1. Long range marketing plans
        2. Annual marketing plans
        3. Marketing plans for new product launches

    B. Frameworks to Improve Marketing Planning
        1. Porter's generic business strategies
            a. cost leadership strategy·
            b. differentiation strategy
            c. cost focus strategy
            d. differentiation focus strategy
        2. Profit enhancement options
            a. increase revenues
            b. decrease costs
            c. do both
         3. Market-product synergies
            a. marketing synergies
                i. market-product concentration
                ii. market specialization
                iii. product specialization
                iv. selective specialization
                v. full coverage
            b. R & D and manufacturing synergies

    C. Some Planning & Strategy Lessons
        1. Guidelines for an effective marketing plan

          a. set measurable, achievable goals
          b. use a base of facts and valid assumptions
          c. utilize simple, but clear and specific, plans
          d. have complete and feasible plans
          e. make plans controllable and flexible
    2. Problems in marketing planning and strategy
          a. plans may be based on very poor assumptions about environmental factors
          b. planners and their plans may have lost sight of their customer's needs
          c. too much time and effort may be spent on data collection and writing the plans
          d. line operating managers often feel no sense of ownership in implementing the plans

III. THE IMPLEMENTATION PHASE OF THE STRATEGIC MARKETING PROCESS

  A. Improving Implementation of Marketing Programs
    1. Communicate goals and the means of achieving them
    2. Have a responsible program champion willing to act
    3. Reward successful program implementation
    4. Take action and avoid "paralysis by analysis"
    5. Foster open communication to surface the problem
    6. Schedule precise tasks, responsibilities and deadlines
          a. action item lists
                i. the task
                ii. name of person responsible for accomplishing task
                iii. the date by which the task is to be finished
          b. program schedules
                i. identify main tasks
                ii. determine the time to complete each task
                iii. arranging activities to meet deadline
                iv. assigning responsibilities to complete each task

  B Organizing for Marketing
    1. Line versus staff and divisional groups
          a. line positions
          b. staff positions
          c. divisional groupings
                i. product line groupings
                ii. functional groupings
                iii. geographical groupings
                iv. market-based groupings
    2. Role of product manager

IV. THE CONTROL PHASE OF THE STRATEGIC MARKETING PROCESS

  A. Marketing Control Process
    1. Measuring results
    2. Taking marketing actions

  B. Sales Analysis

  C. Profitability Analysis

  D. Marketing Audit

You should be able to place these key terms in the outline and be able to discuss them.

action item list	geographical groupings	sales analysis
cost focus strategy	line positions	sales component analysis
cost leadership strategy	market-based groupings	sales response function
differentiation strategy	marketing audit	share points
differentiation focus strategy	product line groupings	staff positions
functional groupings	product or program champion	synergy
generic business strategy	profitability analysis	

QUESTIONS & PROBLEMS

ALLOCATING MARKETING RESOURCES IN PRACTICE

Many firms use share points or percentage points as the basis of comparison to allocate marketing resources effectively.

List the three important types of information a marketing manager must estimate in order to make resource allocation decisions using share points:

1._____

2._____

3._____

Marketing managers must decide how much it would take (in time, money, energy) in order to achieve an additional market share point. This is especially important in companies that have multiple businesses within their own company, since the effort required to gain an additional point in one area may not be the same as the effort required to gain a percentage point in another.

THE PLANNING PHASE OF THE STRATEGIC MARKETING PROCESS

Annual marketing plans deal with the marketing goals and strategies for a product, product line, or entire firm for a single year, whereas long-range marketing plans cover from two to five years into the future.

Identify the following as annual marketing plans or long-range marketing plans:

1. Ford's introduction of the Mercury sport utility vehicle_____

2. McDonald's plans to enter the Mexican food fast food market at all their locations by the year 2000

_____

3. Pepsi's rollout of their new corporate colours_____

4. General Motors plan for new models of Cadillac to appeal to younger buyers_____

MARKET-PRODUCT SYNERGIES

Marketing synergies can act as a framework for relating market segments to products offered or potential marketing actions by a firm. This type of evaluation suggests several alternative strategies. These are:

Market-product concentration
Market specialization
Product specialization
Selective specialization
Full coverage

Indicate which marketing strategies are being used by the following products:

1. Kellogg's--cereals_____

2. Dr. Pepper--soft drinks_____

3. Kraft Foods--food_____

4. Hewlett Packard--printers_____

5. Netscape_____

GUIDELINES OF AN EFFECTIVE MARKETING PLAN

"Plans are nothing; planning is everything." - Dwight D. Eisenhower

List the five basic elements for effective market planning and plans:

1._____

2._____

3._____

4._____

5._____

PROBLEMS IN MARKETING PLANNING, AND STRATEGY

List four common areas where problems can occur in the planning phase of a firm's strategic marketing process:

1._____

2._____

3._____

4._____

THE IMPLEMENTATION PHASE OF THE STRATEGIC MARKETING PROCESS

No magic formula exists to guarantee effective implementation of marketing plans. In fact, the answer seems to be equal parts of good management skills and practices.

List six guidelines for improving program implementation:

1._____

2._____

3._____

4._____

5._____

6._____

ORGANIZING FOR MARKETING

What are the major differences between line positions and staff positions?_____

_____

There are four commonly used organizational groupings:

Product line groupings
Functional groupings
Geographical groupings
Market-based groupings

Match the correct term to the statements listed below:

1. Organization based on the different business activities performed with in the firm, such as marketing, finance, manufacturing_____

2. Organization based upon assigning responsibility for a specific type of customer to a given unit_____

_____

3. Organization based on the geographic region, for example, in terms of sales territory or responsibility___

_____

4. Organization based on specific product offerings_____

CAN YOU PASS THE TEST?

OVERVIEW OF CHAPTER 22: TERMS AND DEFINITIONS (multiple choice)

1. _____ is a plan which deals with the marketing goals and strategies for a product, product line, or entire firm for a single year.
    a. Annual marketing plans
    b. Marketing program
    c. Business portfolio analysis
    d. Marketing strategies
    e. Generic marketing strategy

2. The analysis of a firm's strategic business units (SBUs) as though they were a collection of separate investments is called _____.
    a. Annual marketing plans
    b. Marketing program
    c. Business portfolio analysis
    d. Marketing strategies
    e. Generic marketing strategy

3. _____ is a group of firms producing products which are close substitutes for each other.
    a. Relative market share
    b. Goals
    c. Sales response function
    d. Industry
    e. Share points

4. _____ relates the expense of marketing effort to the marketing results obtained.
    a. Relative market share
    b. Goals
    c. Sales response function
    d. Industry
    e. Share points

5. _____ is a strategy which can be adopted by any firm, regardless of the product or industry involved, to achieve a sustainable competitive advantage.
    a. Annual marketing plans
    b. Marketing program
    c. Business portfolio analysis
    d. Marketing strategies
    e. Generic marketing strategy

6. Percentage points of market share, called _____, is used as the common basis of comparison to allocate marketing resources effectively.
    a. Relative market share
    b. Goals
    c. Sales response function
    d. Industry
    e. Share points

7. The steps, known as _____, which are taken at the product and market levels to allocate marketing resources to viable marketing positions and programs and involve phases of (1) planning, (2) implementation, and (3) control.
    a. Long-range marketing plans
    b. Strategic business units (SBUs)
    c. Market growth rate
    d. Strategic marketing process
    e. Sustainable competitive advantage

8. _____ is a written statement identifying the target market, specific marketing goals, the budget, and timing for the marketing program.
    a. Annual marketing plans
    b. Marketing program
    c. Business portfolio analysis
    d. Marketing strategies
    e. Generic marketing strategy

9. _____ is a firm's strength relative to competitors' strengths in the markets they enter and compete.
    a. Long-range marketing plans
    b. Strategic business units (SBUs)
    c. Market growth rate
    d. Strategic marketing process
    e. Sustainable competitive advantage

10. Precise statements of results sought, quantified in terms of time and magnitude, where possible is known as _____.
    a. Relative market share
    b. Goals
    c. Sales response function
    d. Industry
    e. Share points

11. _____ is a plan which deals with the marketing goals and strategies for a product, product line, or entire firm and covers from two to five years.
    a. Long-range marketing plans
    b. Strategic business units (SBUs)
    c. Market growth rate
    d. Strategic marketing process
    e. Sustainable competitive advantage

12. The annual rate of growth of the specific market or industry in which a given SBU is competing is known as _____.
    a. Long-range marketing plans
    b. Strategic business units (SBUs)
    c. Market growth rate
    d. Strategic marketing process
    e. Sustainable competitive advantage

13. Means by which the marketing goals are to be achieved are called _____.
    a. Annual marketing plans
    b. Marketing program
    c. Business portfolio analysis
    d. Marketing strategies
    e. Generic marketing strategy

14. Tracing sales revenues back to their sources such as specific products, sales territories, or customers is called _____.
    a. Expense-to-sales ratio
    b. Sales component analysis
    c. Contribution margin analysis
    d. Profitability analysis
    e. Sales analysis

15. People in _____ have the authority and responsibility to issue orders to people who report to them.
    a. Action item list
    b. Staff positions
    c. Line positions
    d. Market-based groupings
    e. Marketing audit

16. Measuring the profitability of the firm's products, customer groups, sales territories and regions, channels of distribution, and order sizes is called _____.
    a. Expense-to-sales ratio
    b. Sales component analysis
    c. Contribution margin analysis
    d. Profitability analysis
    e. Sales analysis

17. _____ is an aid to implementing a marketing plan which consists of three columns:(1) the task, (2) the name of the person responsible for completing the task, and (3) the date by which the task is to be finished.
    a. Action item list
    b. Staff positions
    c. Line positions
    d. Market-based groupings
    e. Marketing audit

18. _____ is a form of profitability analysis which spotlights the behaviour of controllable costs and indicates the contribution to profit of a specific marketing factor.
    a. Expense-to-sales ratio
    b. Sales component analysis
    c. Contribution margin analysis
    d. Profitability analysis
    e. Sales analysis

19. _____ are organizational divisions in which a unit is subdivided according to the different business activities, such as manufacturing, marketing, and finance.
    a. Product line groupings
    b. Functional groupings
    c. Geographical groupings
    d. Market-based groupings
    e. Marketing audit

20. _____ is a comprehensive, unbiased, periodic review of the strategic marketing process of a firm or SBU.
    a. Product line groupings
    b. Functional groupings
    c. Geographical groupings
    d. Market-based groupings
    e. Marketing audit

21. _____ in an organization have the responsibility to advise people in line positions but cannot issue direct orders to them.
    a. Action item list
    b. Staff positions
    c. Line positions
    d. Market-based groupings
    e. Marketing audit

22. _____ are organizational divisions in which a unit is subdivided according to the product offerings for which it is responsible.
    a. Product line groupings
    b. Functional groupings
    c. Geographical groupings
    d. Market-based groupings
    e. Marketing audit

23. _____ is a form of ratio analysis in which specific costs or expenses are expressed as a percentage of sales revenue.
    a. Expense-to-sales ratio
    b. Sales component analysis
    c. Contribution margin analysis
    d. Profitability analysis
    e. Sales analysis

24. _____ are organizational divisions in which a unit is subdivided according to geographic location.
    a. Product line groupings
    b. Functional groupings
    c. Geographical groupings
    d. Market-based groupings
    e. Marketing audit

25. _____ is a tool used for controlling marketing programs in which actual sales records are compared with sales goals to identify strengths and weaknesses .
    a. Expense-to-sales ratio
    b. Sales component analysis
    c. Contribution margin analysis
    d. Profitability analysis
    e. Sales analysis

26. _____ is a method or organizing a company which assigns responsibility for a specific type of customer to a unit.
    a. Product line groupings
    b. Functional groupings
    c. Geographical groupings
    d. Market-based groupings
    e. Marketing audit

Chapter 22--Answers

Discussion Questions

Allocating Marketing Resources in Practice

1. market share of the product
2. revenues associated with each point of market share
3. contribution to overhead and profit of each share point

Market-Product Synergies

1. market specialization
2. product specialization
3. full coverage
4. market-product specialization
5. selective specialization

Guidelines for an Effective Marketing Plan

1. measurable, achievable objectives
2. a base of valid assumptions
3. simple, clear, and specific plans
4. complete and feasible plans
5. controllable and flexible plans

Problems in Marketing Planning and Strategy

1. plans may be based on very poor assumptions about environmental factors
2. planners and their plans may have lost sight of their customers needs
3. too much time and effort may be spent on data collection and writing the plan.
4. line operating managers often feel no sense of ownership in implementing the plans.

The Implementation Phase of the Strategic Marketing Process

1. communicate goals and the means of achieving them.
2. have a responsible program champion willing to act.
3. reward successful program implementation.
4. take action and avoid "paralysis by analysis."
5. foster open communication to surface the problems.
6. schedule precise tasks, responsibilities, and deadlines.

Organizing for Marketing

1. functional groupings
2. market-based groupings
3. geographical groupings
4. product line groupings

Sample Tests

1. a	14. b
2. c	15. c
3. d	16. d
4. c	17. a
5. e	18. c
6. e	19. b
7. d	20. e
8. b	21. b
9. e	22. a
10. b	23. a
11. a	24. c
12. c	25. e
13. d	26. d

social forces	technology
value consciousness	cause-related marketing
caveat emptor	code of ethics
Competition Act	ethics

An environmental force that includes inventions or innovations from applied science or engineering research.

The demographic characteristics of the population and its values in a particular environment.

Tying the charitable contributions of a firm directly to the customer revenues produced through the promotion of one of its products.

Consumer concern for obtaining the best quality, features, and performance of a product or service for a given price.

A formal statement of ethical principles and rules of conduct.

A Latin term that means "let the buyer beware."

The moral principles and values that govern the actions and decisions of an individual or group.

Key legislation designed to protect competition and consumers in Canada.

green marketing	IS0 14000
laws	moral idealism
social audit	social responsibility
sustainable development	whistleblowers
back translation	balance of trade

Worldwide standards for environmental quality and green marketing practices.	Marketing efforts to produce, promote, and reclaim environmentally sensitive products.
A personal moral philosophy that considers certain individual rights or duties as universal regardless of the outcome.	Society's values and standards that are enforceable in the courts.
The idea that organizations are part of a larger society and are accountable to society for their actions.	A systematic assessment of a firm's objectives, strategies, and performance in the domain of social responsibility.
Employees who report unethical or illegal actions of their employers.	The practice of conducting business in a way that protects the natural environment while making economic progress.
The difference between the monetary value of a nation's exports and imports.	The practice of retranslating a word or phrase into the original language by a different interpreter to catch errors.

consumer ethnocentrism	countertrade
cross-cultural analysis	cultural symbols
currency exchange rate	customs
direct investment	dumping
economic infrastructure	exporting

Using barter rather than money in making international sales.	The tendency to believe that it is inappropriate, indeed immoral, to purchase foreign-made products.
Things that represent ideas and concepts.	The study of similarities and differences between consumers in two or more nations or societies.
Norms and expectations about the way people do things in a specific country.	The price of one country's currency expressed in terms of another country's currency.
When a firm sells a product in a foreign country below its domestic price.	In global marketing, a domestic firm actually investing in and owning a foreign subsidiary or division.
Producing goods in one country then selling them in another country.	A country's communication, transportation, financial, and distribution systems.

global competition	global consumers
global marketing strategy	grey market
gross domestic product	ISO 9000
joint venture	multidomestic marketing strategy
protectionism	quota

Customer groups living in many countries or regions of the world who have similar needs or seek similar features and benefits from products and services.	A competitive situation that exists when firms originate, produce, and market their products and services worldwide.
A situation in which products are sold through unauthorized channels of distribution; also called parallel importing.	The practice of standardizing marketing activities when there are cultural similarities, and adapting them when cultures differ.
International standards for registration and certification of a manufacturer's quality management and quality assurance system.	The monetary value of all goods and services produced in a country during one year.
A firm's worldwide marketing strategy that offers as many different product variations, brand names, and advertising programs as countries in which it does business	In international trade, an arrangement in which a foreign company and a local firm invest together to create a local business.
In international marketing, a restriction placed on the amount of a product allowed to enter or leave a country.	The practice of shielding one or more sectors of a country's economy from foreign competition through the use of tariffs, or quotas.

semiotics	strategic alliances
tariff	trade feedback effect
values	World Trade Organization

Agreements between two or more independent firms to cooperate for the purpose of achieving common goals.	The field of study that examines the correspondence between symbols and their role in the assignment of meaning for people.
A country's imports affect its exports and exports affect imports.	In international marketing, a government tax on goods or services entering a country.
An institution that sets rules governing trade among its members through a panel of experts.	The beliefs of a person or culture; when applied to pricing, the ratio of perceived quality to price (Value = Perceived benefits/Price).

brand equity	brand name
branding	co-branding
downsizing	euro-branding
generic brand	licensing
manufacturer branding	market modification

Any word or device (design, shape, sound, or color) that is used to distinguish one company's products from a competitor's.	The added value a given brand name provides a product.
The pairing of two brand names of two manufacturers on a single product.	Activity in which an organization uses a name, phrase, design, or symbol, or a combination of these, to identify its products and distinguish them from those of a competitor.
The strategy of using the same brand name for the same product across all countries in the European Community.	The practice of reducing the content of package without changing package size and maintaining or increasing the package price.
A contractual agreement where by a company allows another firm to use its brand name, patent, trade secret, or other property for a royalty or fee.	A branding strategy that lists no product name, only a description of contents.
Attempts to increase product usage by creating new-use situations or finding new customers.	A branding strategy in which the brand name for a product is designated by the producer, using either a multiproduct or multibranding approach.

mixed branding	multibranding
multiproduct branding	packaging
private branding	product class
product form	product life cycle
product modifications	trade name

A manufacturer's branding strategy in which a distinct name is given to each of its products.	A branding strategy in which the company may market products under their own name and that of a reseller.
The container in which a product is offered for sale and on which information is communicated.	A branding strategy in which a company uses one name for all products; also called blanket or family branding.
An entire product category or industry.	When a company manufactures products that are sold under the name of a wholesaler or retailer.
The life of a product over four stages: introduction, growth, maturity, and decline.	Variations of a product within a product class.
The commercial name under which a company does business.	Strategies of altering a product characteristic, such as quality, performance, or appearance.

trademark	trading down
trading up	capacity management
customer contact audit	four I's of service
gap analysis	idle production capacity
internal marketing	off-peak pricing

Reducing the number of features, quality, or price of a product.	Legal identification of a company's exclusive rights to use a brand name or trade name.
Managing the demand for a service so that it is available to consumers.	Adding value to a product by including more features or higher quality materials.
Four unique elements to services: intangibility, inconsistency, inseparability, and inventory.	A flow chart of the points of interaction between a consumer and a service provider.
A situation where a service provider is available but there is no demand.	An evaluation tool that compares expectations about a particular service to the actual experience a consumer has with the service.
Charging different prices during different times of the day or days of the week to reflect variations in demand for the service.	The notion that a service organization must focus on its employees, of internal market, before successful programs can be directed at customers.

service continuum	services
average revenue	barter
break-even analysis	break-even chart
break-even point (BEP)	demand curve
demand factors	fixed cost

Intangible items such as airline trips, financial advice, or telephone calls that an organization provides to consumers in exchange for money or something else of value.

A range from the tangible to the intangible or good-dominant to service-dominant offerings available in the marketplace.

The practice of exchanging goods and services for other goods and services rather than for money.

The average amount of money received for selling one unit of a product.

A graphic presentation of a break-even analysis.

An analysis of the relationship between total revenue and total cost to determine profitability at various levels of output.

The summation of points representing the maximum quantity of a product consumers will buy at different price levels.

Quantity at which total revenue and total cost are equal and beyond which profit occurs.

Factors that determine the strength of consumers' willingness and ability to pay for goods and services.

Factors that determine the strength of consumers' willingness and ability to pay for goods and services.

marginal analysis	marginal cost
marginal revenue	price elasticity of demand
price	pricing constraints
pricing objectives	profit equation
total cost	total revenue

The change in total cost that results from producing and marketing one additional unit.	Principle of allocating resources that balances incremental revenues of an action against incremental costs.
The percentage change in quantity demanded relative to a percentage change in price.	The change in total revenue obtained by selling one additional unit.
Factors that limit a firm's latitude in the price it may set.	The money or other considerations exchanged for the purchase or use of the product, idea, or service.
Profit=Total revenue-Total cost.	Goals that specify the role of price in an organization's marketing and strategic plans.
The total amount of money received from the sale of a product.	The total expense a firm incurs in producing and marketing a product, which includes fixed cost and variable cost; in physical distribution decisions, the sum of all applicable costs.

value pricing	value
variable cost	above-, at-, or below-market pricing
basing-point pricing	bundle pricing
cost-plus pricing	customary pricing
everyday low pricing	experience curve pricing

Specifically, value can be defined as the ratio of perceived quality to price (Value = Perceived benefits/Price).

The practice of simultaneously increasing service and product benefits and decreasing price.

Pricing based on what the market price is.

An expense of the firm that varies directly with the quantity of product produced and sold.

The marketing of two or more products in a single "package" price.

Selecting one or more geographic locations (basing point) from which the list price for products plus freight expenses are charged to buyers.

A method of pricing based on a product's tradition, standardized channel of distribution, or other competitive factors.

The practice of summing the total unit cost of providing a product or service and adding a specific amount to the cost to arrive at a price.

A method of pricing where price often falls following the reduction of costs associated with the firm's experience in producing or selling a product.

The practice of replacing promotional allowances given to retailers with lower manufacturer list prices.

flexible-price policy	**FOB origin pricing**
loss-leader pricing	**odd-even pricing**
one-price policy	**penetration pricing**
price fixing	**prestige pricing**
price discrimination	

A method of pricing where the title of goods passes to the buyer at the point of loading.	Offering the same product and quantities to similar customers, but at different prices.
Setting prices a few dollars or cents under an even number, such as $19.95.	Deliberately pricing a product below its customary price to attract attention to it.
Pricing a product low in order to discourage competition from entering the market.	Setting the same price for similar customers who buy the same product and quantities under the same conditions.
Setting a high price so that status-conscious consumers will be attracted to the product.	A conspiracy among firms to set prices for a product.
	The practice of charging different prices to different buyers for goods of like trade and quality

price lining	product line pricing
promotional allowance	quantity discounts
skimming pricing	standard markup pricing
target pricing	target profit pricing
target return-on-investment pricing	target return-on-sales pricing

The setting of prices for all items in a product line.	Setting the price of a line of products at a number of different specific pricing points.
Reductions in unit costs for a larger order quantity.	The cash payment or extra amount of "free goods" awarded sellers in the channel of distribution for undertaking certain advertising or selling activities to promote a product.
Setting prices by adding a fixed percentage to the cost of all items in a specific product class	A high initial price attached to a product to help a company recover the cost of development.
Setting a price based on an annual specific dollar target volume of profit.	The practice of deliberately adjusting the composition and features of a product to achieve the target price to consumers.
Setting a price to achieve a profit that is a specified percentage of the sales volume.	Setting a price to achieve a return-on-investment target.

uniform delivered pricing	yield management pricing
brokers	cash and carry wholesaler
channel captain	channel partnership
direct marketing	direct marketing channels
disintermediation	drop shipper

The charging of different prices to maximize revenue for a set amount of capacity al a given time.

A geographical pricing practice where the price the seller quotes includes all transportation costs.

A limited-service merchant wholesaler that takes title to merchandise but sells only to buyers who call on it and pay cash for and transport their own merchandise.

Channel intermediaries that do not take title to merchandise and make their profits from commissions and fees by negotiating contracts or deals between buyers and sellers.

Agreements and procedures among channel members for ordering and physically distributing a producer's product through the channel to the ultimate consumer.

A marketing channel member that coordinates, directs, and supports other channel members; may be a manufacturer, wholesaler, or retailer.

Allow consumers to buy products by interacting with various advertising media without a face-to-face meeting with a salesperson.

A promotional alternative that uses direct communication with consumers to generate a response in the form of an order, a request for further information, or a visit to a retail outlet.

A merchant wholesaler that owns the merchandise it sells but does not physically handle, stock, or deliver; also called a desk jobber.

The practice whereby a channel member bypasses another member and sells or buys products direct.

dual distribution	exclusive distribution
franchising	general merchandise wholesaler
indirect channel	industrial distributor
intensive distribution	electronic marketing channels
manufacturer's agents	marketing channel

A distribution strategy whereby a producer sells its products or services in only one retail outlet in a specific geographical area.

An arrangement by which a firm reaches buyers by employing two or more different types of channels for the same basic product.

A full-service merchant wholesaler that carries a broad assortment of merchandise and performs all channel functions.

The contractual agreement between a parent company and an individual or firm that allows the franchisee to operate a certain type of business under an established name and according to specific rules.

A specific type of intermediary between producers and consumers that generally sells, stocks, and delivers a full product assortment.

A marketing channel where intermediaries are situated between the producer and consumers.

Channels that employ the Internet to make goods and services available for consumption or use by consumers or industrial buyers.

A distribution strategy whereby a producer sells products or services in as many outlets as possible in a geographic area.

People and firms involved in the process of making a product or service available for use or consumption by consumers or industrial users.

Individuals or firms that work for several producers and carry noncompetitive, complementary merchandise in an exclusive territory; also called manufacturer's representatives.

rack jobber	selective distribution
selling agent	specialty merchandise wholesaler
strategic channel alliances	truck jobber
vertical marketing systems	customer service
freight forwarders	intermodal transportation

A distribution strategy whereby a producer sells its products in a few retail outlets in a specific geographical area.

A merchant wholesaler that furnishes racks or shelves to display merchandise in retail stores, performs all channel functions, and sells on consignment.

A full-service merchant wholesaler that offers a relatively narrow range of products but has an extensive assortment within the products carried.

A person or firm that represents a single producer and is responsible for all marketing functions of that producer.

Small merchant wholesalers that usually handle limited assortments of fast-moving or perishable items that are sold directly from trucks for cash.

A practice whereby one firm's marketing channel is used to sell another firm's products.

The ability of a logistics system to satisfy users in terms of time, dependability, communications, and convenience.

Professionally managed and centrally coordinated marketing channels designed to achieve channel economies and maximum marketing impact.

Combining different transportation modes in order to get the best features of each.

Firms that accumulate small shipments into larger lots and then hire a carrier to move them, usually at reduced rates.

just-in-time (JIT) concept	lead time
logistics management	materials handling
quick response	reverse logistics
supply chain	supply chain management
third-party logistics providers	total logistics cost

Lag from ordering an item until it is received and ready for use.	An inventory supply system that operates with very low inventories and requires fast, on-time delivery.
Moving goods over short distances into, within, and out of warehouses and manufacturing plants.	The practice organizing the cost-effective flow of raw materials, in-process inventory, finished goods, and related information from point-of-origin to point-of-consumption to satisfy customer requirements.
The process of reclaiming recyclable and reusable materials, returns and reworks from the point-of-consumption to use for repair, remanufacturing, or disposal.	An inventory management system designed to reduce the retailer's lead time for receiving merchandise.
The integration and organization of information and logistic activities across firms in a supply chain for the purpose of creating and delivering goods and services that provide value to customers.	A sequence of firms that perform activities required to create and deliver a good or service to consumers or industrial users.
Expenses associated with transportation, materials handling and warehousing, inventory, stockouts, and order processing.	Firms that perform most or all of the logistics functions that manufacturers, suppliers, and distributors would normally perform themselves.

vendor-managed inventory	breadth of product line
central business district	community shopping centre
depth of product line	form of ownership
hypermarket	level of service
merchandise line	off-price retailing

The variety of different items a store or wholesaler carries.

An inventory management system whereby the supplier determines the product amount and assortment a customer (such as a retailer) needs and automatically delivers the appropriate items.

A retail location that typically has one primary store (usually a department store branch) and 20 to 40 smaller outlets and serves a population base of about 100,000.

The oldest retail setting; the community's downtown area.

Who owns a retail outlet. Alternatives are independent, corporate chain, cooperative, or franchise.

The assortment of each item a store or wholesaler carries.

The degree of service provided to the customer by the retailer: self, limited, or full.

A large store (over 200,000 square feet) offering a mix of food products and general merchandise.

Selling brand name merchandise at lower than regular prices.

The number of different types of products and the assortment a store carries.

power centre	regional shopping centres
retail positioning matrix	retailing
retailing mix	scrambled merchandising
shrinkage	strip location
telemarketing	advertising

Suburban malls with up to 100 stores that typically draw customers from a 8- to 16-km radius, usually containing one or two anchor stores.

Large strip malls with multiple anchor (or national stores), a convenient location, and a supermarket.

All the activities that are involved in selling, renting, and providing goods and services to ultimate consumers for personal, family, or household use.

A framework for positioning retail outlets in terms of breadth of product line and value added.

Offering several unrelated product lines in a single retail store.

The strategic components that a retailer manages, including goods and services, physical distribution, and communication tactics.

A cluster of stores that serves people who live within a 5- to 10-minute drive in a population base of under 30,000.

A term used by retailers to describe theft of merchandise by customers and employees.

Any paid form of nonpersonal communication about an organization, good, service, or idea by an identified sponsor.

Involves the use of the telephone to interact with and sell directly to consumers.

channel of communication	communication
decoding	direct marketing
encoding	feedback
field of experience	integrated marketing communications
noise	personal selling

The process of conveying a message to others. Six elements--a source, a message, a channel of communication, a receiver, and the processes of encoding and decoding—are required for communication to occur.

The means (e.g., a salesperson, advertising media, or public relations tools) of conveying a message to a receiver.

A promotional alternative that uses direct communication with consumers to generate a response in the form of an order, a request for further information, or a visit to a retail outlet.

The process of having the receiver take a set of symbols, the message, and transform them back to an abstract idea.

The communication flow from receiver back to sender; indicates whether the message was decoded and understood as intended.

The process of having the sender transform an abstract idea into a set of symbols

The concept of designing marketing communications programs that coordinate all promotional activities-advertising, personal selling, sales promotion, and public relations-- to provide a consistent message across all audiences.

A person's understanding and knowledge; to communicate effectively, a sender and a receiver must have a mutually shared field of experience.

The two-way flow of communication between a buyer and seller, often in a face-to-face encounter, designed to influence a person's or group's purchase decision.

Extraneous factors that work against effective communication by distorting a message or the feedback received.

promotional mix	public relations
publicity	pull strategy
push strategy	receivers
sales promotion	source
hierarchy of effects	percentage of sales budgeting

A form of communication management that seeks to influence the feelings, opinions, or beliefs held by customers, stockholders, suppliers, employees, and other publics about a company and its products or services.

The combination of one or more of the promotional elements a firm uses to communicate with consumers. The promotional elements include: advertising, personal selling, sales promotion, and publicity.

Directing the promotional mix at ultimate consumers to encourage them to ask the retailer for the product.

A nonpersonal, indirectly paid presentation of an organization, good, or service.

The consumers who read, hear, or see the message sent by a source in the communication process.

Directing the promotional mix to channel members or intermediaries to gain their cooperation in ordering and stocking a product.

A company or person who has information to convey.

A short-term inducement of value offered to arouse interest in buying a good or service.

Allocating funds to advertising as a percentage of past or anticipated sales, in terms of either dollars or units sold.

The sequence of stages a prospective buyer goes through from initial awareness of a product to eventual action (either trial or adoption of the product). The stages include awareness, interest, evaluation, trial, and adoption.

competitive parity budgeting	all-you-can-afford budgeting
objective and task budgeting	direct orders
lead generation	traffic generation
consumer-oriented sales promotion	cooperative advertising

Allocating funds to advertising only after all other budget items are covered.

Matching the competitors' absolute level of spending or the proportion per point of market.

The result of direct marketing offers that contain all the information necessary for a prospective buyer to make a purchase and complete the transaction.

A budgeting approach whereby the company (1) determines its advertising objective, (2) outlines the tasks to accomplish the objectives, (3) determines the advertising cost of performing these tasks.

The outcome of a direct marketing offer designed to motivate people to visit a business.

The result of a direct marketing offer designed to generate interest in a product or a service, and a request for additional information.

Advertising programs in which a manufacturer pays a percentage of the retailer's local advertising expense for advertising the manufacturer's products.

Sales tools used to support a company's advertising and personal selling efforts directed to ultimate consumers; examples include coupons, sweepstakes, and trading stamps.

cost per thousand (CPM)	frequency
full-service agency	gross rating points (GRPs)
infomercials	in-house agency
institutional advertisement	limited-service agency
post-tests	pretests

The average number of times a person in the target audience is exposed to a message or advertisement.

The cost of reaching 1,000 individuals or households with an advertising message in a given medium.

A reference number for advertisers, created by multiplying reach (expressed as a percentage) by frequency.

An advertising agency providing a complete range of services, including market research, media selection, copy development, artwork, and production.

A company's own advertising staff which may provide full services or a limited range of services.

Program length advertisements, often 30 minutes long, that take an educational approach to communicating with potential customers.

An agency that specializes in one aspect of the advertising process such as providing creative services to develop the advertising copy or buying previously unpurchased media space.

Advertisements designed to build goodwill or an image for an organization, rather than promote a specific good or service.

Tests conducted before an advertisement is placed to determine whether it communicates the intended message or to select between alternative versions of an advertisement.

Tests conducted after an advertisement has been shown to the target audience to determine whether it has accomplished its intended purpose.

product advertisements	product placement
publicity tools	rating (TV or radio)
reach	trade-oriented sales promotions
account management policies	adaptive selling
conference selling	consultative selling

Advertising media alternative in which the manufacturer pays for the privilege of having a brand name product used in a movie.	Advertisements that focus on selling a good or service and take three forms: (1) pioneering (or informational), (2) competitive (or persuasive), and (3) reminder.
The percentage of households in a market that are tuned to a particular TV show or radio station.	Methods of obtaining nonpersonal presentation of an organization, good, or service without direct cost. Examples include news releases, news conferences, and public service announcements.
Sales tools used to support a company's advertising and personal selling efforts directed to wholesalers, distributors, or retailers. Three common approaches are allowances, cooperative advertising, and salesforce training.	The number of different people or households exposed to an advertisement.
A need-satisfaction sales presentation involving adjusting the presentation to fit the selling situation.	Policies that specify whom salespeople should contact, what kinds of selling and customer service activities should be engaged in, and how these activities should be carried out.
A need-satisfaction sales presentation where the salesperson focuses on problem definition and serves as an expert on problem recognition.	A form of team selling where a salesperson and other company resource people meet with buyers to discuss problems and opportunities.

emotional intelligence	formula selling presentation
major account management	missionary salespeople
need-satisfaction presentation	order getter
order taker	partnership selling
personal selling process	personal selling

The selling format that consists of providing information in an accurate, thorough, and step-by-step manner to persuade the prospect to buy.

The ability to understand one's own emotions and the emotions of people with whom one interacts on a daily basis.

Sales support personnel who do not directly solicit orders but rather concentrate on performing promotional activities and introducing new products.

The practice of using team selling to focus on important customers to build mutually beneficial long-term, cooperative relationships.

A salesperson who sells in a conventional sense and engages in identifying prospective customers, providing customers with information, persuading customers to buy, closing sales, and following on customer experience with product or service.

A selling format that emphasizes probing and listening by the salesperson to identify needs and interests of perspective buyers.

The practice whereby buyers and sellers combine their expertise and resources to create customized solutions, commit to joint planning, and share customer, competitive, and company information for their mutual benefit, and ultimately the customer.

A salesperson who processes routine orders and reorders for products that have already been sold by the company.

The two-way flow of communication between a buyer and seller, often in a face-to-face encounter, designed to influence a person's or group's purchase decision.

Sales activities occurring before and after the sale itself, consisting of six stages:
(1) prospecting, (2) preapproach, (3) approach, (4) presentation, (5) close, and (6) follow-up.

relationship selling	sales engineer
sales management	sales plan
salesforce automation	seminar selling
stimulus-response presentation	team selling
workload method	action item list

A salesperson who specializes in identifying, analyzing, and solving customer problems and who brings technological expertise to the selling situations, but does not actually sell goods and services.

The practice of building ties to customers based on a salesperson's attention and commitment to customer needs over time.

A statement describing what is to be achieved and where and how the selling effort of salespeople is to be deployed.

Planning, implementing, and controlling the personal selling effort of the firm.

A form of team selling where a company team conducts an educational program for a customer's technical staff describing state-of-the-art developments.

The use of technology designed to make the sales function more effective and efficient.

Using a group of professionals in selling to and servicing major customers.

A selling format that assumes the prospect will buy if given the appropriate stimulus by a salesperson.

An aid to implementing a market plan, consisting of three columns: (1) the task, (2) the name of the person responsible for completing the task, and (3) the date by which the task is to be finished.

A formula-based method for determining the size of a salesforce that integrates the number of customers served, call frequency, call length, and available time to arrive at a salesforce size.

cost focus strategy	**cost leadership strategy**
differentiation focus strategy	**differentiation strategy**
functional groupings	**generic business strategy**
geographical groupings	**line positions**
market-based groupings	**marketing audit**

Using a serious commitment to reducing expenses that, in turn, lowers the price of the items sold in a wide range of market segments.	Involves controlling expenses and, in turn, lowering prices, in a narrow range of market segments.
Using innovation and significant points of difference in product offerings, higher quality, advanced technology, or superior service in a wide range of market segments.	Using significant points of difference in the firm's offerings to reach one or only a few market segments.
Strategy that can be adapted by any firm, regardless of the product or industry involved, to achieve a competitive advantage.	Organizational groupings in which a unit is subdivided according to the different business activities within a firm, such as manufacturing, marketing, and finance.
People in line positions, such as group marketing managers, have the authority and responsibility to issue orders to the people who report to them, such as marketing managers.	Organization groupings in which a unit is subdivided according to geographical location.
A comprehensive, unbiased, periodic review of the strategic marketing process of a firm or a strategic business unit (SBU).	Organizational groupings that assign responsibility for a specific type of customer to a unit.

product (program) champion	product line groupings
profitability analysis	sales analysis
sales component analysis	sales response function
share points	staff positions
synergy	

Organizational groupings in which a unit is responsible for specific product offerings.

A person who is able and willing to cut red tape and move a product or program forward.

A tool for controlling marketing programs where sales records are used to compare actual results with sales goals and to identify strengths and weaknesses.

A means of measuring the profitability of the firm's products, customer groups, sales territories, channels of distribution, and order sizes.

The relationship between the expense of marketing effort and the marketing results obtained. Measures of marketing results include sales revenue. profit, units sold, and level of awareness.

A tool for controlling marketing programs that traces sales revenues to their sources such as specific products, sales territories, or customers.

People in staff positions have the authority and responsibility to advise people in the line positions but cannot issue direct orders to them.

Percentage points of market share; often used as the common basis of comparison to allocate marketing resources effectively.

The increased customer value achieved through performing organizational functions more efficiently.